Split Up by the Sea

A Vietnamese refugee's

memoir of

survival and hope

LEN TRAN

Split Up by the Sea

Copyright © 2022 by Len Tran

All rights reserved. No part of this publication may be reproduced, stored in a retrieval system, or transmitted, in any form or by any means, electronic, mechanical, photocopying, recording, or otherwise, without the prior permission of the publisher and copyright owner.

First edition October 2022

Jacket design by Virginia McKevitt

Manufactured in the United States of America

ISBN: 979-8-9850905-5-0 (paperback)

ISBN: 979-8-9850905-6-7 (hardback)

Library of Congress Control Number: 2022918235

DEDICATION

In Loving Memory of Ong Noi and Ba Noi

To Ba, Ma, Chi Trang, Trinh, Anh, Vu, Ly, Phong, and Edgar

To all the Vietnamese refugees who took a daring journey so their lives can change.

ACKNOWLEDGMENTS

This book would not be completed without the support of my beautiful and lovely wife, Kelly (Phuong Linh) Tran. Thank you for always believing in me! To my daughter, Lara, and my son, Leo. Thank you for being patient while I was writing this memoir.

To my best friends, Kevin Kerns and Diane Mizrahi, for listening to my stories for the past two decades and helping me gather my thoughts during the writing process.

Thanks to Amy M. Le for guiding and showing me the life of an author. You are an amazing writing coach!

To my karate students (Virginia Shorin Ryu) for allowing me to take writing breaks and do karate when I have writer's block.

Author's Note

My life continues to be influenced by my family's story of survival and hope, beginning on a boat on the shore of Thuan An, Hue, Central Vietnam. After the Vietnam War, our freedom was lost, and the only way to find freedom was to risk our lives on a small fishing boat hoping to be rescued by an American ship. In April 1982, my father and I, along with twenty-three other people, were lost in the South China Sea in search of this freedom. I knew nothing of what lay ahead—or even if we would survive. All I knew was that I was with the person I trusted most in this world and that with him, no harm would come to me. This is our story. It would have been impossible to record the events and conversations exactly as they occurred when they occurred, so in writing this memoir, I strove for emotional truth, recreating my memories as best I could and using the stories told to me. Consequently, some of the conversations are representational, some events have been compressed, and some names have been changed.

In the midst of danger and despair,
Random thoughts of surrendering bring me to tears,
But I remember there is such a thing as "hope"
That echoes between my ears.

Len Tran

CONTENTS

Introduction I
1 The Beginning of the Journey 1
2 South China Sea 11
3 "Jellyfish" Island 22
4 The Barge 30
5 Hong Kong Refugee Camp 37
6 Bataan, Philippines 45
7 New York City 53
8 Welcome to the Bronx 59
9 Treasure Hunting 66
10 Time for School 73
11 The TV 82
12 My Friends 91
13 Third Grade Awakening 98
14 The Change 106
15 Living Together 118
16 Birth 125
17 Karate 134
18 The Separation 144
19 Astoria, Queens 152
20 The Summer Job 163
21 The Phone Call 172
22 The Reunion 180
23 The Pair of Gloves 191
24 New Home 199
25 The College Years 208
26 Last Year of CCNY 220
27 The Meet-up 231
28 The Move: Virginia 243
29 Building My Own Family 258
30 The Conflict 269
31 The Moment 280
Afterword On Hope 296
Reflection by Veronica McKeever 298

Introduction

On the fifth day of our journey to find freedom, we were still lost at sea. I sat next to my dad on a small fishing boat with twenty-three other people. In the distance, a dark ominous cloud approached us. I felt uneasy looks of confusion spread on the faces of the men who were in charge of the boat. As these men became quieter, I suspected something horrifying was about to happen. I looked at Dad's face and saw fear in his dilated pupils. Without saying a word to me, he placed both of his trembling hands together and chanted the Buddhist praying mantras. I looked to my left and right—everyone did the same. Immediately, I placed both palms together in front of my chest and tried to slow down my breathing as I prayed to our divinity. The ominous cloud got closer, and I knew our prayers would be heard momentarily. In the meantime, the wind picked up, and the only option left was to hold onto the arms of our loved ones.

  Dad was my only hope, my savior, my hero. He brought me along this journey I did not request. I wanted a vacation with Dad, not be on a boat that was about to capsize by the wind, rain, and horrendous waves that were smacking vociferously onto the sides of the boat. Tears fell from the adults' cheeks and children screamed cries of fear. The treacherous sea showed no sign of forgiveness—the salty water continued to splash onto our faces. Haven't our prayers been heard? Are the wind and waves too deafening? At that moment, the ominous cloud was between us and the beautiful blue sky that symbolized hope. Death was imminent.

We braced for death. The wind blew stronger. The salty water splashed and covered my entire face. It was hard to open my eyes—all I heard was the sound of mother nature about to destroy twenty-five lives. Suddenly, a cloudburst poured upon us from the sky. After five days of exhaustion, everyone on the boat needed the rainwater. I cupped my hands together tightly, leaving no gap between my fingers for the water to escape, and gulp as much as I could. Everyone on the boat got the precious water. After five minutes of rain, the ominous cloud continued on its path. The bright blue sky appeared above our heads with the sun beaming beautiful rays that reflected off the sea. In the instant, someone on the boat softly said, "The divine will always listen to our prayers if we remain faithful." Our journey continued from one island to another until we found hope twenty-one days later.

The ordeal of finding freedom taught me a valuable life lesson. If you want to achieve your dreams, expect obstacles to be waiting for you along the way. However, obstacles are made for us to transform into better versions of ourselves. During the journey at sea, I learned the values of perception and persistence, and to be ready for perspiration. Dad taught me that changing my perception allowed me to see the positivity in this world and that hope was on our side. He taught me being persistent was the key to getting closer to hope. In the process of reaching hope, he taught me the value of hard work—perspiring during each step. If life was easy, then achieving our dreams would be within reach, but it doesn't work that way. If you want to achieve your dreams badly enough, the obstacles ahead are not meant to stop you, but to start you.

My purpose in writing this book was to share a story of a young boy born in the countryside of Hue, Vietnam, just before the Vietnam war ended. Although the war had ended, my family was still living in famine, eating whatever was given to us by the fishermen, or the cactus leaves grown in the sand between our house and the beach. However, all that changed because Dad decided to bring me along on his journey to find freedom. The journey at sea was tough, but the adaptation to the new world, America, was even tougher and longer. Through changing our perception, being persistent, and being ready for perspiration from hard work, our lives have changed.

In this book, I hope to immerse you in the story of hardship and show how overcoming obstacles can lead to achieving dreams. Enjoy, and see you at the end of my journey!

1 The Beginning of the Journey

The beautiful ocean was less than two hundred feet away from our house. Even though we lived so close to it, Ong Noi (*Grandfather in Vietnamese*) had ingrained in our heads that it was dangerous and forbade any of us from going anywhere near it. Ba (*Father in Vietnamese*) told us many times about the story of how his older sister, O (*Aunt in Vietnamese*) Tai, had drowned years ago when she was in her teens. Since then, Ong Noi set a strict rule with his descendants to prevent another tragedy.

One time, Chi (*Older sister*) Trang and I were going to the beach to hang out with her friends. It was a sweltering day with the sun shining over our heads, slowly darkening our skin. A gentle breeze blew as we ran around on the fine sand playing catch. After a couple of rounds of chasing each other, we all gave up and decided to rest under the shade of a palm tree. There was a moment of silence where we all collectively looked out at the ocean. Sunlight glimmering over the waves made it look so inviting, enticing us to inch farther and farther toward it.

"Let's go play in the water," one of Chi Trang's friends suggested.

"Good idea, since it's so hot," another replied.

Everyone got up and ran towards the ocean. I turned to Chi Trang and saw the hesitation in her eyes as she watched her friends unwaveringly bolt for the water. She was about to make a decision that would get herself in trouble if Ong Noi found out.

"Em (*Younger brother*), stay here, and don't you dare go in the water," she warned me.

"But Ong Noi said no one is allowed to go in the ocean. You shouldn't be going there."

"I know, but I don't want to be embarrassed in front of my friends," she whispered in my ear.

Immediately, she left me there and rushed to join her friends. I didn't have a chance to stop her from disobeying Ong Noi. I stood there alone, looking at the ocean, debating if I should be bold and go against Ong Noi's admonition like Chi Trang, who was laughing and splashing water at her friend. The more I looked at the ocean, the more Ong Noi's words disappeared in my head and the more my feet began to move. Chi Trang and her friends were completely under now with only their heads above the water. They looked like they were having so much fun, and suddenly, my toes were met with a cold, yet gentle wave. Admittedly, it felt nice, cooling me down from the heat. Unable to resist the temptation, I took a few more steps until the water was up to my calves. The waves did not seem as dangerous as Ba and his father had exaggerated. It wouldn't hurt to take another step. I went farther and farther until a rip current grabbed me by the ankles and pulled me under. Within a split second, my body was completely submerged, and I was dragged farther away from the shore. As I panicked and tried to reach for air, I realized how the ocean's beauty deceived me. It was dangerous indeed. I did not know how to swim, but I attempted to gather all my strength, kicking my legs as hard as I could, hoping I could raise my head above the water just to catch one breath of air. However, the more I tried, the more I felt like my body was sinking. I thought I was going to die.

They say that when you think death is near, your life passes before your eyes. As I was holding air in my lungs and desperately fighting for one more breath, images of my family played in my mind as if I were flipping through a photo album. I saw their smiling faces as they waited for me to come home. At that moment, I was not ready to say goodbye. With all my might, I paddled with my arms and kicked viciously hoping to be buoyant for a gasp of air. Instead, I gulped salt water, and this time, I was out of strength to fight the waves. With my arms and legs coming to a halt, I was about to accept my fate. I was seconds from losing air when I felt a hand grab my arm. I instantly reached and held on tight. An unimaginable force pulled me closer to their shoulder. I gasped to take a big breath as my head was finally out of the water. I opened my eyes and tried to look for my savior. It was one of Chi Trang's friends. He saved me from the violent waves. He held me over his shoulder as he walked and placed me on the sand. Being able to breathe again, I understood why Ong Noi was so strict about staying away from the ocean. He did not want to risk another one of his family members having the same fate as his daughter.

Chi Trang told no one about the incident after we got home. She did not have to remind me how angry and disappointed Ong Noi would be if he ever found out. I kept quiet and promised myself to stay away from the water. Yes, the ocean was beautiful, but on that day, I learned it could be vicious and deadly.

My family lived in a small village called Thon Twelve (*Province 12)* of Thuan An, Central Vietnam. My name is Tran Vinh Linh, and I was seven years old. I had three sisters, one brother, and one more sister on the way. My older sister, Tran Thi Thuy Trang, was four years older than me; my sister, Tran Thi Thuy Trinh, was two years younger; and Tran Diem Hoang Anh, was three years younger. My brother, Tran Vinh Thien Vu, was five years younger. Together with our parents, Ba (*Dad in Vietnamese*), Tran Vinh Thuy, Ma (*Mom in Vietnamese*), Tran-Le Kim An, Ong Noi, and Ba Noi (*Grandmother in Vietnamese*), all nine of us lived in a small house. No walls separated the rooms—the house was one open space where we did everything—eating, sleeping, and even praying to our ancestors. There were two sets of beds on both ends of the room. My parents and we kids slept on the wooden platform on one side, and my grandparents slept on the other side.

The kitchen was separated from the rest of the house, at least twenty feet away, which was not unusual for houses in Thuan An. It was an open kitchen, so when I helped Ma collect wood to start a fire, I had to be incredibly careful because the fire could spread quickly on a windy day. And that was something we never wanted to witness. Our kitchen stove was made with bricks while a rack was on top with dry wood inside to create a fire. The kitchen was made of wooden frames, but the walls and roof were hay stacked on top of one another. If a fire caught the dry hay, it would burn down the entire kitchen within minutes.

A barn next to the kitchen held our two beastly pigs. They ate so much of our leftover vegetable stems and other food scraps that it was not long before they grew to twice my size. Whenever I helped Ma cook rice, I fed them the leftover water from cleaning the rice. I despised that task the most. I did not mind helping Ma with rinsing and cleaning the rice but hauling a bucket of dirty rice water to the muddy, smelly pigs was the worst part of my day. On top of that, I had to fight off the flies that swarmed them and attacked me.

Next to the barn, Ong Noi had plowed the land and created a vegetable garden. We grew watercress, bitter melons, squash, cilantro, and scallions. One of my daily jobs was to go with Chi Trang every morning and late afternoon to the well, which was a third of a mile from the house, to collect water and pour it into a large drum for washing, gardening and cooking. We would fill two buckets of water, approximately three gallons each, and have them hung onto a wooden rod. Chi Trang would carry one end on the shoulder while I carried the other end. We had to go back and forth so many times until the drum was full. With nine people living in the house, we had to make several trips each day.

Even though we had two pigs and a bunch of chickens running around, it was extremely rare for us to have any sort of meat during our everyday meals. Only on special occasions, such as New Year or to commemorate our ancestors, Ma would prepare a dish with one of our chickens. Our main source of meat was the ocean right in front of our home. Every time we saw fishing boats come to dock at the shore, my sisters and I would run out to meet them and open our hands hoping they would spare us some of their catch. If we were lucky, they would toss us one or two mackerel. We would rush home and help Ma scrape off their scales, clean their insides, and slice them proportionately for our whole family. Ma would add her special seasoning of fish sauce, onions, chili peppers, and salt to make her signature dish. Ma cooked fish so often that she became an expert at it. One time, I was cutting the chili peppers that we grew in the garden to help Ma prepare for dinner. I accidentally rubbed my eyes with the same hand that I used to cut the pepper with. The burn was unbearable, and I cried so much. Ma would tell me to rub my eyes on her hair as this was the remedy to wipe away the hot oil from the chili peppers. Surprisingly, it worked!

Ba was the youngest son among his four siblings. He had two older sisters, O Chat and O Tai, and an older brother, Bac (*Uncle in Vietnamese*) Thanh. Ong Noi was a well-known carpenter in the village, and fishermen would ask him to build boats for them. Although he made little money, he understood the value of education. He saved his money so that all his children would be able to travel to the city to continue studying since the village was limited to the elementary school level. However, O Chat got married at a young age and wanted to stay in the village. O Tai drowned in her teens, so only Ba and Bac Thanh were sent to the city. Years later, Bac Thanh quit school, got married, and decided to live in the city with his new family. Ba was the only one left in the family determined to get an education so that one day he could become a doctor. He spent most of his time studying and rarely did anything else.

When Ba was almost twenty years old, Ong Noi chose Ma for him. Although it wasn't a prearranged marriage, they knew each other since childhood. Ong Noi thought since both families knew each other for so long, having both of them become married to each other was the best match. After Ba and Ma got married, they had Chi Trang within the same year. However, since Ba was still in school, he continued to stay in the city while the rest of the family lived in the village. He only visited during his breaks. After I was born in 1975, Ba couldn't continue his education due to the fall of Saigon.

Nevertheless, since Ba learned and practiced his medical education in the city, he was considered the expert in the village. People would come to our house and ask for medical advice. At times, I would see Ba administer drugs to his patients and go to houses in the village to do regular check-ups. Chi Trang and I did our regular duties of going to his patients' homes to collect money. Sadly, there were times we came back empty-handed.

Chi Trang said, "Ba, they said they don't have money."

"It's okay. They have their difficulty," Ba said.

Ba knew everyone in the village was poor, so he didn't expect much but felt cheerful to help them.

One afternoon, after I got home from playing on the beach with my friends, Ba stopped me in the front yard and asked if I wanted to take a walk with him. Ba was always busy with his studying and hardly had time for a stroll like this. Although he couldn't continue with his studies, I always found him immersed in books. I happily agreed, since I could spend time with Ba. We took a walk toward the beach. Ba asked me how I was doing in school, but he seemed unfocused. As we were walking back to the house, Ba looked out at the sea and paused for a while before he asked, "Linh, do you want to go visit Bac Thanh?"

Bac Thanh still lived in the city, which was thirty kilometers away from our village. The trip to Bac Thanh's house would take at least half a day by ferry, followed by a xe lam, which is a three-wheeled, motorized version of a pulled rickshaw that can hold up to ten passengers.

We rarely went to visit Bac Thanh because the fare was quite expensive. Most of the time, it would be just Ba and Ma, but only for special occasions. So of course, I didn't want to miss the chance to finally go.

"Yes, Ba," I answered with joy. "Are my siblings going too?"

"No, only the two of us," Ba answered.

I was confused by Ba's response. I knew bringing the entire family would be expensive, but not even Ma? I felt strange. I glanced over at Ma and my siblings, who were busy cooking in the kitchen. I wondered why he only took me this time. However, I was so happy that I got to go since I had been hearing many wonderful things about the city. I didn't want to ask too much, afraid that Ba would change his mind.

"When are we leaving?" I asked.

"This afternoon," Ba answered.

I couldn't wait to leave as I was looking at the pigs. Finally, I could take a break from a task that I disliked the most but had to do as the oldest son in the family. I couldn't help but smile, thinking that I wouldn't have to smell them and clean myself from the muddy soil after feeding them for a while.

That late afternoon with the sun about to set, Ba held my hand as we walked along the beach. We carried nothing with us, which made me wonder how long we were going to stay at Bac

Thanh's. I wanted to ask Ba, but every time I would face him to talk, he would be gazing elsewhere, looking conflicted. I didn't want to bother him, so I kept on walking. It was a long walk—about two miles—and we walked in silence. I did not know what was on Ba's mind. I was wondering if he was worried that Ma would be mad because he did not take her or he did not tell her where we were going. But then again, I was sure that Ba would have told her. I figured I was just overthinking.

After what seemed like forever, we approached a small house like ours along the beach. It was not Bac Thanh's house, but instead, it was one of Ba's friend's house. As Ba looked at the house, he had a very unusual expression on his face. I could not tell if he was sad or happy.

"We're stopping here, Linh. We're having dinner with some of my friends tonight," Ba told me.

"And we go visit Bac Thanh after dinner?"

"No, we are going there early tomorrow morning."

"Then we are going home after dinner here?"

"No, we will sleep here tonight and will leave in the morning."

We walked inside the house and saw a group of people—about twenty of them—men, women, and even kids. Ba told me this was his friend's house, but I had never seen any of them before. Like most homes in the rural parts of Vietnam, and like ours, this one had one large open space for both eating and sleeping. There were two big wooden beds on each side of the walls of the house with people sitting there. Ba and I walked up to one of the beds, sat down, and had dinner with them. We continued to eat with minimal conversations. Everyone seemed to focus on eating their food, instead of the usual loud interactions when a large group gets together. As soon as everyone finished, we cleaned up the bed, put out the pillows and blankets, and got ready to go to sleep. The whole thing seemed very strange to me. I couldn't understand the quiet dinner, then having to sleep earlier than usual, but I did not want to ask. Maybe Ba wanted us to rest before heading to see Bac Thanh early in the morning. I laid down next to Ba and tried to fall asleep.

In the middle of the night, I was sweating and couldn't feel my legs. I turned over to Ba and wanted to tell him. However, my entire body was paralyzed, except my head. As I opened my mouth to call Ba, nothing was coming out. I tried to scream, but I couldn't make a sound. I turned my head back to the middle and saw someone standing at the end of the bed looking at me. I screamed, but again, I was muffled. Suddenly, that face was within inches of mine. I was lying there helpless, sweaty, and horrified. I clenched my fist and forced out a loud scream that suddenly woke me up. As I opened my eyes, Ba was tapping on my shoulder trying to calm me, "It's okay, Con. It was only a bad dream." (*Con is a loving Vietnamese term for a child.*)

As I laid back down, I remembered what Ba Noi always told me. Every time when I had a nightmare, Ba Noi would have me chant the Buddha's mantra, *Nam Mo A Di Da Phat*, praising Buddha and asking for his blessing. I closed my eyes and kept on chanting. Within moments, I drifted away.

Shortly before dawn, while settled into a restful sleep, someone grabbed me by the arms and covered my mouth. I tried to shout and kick, but the voice of the person holding me down whispered, "Be quiet or you will get us killed!"

I was in shock and could not process what exactly had just happened. Without knowing who this strange man was, I followed his command and stayed quiet. I wanted Ba, but he wasn't around. I did not know where he was. The strange man threw me over his shoulder and carried me along the beach. I saw other people running in a hurry. Tears rolled down my cheek as I asked the man, "Where is Ba?"

"You will see him soon. Shut up!" the man snarled.

"I want Ba," I cried.

"Just shut up!" He was even angrier.

The man huffed and tossed me onto a boat with a bunch of other people. I was so scared. I tried to climb over the side of the boat. As one of my legs was over the edge and I was about to jump, I heard a familiar voice calling my name, I turned around and there was Ba. I faced him and wailed. I did not understand what was going on or who the cruel stranger was that threw me into the boat. However, I felt better now knowing Ba was with me.

"Ba, where are we going?" I asked.

"Just sit still. I will be right there," he whispered.

Ba jumped off and helped the other men push the boat out into the water... into the sea that once nearly devoured me. As I regained my composure, I saw women and kids whom I met the night before sitting in silence. The empty looks on their faces scared me even more. I wanted Ba to jump into the boat beside me or Ma to appear and hold me. As the boat gained some buoyancy and drifted into the water, the men jumped in. I clutched Ba's arm tightly.

"Why are we in this boat, and where are we going, Ba?" I lowered my voice out of fear of being yelled at by the cruel man.

Ba looked at the shore and did not reply. The captain turned on the engine and took the boat farther out to sea. As I realized how far we were from the shore, I started to panic. I remembered Ong Noi's warning of the deep sea and held tightly to Ba's arm. I wondered what Ong Noi would do or say to us if he found out where Ba and I were now.

The ocean that Ong Noi had warned us all about so many times was now under me again, with just a small wooden fishing boat keeping us from drowning. There were twenty-five of us barely fitting into it with men, women, and children. We were all crammed together in a boat no more than six feet wide and about twenty-five feet long. I stopped asking Ba where we were going with all these people we did not know. I tried to keep my rollercoaster of emotions to myself.

I sat in my spot in the mid-section of the boat, too afraid to move or make a sound. The men were screaming and shouting to be heard over the engine noise while the wind was blowing at us. They were scrambling to stow jars of cooked rice and plastic gallon jugs of fresh water into the storage area just underneath a wooden platform near where I sat.

"Where is the other boat?" the captain shouted. "They were supposed to meet us out here and they have the compass."

"Dammit, we lost them," one of the men said.

"Let's just keep going. I'll have to use the sun as direction," the captain said.

Ba later explained to me that the plan was to have both boats evenly divided with twenty-five people. It was agreed that whichever boat left first would have to wait for the other boat at sea and then go together. However, during the chaotic morning and due to the lack of coordination, the other boat panicked and left.

About an hour later out on the open sea, I couldn't see land anymore; only water everywhere I looked. I leaned over and looked down at the ocean. I wondered how deep it actually was. Fear struck through my body as I was reminded of the time the ocean almost took my life with its treacherous waves. Instinctively, I sat back and shifted my focus elsewhere. The people in the boat became quiet now; no more screaming or shouting. There was sadness on everyone's faces as they turned to look at the land that was farther and farther away from us. Tears brimmed in their eyes, but none were shed. The captain shut off the engine and walked to the front of the boat. He took a long look at the land, then with tear-filled eyes, he turned to us and made his speech. "Everyone, there is no turning back now. We just left our country for good. We don't know if we'll ever see Vietnam again. Let's all pray for our safety."

I was shocked. What did he mean by leaving our country for good? What about Ma? What about Chi Trang, Trinh, Anh, Vu, Ong Noi, and Ba Noi? Would I ever see them again? I thought we were going to visit Bac Thanh. Tears rolled down my face as I turned to Ba and asked, "Where are we going, Ba?"

With sadness streaked across his face and a single tear cascading down his cheeks, leaving tracks of salty tears, he grabbed my face and whispered, "We are going to find freedom!"

2 South China Sea

At six in the morning, the bright sun woke me up. Habitually, I was ready to tend the roosters in our coop, as they would usually wake us up at this time. However, the smell of saltwater reminded me of where I was. I wondered if Ma, Ong Noi, and Ba Noi were worried that Ba and I didn't come home last night. I could imagine them running around the village looking for us. Ma especially, as she was very emotional. I wished all this was a dream so Ma wouldn't be overexerting herself with tears and worries since she was pregnant.

A few men walked by me to go to the back end of the boat to talk to the captain who was controlling the steering wheel. After a brief moment of exchanging words, I saw an uncertain look on the captain's face.

"There are no signs of the other boats. We are on our own now," the captain announced.

"They have most of the rice, water, and gas," one of the men replied.

Everyone was worried. We couldn't survive for long since our food preserves were on the other boat, and we didn't have the compass with us. Panic arose. I sat there listening to the multiple conversations, but I had no idea what they were planning to do. Suddenly, in the corner of my eye, I saw Ba stand up and raise his hand to signal everyone to calm down.

"Let's just keep going. We have no other choice, and we may see them," Ba said.

The captain nodded his head as he agreed with Ba. To reassure everyone, he said he would try to speed up hoping we could catch up to the other boats. Everyone was reassured after hearing the captain. Some of the ladies, who looked to be Ma's age, took out a large pot. They grabbed handfuls of rice from it and rolled it into the shape of a rod to pass around. They kept doing this until we each got our rolls of rice. Once again, we ate in silence and all I could hear was the sound of the gentle waves hitting on the side of the boat. As we gobbled down the food, I noticed tears running down Ba's face. One by one others started to cry while they were chewing their rice. I just could not tell what was on their minds.

"Does Ma or Ong Noi know that we are leaving the country, Ba?" I asked.

"They don't, but I left them a letter." Ba struggled to say.

I wondered what Ba wrote in the letter. Did he tell them we were going to see Bac Thanh, or that we were going to find freedom as he told me? I was confused, but I did not want to keep bombarding Ba with so many questions. With all the obstacles we were faced with, I did not want to provoke Ba any further. On the other hand, I couldn't imagine how Ma and my grandparents would react. I was uncertain whether or not we would ever see each other. Overwhelming pain consumed me.

The boat moved slowly, partly due to the overweighting capacity, but also because every fifteen minutes or so, we had to let people who were queasy throw up over the edge. Luckily, I didn't throw up often since I didn't eat much, or maybe I wasn't as seasick as the others. Although, the heat from the sun bothered me more. Fortunately, the water was less than two feet below us, so I could splash the water up into my face whenever I needed to refresh myself.

After lunch, there was not much movement since everyone was tired after an early morning full of chaos. Some were taking naps, and some were just laying down, probably to think of their own families. The captain conserved fuel by slowing down and making random stops in the middle of the ocean to assess the direction of where to head next. There was still no sign of the other boat. At this point, the only hope, with no compass to guide us, was to be found by rescuers, or at least to have sight of land other than Vietnam.

Whether it was people's nature or just the people on my boat, they panicked when it was too quiet. Making noise to distract them from thinking of the unknown was their plan, I guess.

"Where is the other boat?" one man asked.

"Are we going to be found?" another one added.

"We are going to die here!" one screamed.

"No, we won't die here. Someone will find us, and we will be rescued." The captain sternly spoke.

The captain patiently reassured everyone. He knew having people be terrified would do us more harm than anything else at that moment. For the captain, the safety of everyone on board was his priority. Although he sounded like he was certain with his words, his underlying facial expressions revealed otherwise. Ba seemed to catch on while others were still busy with their doubtful thoughts. As the boat idled in the middle of the ocean, Ba walked up to the captain as he was discussing with other men near the engine. He removed his *Citizen* watch and gave it to the captain. Ong Noi had given that watch to Ba when he was accepted to medical school, and Ba always cherished that gift the most. Ong Noi, who was a carpenter, had to build extra boats to buy him that watch. I had never seen Ba take it off, and I did not understand why he was giving it away. It was probably the last gift he would ever receive from his father.

After about an hour, we spotted a fisherman's boat. The captain turned off the engine, removed his white shirt, and waved it in the air. I learned later on that it was a sign of surrender and that we were of no harm. The captain must have known the rules of the South China Sea when seeking help. The fisherman's boat came near us, and after a short exchange of words, the captain gave them Ba's watch in exchange for what looked like a new engine propeller. Due to the captain's hunch that the propeller would fail, Ba, prepared like always, gave him the watch for the chance of something like this happening.

It did not take long for the captain's hunch to come true. Soon after the fisherman's boat left, the captain announced that there was something wrong with the engine. Everyone was worried as we had encountered our first hindrance. The captain turned off the engine and asked three men to dive into the water to check on the propeller. They plunged deep into the ocean for a while, and when they surfaced, they told us the propeller was broken. The captain gave them the new one to replace. I sat at the side of the boat and watched the men underwater, which felt like more than five minutes. As I sat there, I looked at the ocean, and oddly enough, I found the water that I had once almost drowned in to be quite beautiful. It was a vibrant blue, and the sun reflecting on the water created tiny sparkles that looked like glitter. As the men were changing the propeller, I noticed how calm the water was, and at that moment, I wanted to dangle my feet into it. I wondered if I could float on top of it, like these men, and feel the buoyancy of my body on top of the water. They were taking turns as one would get up to gasp enough air and rest while the other two were underwater fixing the propeller. It was an unbelievable sight to see someone brave and skilful enough to swim into what Ong Noi had described as a death trap. After thirty minutes or so, the three men got up with good news announcing that the new propeller was replaced and that we were good to go. Everybody looked relieved, especially the captain. He told everyone that Ba had saved our lives. The boat was moving smoother with the new propeller, easing those who were previously panicked.

As the sun went down, all the women on the boat began to roll the rice to pass it out for dinner. I thought about Ma and my siblings. Trinh and Anh would be setting up the table, and Chi Trang and I would help Ma bring out the rice and food. Vu would walk Ba Noi to the table since she was blind. Although our dinners were simply rice and fish, we enjoyed our time as the three generations sat under one roof sharing a meal. I wondered if they were having dinner right now as well and if they were missing us as much as I missed them.

When night came at sea, it would be completely dark, except for the moon and the stars. Nothing but the sound of the waves and the smell of the saltwater. I reminisced about all the times my siblings and I would stargaze after dinner.

Breaking the silence, a man jumped up and started singing a traditional song. I had heard this song many times before when Ong Noi and his friends sat by the beach during late afternoons. I would be flying kites with my friends, and it wouldn't be long until Ong Noi and his friends would start singing. Soon, everyone on the boat started to chime in and the sound of laughter filled the emptiness that many of us felt. As a sense of peace was established, I felt less afraid, and it seemed like everyone felt that, too. Still, I wondered why this trip was taking such a long time. We were supposed to go visit Bac Thanh, but instead, we had been stuck traveling on this boat to nowhere for hours and none of us knew where to go. When the singing ended, the adults were teary-eyed again. One man screamed, "We're on the path to freedom! No more communism!"

Sleeping that first night was tough. I thought I wasn't seasick like everyone else, but I ended up throwing up over the edge of the boat, nauseous for the whole night. Other kids were having the same problem, but all we could do was close our eyes and force ourselves to try to sleep. Besides the ocean sickness, images of dead bodies washed up on the shore flashed in my mind every time I closed my eyes. I remembered the times Ma and I walked along the beach to my aunt's house, who lived a town away. At least two separate times we witnessed dead bodies washed up on the beach. I didn't know what happened to them. At the time, I thought they were fishermen who fell off their boats, but I pieced together in my head that those must have been the bodies of people who had tried to escape by boat like us. They just could not make it. It was hard getting good rest, thinking that that could be us at any moment.

The word "freedom" popped into my head. Was it freedom that those individuals were seeking? Was "freedom" that important to make people desperately leave Vietnam and their loved ones behind? I was deep in my thoughts until I heard another commotion arise.

"Let's head back and find a place to hide the wives and kids, and we men can go to prison," one man shouted.

"We made a decision and accepted death. Why go back and be tortured by them?" another man argued back.

It was a night of disagreement. There were debates on whether or not to continue moving forward or to go back to Vietnam and accept imprisonment. I sat there alone as Ba was also part of the commotion. I wanted to be held like other kids by their mothers as I watched these men scream from the top of their lungs. I didn't understand why these men kept shouting about the same thing.

"We are now lost. I don't know where we are either. But everyone please calm down because it won't help if we keep fighting. Hopefully, we will see land or be rescued soon. Just let fate decide for us." The captain brought the noise to a halt.

After he finished talking, the captain walked back to the engine with his head down. The crew became quiet again as everyone tried to process the unsettling news. What we had been afraid of had happened. No one was in the mood to scream or shout anymore as they were worried about what would come next now that we were lost. The captain turned off the engine and decided to let the boat drift. We were uncertain of where to go, and we could not see anything either. Everyone decided to rest although it was not easy.

At daybreak, the captain turned on the engine and moved forward for the second day of our journey. Soon after everyone woke up, the arguments started again. They were debating about which direction we should be going since we did not have a compass. After minutes of bickering, they decided we should use the direction of the sun and go north. We all agreed that as long as we were going farther and farther away from Vietnam, we would be fine. Ba eventually told me later that the goal was to reach Hong Kong, which was still under British rule during the 1980s.

Right after we settled on which direction to go, the engine started sputtering. We were running low on gasoline. Understanding everyone's tendency to panic, the captain assured us that we would be fine. There were many fishermen on the South China Sea that we could ask for help. It appeared that these fishermen had seen so many Vietnamese boat people out on the ocean that they knew what we needed and were willing to assist us. These fishermen were not Vietnamese—they were either from Mainland China or Hainan, an island that belonged to China. Shortly, we spotted a boat coming toward us. The captain used his white shirt and called for help. Although a couple of them didn't respond to his white shirt, we were lucky as the third one stopped and helped us. They gave us some gasoline that they had left on their boat but didn't ask for anything in exchange.

Even though we got some fuel, it wasn't enough to last us for long. We needed to seek more help. Luckily that afternoon, we spotted land, but we were afraid to get too close. From afar, I saw palm trees and the same huts—wood with hay for roofs, the same type of homes as ours. We thought we were back in Vietnam. The captain was hesitant and slowed down the engine as he assessed the location of this island. While some people were happy to see land, hoping to return to Vietnam and leave this trip, others were afraid to be back, being imprisoned, and enduring the hardship under communism.

As the captain got closer to the land, gobs of seaweed floated on the water near the shore and stuck into every crevice of the boat. He looked at the beach and could not tell if we were in another area of Vietnam. However, we were desperate and needed to stop at this beach. Everybody was tired after two days of throwing up and sitting in a tight space. We all needed to stretch our bodies and take a break from the rocking sensation of the boat. Besides, we could ask the people there for more fuel. The risk of being stuck in the middle of the ocean was the last thing we wanted to take. We got closer to the shore, and everyone agreed to let Buddha decide our fate. If we were back in Vietnam, then we would accept that our journey stopped here. The captain moved our boat nearer to the shore and saw a bunch of people running toward us. We sat motionless while anticipating being back home and accepting months or years of imprisonment. Finally, these people approached the boat and spoke a language that we did not understand. The sound of the unrecognizable language sent everyone into a state of relief. They were Hainanese.

After communicating with their hands, the captain and the Hainanese people signaled us to follow them. It seemed like we weren't the first group who stopped by and sought help because they knew who we were and what we needed. Everyone got off the boat, having a challenging time walking, knees locked and legs wobbly. It took me a few seconds to re-learn how to walk again after all the sitting.

Thankfully, the Hainanese people were friendly and offered us hospitality. Their homes were exactly like ours back in the village—one open room with barely any furniture. They served us congee, a rice soup with ground meat, which is a quite common Asian dish. After eating only dry rolled rice for the last two days on the boat, I was ready to eat a full meal. Nothing was more satisfying than eating while on the brink of starvation. The first taste of the hot soup was refreshing. I did not hesitate to ask for a second bowl nor did everyone else. We were thankful for a satisfying meal that helped us regain our energy.

As the night came, using their hands and other motions again, the Hainanese asked if we wanted to spend the night at their homes. Everyone was exhausted and didn't want to go back to the cramped space on the boat to sleep so we accepted the offer. I saw the captain ask them for fuel. They were generous enough to fill up our fuel tank and also give the captain some extra gallons of fuel in containers. We were all ready to finally get a decent night of sleep, however, in the middle of the night, the captain ordered us to head back to the boat. He did not want to take any chances of the women or children being kidnapped. We did not know if we could trust these people at night but were grateful for everything that they had given us.

Without making a sound, the men pushed the boat away from the shore. One by one, we all quietly slipped into the boat, and soon we drifted away from the island. Once we were a few hundred feet away, the captain turned on the engine and we continued our journey.

Everyone was exhausted after two days on the ocean and awakened at night. Even though we had no blankets or anything to cover us from the chilly night wind, everyone was deep in their sleep, dreaming of the land of "freedom" that we were going to find. As the boat was drifting in the water, it suddenly rocked, splashing water onto my face, waking me up. This occurred several times, and each time the water hit my face, Ong Noi's words ran through my mind about the dangers of the sea. I couldn't go back to sleep, thinking about what might come to harm us. I looked around, as everyone was agitated by that bothersome water as well. It seemed like the ocean wanted to wake us up and bring us back to the reality that we were still stuck on the boat in the middle of the ocean, waiting to be rescued.

On the third day, we became weak from lack of food and sleep. The congee we had eaten the previous night didn't sustain us for very long. Our energy ran low again. Around noon time, the women were passing out rice rolls for everyone, but this time, not many of us were able to swallow them. The rice had hardened and was impossible to chew. Ba sprinkled salt on my rice to bring out the flavor, and it helped me generate enough saliva so I could slowly ingest it. However, it was still so dry and cold. I turned to Ba and asked for some water thinking it would help me to gulp it down. We found out there was not much water left and everyone needed to drink it sparingly. They gave us a small cup of water that was enough for one sip. Ba gave it to me to drink as he just tried to swallow his saliva. On top of the hardened rice and the lack of water, the heat from the sun was like the last strike beating us down. It was excruciating and we had nowhere to look for shade. Our little boat wasn't fancy enough to have a cover to block the sun's rays. Some of the men removed their shirts to cover their heads, but their bodies were still exposed. Hopelessly, we sat there and endured the cruel sun. The longer we were out in the open sea with the sun constantly beating down on us, the thirstier we became.

    We stayed like that for a long time until one of the Chinese fisherman's boats spotted us and came closer to give us some food and water. It was a ray of light in the hour of despair, and we hurriedly grabbed the items with gratitude. There was no exchange of conversation. They gave us the food and clasped their hands as a sign of good luck—they could tell that we were desperate. More than half of the people on the boat were sitting in a daze with our dried mouths, but thanks to the food and water from the Chinese fishermen, we became alive again. As soon as the energy was back, so was the bickering. While all this arguing went on, Ba and I sat quietly. I thought about home again. For the very first time, I wanted to be near the pigs and feed them. I just wanted to go back home with my family.

    The temperature was extremely hot on the fourth day. The little water that we had left in the containers became too salty as we got hit by big waves the night before. It was impossible to drink it even if we tried. We had no choice but to dump it into the ocean. We watched one of the men pour the water out as we threw away one of our modes of survival. It was painful to see it disappear right in front of our eyes. That early afternoon, we became dehydrated and desperate for water. Even generating saliva was extremely hard with a dry throat and lips. The sun was ruthless, leaving us with scorching burns. One of the kids my age was crying out of thirst, and in a moment of despair, the father had to urinate in a container and give it to his son to drink to save him from dying of dehydration.

"Let's just turn around and go back home," still that same man screamed.

"How do we go back? We don't even know where we are right now," another argued.

"We're going to die. We're all going to die," another one violently sobbed.

By now, I got used to all the back-and-forth screaming. I did not think they wanted to argue; they just needed something to keep them occupied and not to face another day lost at sea. I looked away and into the water, wondering how much longer we could endure until we reached freedom.

As the fifth day came, we had no food, no water, and no sense of direction. We were very much on the brink of losing a fight against the ocean. We were alive but felt dead inside. The heat took a toll on everyone—enough to make some murmur, "Just let me die." The captain had indeed lost his motivation to continue. We could see in his face how he did not want to take control of the steering wheel. He stopped the engine and simply let the boat float. Everyone sat there in silence, feeling defeated, not knowing what to do.

"Nam Mo Quan The Am Bo Tat (*Buddha bless us*)," one man chanted.

At this point, we had nothing to lose, as we lost everything. One by one, out of despair, we collectively joined him. We pressed our hands together, closed our eyes, and chanted the same prayer. Soon enough, everyone on the boat was praying for help. I remembered Ba Noi once told me about Quan The Am Bo Tat (*The Goddess of Mercy*), one of the Bodhisattva, who was known as the pinnacle of mercy, compassion, kindness, and love. She, who had earned to leave the world of suffering and was destined to become a Buddha, had forgone the bliss of nirvana with a vow to save all people who asked for her help. Ba Noi also said, whenever I felt like I was in danger and in need of protection, I should call her name, Quan The Am Bo Tat.

"Nam Mo Quan The Am Bo Tat," we prayed. "Nam Mo Quan The Am Bo Tat."

Dark ominous clouds appeared. The chanting stopped as everyone looked up. The sun died down and the air became moist. A sign of an intense storm was heading our way. I felt a wave of fear rush within me and imagined our boat being blown away. Most of us began to cry thinking of how devastating it would be to have our last moments at sea. I was so scared as my heart pounded fast, aware that this could be the end of our journey. Everyone was on their knees and the chanting escalated.

In that split second, I felt a raindrop on my forehead, thinking this was it. Finally, this beautiful but vicious ocean will take me under, and Chi Trang's friend wouldn't be there to save me. The image of my family flipped through my mind. I closed my eyes and was ready to accept my fate. Suddenly, I heard someone scream, "It's raining. It's raining."

I opened my eyes and looked up at the sky. The dark clouds were still there, but no wind, no storm… only the rain pouring down. Everyone was laughing, cheering, and hugging each other. Some had their heads down, saying thank you to Quan The Am Bo Tat for blessing us with the rain. Some were scuttling around finding all the jars and containers to fill the rainwater for the days ahead. I just stood there with my mouth wide open. I wanted to enjoy every drop of this precious water.

After five more minutes of rain, the dark clouds faded, and the sun began to shine again. We captured enough water in the containers to last us another day. Our prayers worked. I would never forget that moment. Buddha heard our prayers and gave us life in the form of raindrops that fell from the sky.

3 "Jellyfish" Island

In the morning of the sixth day, as we continued to drift, someone spotted land. However, the site did not look like the one we saw on our second day at the Hainanese village. There were no palm trees or houses like ours back home. We were also fairly sure it wasn't Vietnam since we had been going North towards Hong Kong. This time, we weren't afraid of being imprisoned by the Vietnamese communists. We were afraid of what all the boat people wouldn't want to encounter – Pirates.

The stories of the pirates, who lived on islands along the shore waiting to capture the boat people, had been shared among us on the first day I onboarded. Pirates would chase after them and get on their boats, take their valuables, rape the women, and kidnap the children to sell them. Besides the dangerous storms, the pirates were the second thing that boat people like us never wanted to experience. With that in mind, the captain slowly steered the boat parallel to the land to see if anyone was waiting to come after us.

After about thirty minutes as the captain assessed the area, he saw no signs of pirates. He decided to pull closer to the shore. When we got a bit closer, someone screamed, "Jellyfish!" We made it to the island with lots of jellyfish. We finally found another food source. The captain got us closer to the shallow water, took another look for his last evaluation, then decided that we should stay here for a short break since everyone was stuck on the boat for quite some time. All the men jumped off the boat and helped pull the boat onto the sand.

From the exhausted look on everyone's faces, no one disagreed with him. We got off the boat and walked to the beach. Everyone lay down on the soft sand, feeling at ease with the soft morning breeze. I finally could stretch out my arms and legs without touching anyone else. I had laid down on the sand before, as my house was right on the beach, but I had never felt this relaxed and relieved, for I hadn't been able to stretch out my limbs in days. While closing my eyes for a quick nap, I could still feel the boat rocking back and forth, although I was on land.

While everyone was relishing the comfort of laying down on the beach, taking our minds off the unwanted reality, one of our men spotted a few people coming toward us. Immediately, he alerted everyone, urging everybody to get on their feet in case we had to evacuate. Panic arose, as people feared they would be pirates. We all desperately turned to the captain, hoping he would have a plan. However, the captain was just as scared and clueless as we were. The people walked closer to us, and to our surprise, these people were not pirates but the local people of this island. They came and greeted us in Chinese. Once again, one of our men responded in Vietnamese and used hand signals as we did with those fishermen on the sea. Without needing to say or do more, they knew that we were boat people from Vietnam and that we needed help. It appeared we were not the first group that stopped by on this island and sought help.

They left after talking to our men, and I wasn't sure if they understood us. However, they came back after a while with food and water. We were happy and thanked them as well as our men for being experts with "hand signals" that helped us have another meal. After lunch, the captain asked Ba and a couple of men to walk with him to check the area while everyone else rested on the sand. When they came back, the captain announced, "Let's stay here for the night. It's better than floating in the middle of the ocean."

We all quickly got together and tried to prepare food. The women went back to the boat to get pots and pans that they had brought along, while the men roamed further inland to collect wood to create a fire. Some went to catch the jellyfish that we saw earlier so we could have some meat, which we had been craving for the last six days. Luckily, we still had some rice left in the container – enough to make congee for dinner.

After a couple of hours of preparing and cooking a simple dish – congee and jellyfish filled our tummies. We were happy that we didn't have to eat the hardened rice roll again. As the night came, we all sat around the fire that we made for cooking earlier and shared stories of "finding freedom." Some were there with their entire families, some were there with a son or a daughter like us, and some were there alone. We all had different backgrounds and situations, but we all had one thing in common: we had no idea where or how to find "freedom." All we knew was that if we took the boat out to sea, eventually someone would come to rescue us. Sadly, it was already the sixth day, and we still hadn't been rescued.

That night, sleeping on the beach, I remembered the time my siblings and I were laying on the sand under the moon in front of our house. We asked each other what we wanted to be when we grew up. We teased each other for choosing professions we knew nothing about. Our laughter filled the house, inviting Ong Noi to come and join the fun with his beloved grandkids. Ong Noi would tell us the stories of how he became a carpenter until we were all tired and fell asleep. I wondered what my siblings were doing. Were they sleeping on the beach and looking at the same moon that I was looking at, missing me just like I was missing them? Deep in my thoughts, I fell asleep with a beautiful dream that I was back at home with my loved ones.

I woke up early in the morning of the seventh day feeling well-rested thanks to a satisfying meal the day before and the dream that eased my mind the night before. I looked around and saw a few of our men holding fishing nets that we had on our boat. They walked toward the ocean and jumped in. I ran over to see what they were doing. After a few minutes of swimming, they pulled up the nets and it was filled with small fish. I looked at the fish and it reminded me of the time when Chi Trang and I went to ask for fish from the fishermen so Ma could make her signature dish. I swallowed my saliva as the spicy taste of the chili pepper was still tingling on my tongue. I wondered which of my siblings would help Ma cut it now that I was not around.

Shortly after everyone woke up that morning, the captain told us to gather around as he had news and wanted to share it with us. After checking on the boat that morning, he found that the two-cylinder engine had failed. However, he assured us we were in good hands since we had a mechanic on board with us, Chu Tien. He had brought spare parts in case something like this happened.

We thought Chu Tien could get the boat fixed by the afternoon, then we would hop back on and continue our way. Anyhow, it took longer than we expected. We ended up staying on that beach for the next four days. Since we ran out of rice, the women and children had to go inland to beg for food. Fortunately, we met those local people who helped us before, and they gave us rice and vegetables. We continued to have the same meal every day, but nobody bothered to complain due to starvation.

On the eleventh day, after four days of working hard fixing the engine without proper tools, Chu Tien gave us the good news that we could continue our journey after lunch. Everyone was happy that we could get back on the boat, but at the same time, we were hesitant due to the fear of the sea's uncertainty. However, this island wasn't what we set out to find. We cleared the site and got back on the boat. Thanks to the kindness of the inland people, they gave us some dried food and a few more gallons of water and fuel to get back on our journey. We departed that afternoon and headed for the unknown that awaited us.

The captain had a new plan this time. Instead of going farther out into the ocean, he decided to go along the shore. From what Ba told me later, the captain was worried that the engine might fail again, and he would rather be close to land and get help than be stranded in the middle of the ocean. The other reason was that if we followed the coastline of China, eventually we would be closer to Hong Kong, which at the time was under the British government, and our chances for rescue would be higher.

For the next two days, we made sure to keep sight of land on our left side as we headed northeast along the coast of China. Although we kept on going, at times the captain would turn off the engine to conserve fuel and optimistically hope to be rescued while idling. We were lucky that there hadn't been any storms or big waves ever since we got back on the boat. However, the nights at sea always frightened me. It was pitch black in the middle of the ocean and I couldn't see who was sitting close to me. That same scary feeling at Ba's friend's house the night we left Vietnam crept up on me every time. The constant ocean waves hitting the side of the boat made me dizzy until I fell asleep. I dreamt of the boat being beaten away and the water would eventually penetrate the side of the boat and kill us all. I woke up and was relieved that it was only a dream. I closed my eyes and called for Buddha's name once again to bring us safety.

The next morning, I was feeling fearful and weary since I could not go back to sleep after that scary dream. I looked around to see those familiar faces that I'd been with… they all had lost weight after two weeks on this journey to freedom. Their faces were darker, and I could see their cheekbones more pronounced from lack of food and sleep and being under the sun.

Although Chu Tien had fixed the cylinders, the engine kept on sputtering. Due to the lack of actual tools, he couldn't get it all fixed last time. He suggested to the captain that we look for another place to stop so he could take a look at it again. By the afternoon, we passed by a shore and the captain decided to make another stop so Chu Tien could fix the engine and we could find food. One of the ladies who had been taking care of the food declared that we were running short. At this point, everyone was exhausted. They did not care whether the captain wanted to continue or stop to fix the engine or even find food.

Albeit we had been lucky to have not come across those pirates yet, the captain was always cautious every time he tried to approach any island. He would assess the site to make sure there was no suspicious activity or any sign of those bandits. Just like usual, the captain slowed down the boat but had one of our men ready to pick up the speed in case we were under attack. However, as the boat got a bit closer, we saw people working on the beach drying mackerels. Seeing no signs of danger or abnormalities, the captain signaled our men to have the boat move in toward the shore.

"Do you think it's safe to stop here?" Ba asked the captain

"We are desperate. The engine is dying, and we need to find food," the captain responded. "These people seem fine."

And just like the captain predicted, as these people saw our boat coming in, they ran toward us and helped to pull the boat to shore. Surprised by their kind gestures, we did not doubt that we were in a safe place. Once again, with our hand signals, we rubbed our stomachs as a sign to show our starvation. They nodded their heads with a smile and motioned us to get off the boat. We followed them and walked past trays of dried mackerel. The smell of the dried fish made us even hungrier. Some of our ladies joked that she wouldn't mind staying here eating these fishes forever.

After a few yards of walking, they took us back to their working site. There was a big space with a hay roof but no walls around and some wooden platforms inside. I guessed it must've been their resting area. They had us sit on those platforms and some of the men brought us rice and dried mackerels. At that moment, nothing tasted better. We peeled through the skin of the fish and the dry meat was simply perfect with a bowl of hot rice. We were so hungry, and the food was tasteful that we didn't hesitate to ask for even a third bowl. As we were still eating and enjoying the flavor of the dried fish, we saw a group of men in uniform walking quickly toward us. Everyone stopped eating and sat in silence.

"I think they are policemen," one of our men whispered.

"Just try to act normal and don't alert them," the captain whispered back.

We listened to the captain and stopped looking their way. We started to eat again but tried not to make noise either. We acted as normal as we could. One of the men that brought us food walked to those policemen and greeted them. We didn't want to draw any attention to the policemen, so we just glanced over sometimes to see what they were doing. The distance was a bit far for us to hear them, but the man pointed to our boat, then pointed to us as he tried to explain something. Those policemen quietly listened then all left and the man slowly headed back. The situation wasn't good. We all looked at the captain and waited for his foresight.

"Tien, can you take a look at the engine and see if it can be fixed quickly?" the captain asked.

"Let me see what I can do," Tien said.

"Once you get it done, we'll be out of here instantly," the captain said.

Chu Tien and one of our men immediately ran back to the boat and inspected the engine. After a few minutes, the man came back to deliver the news that Chu Tien needed to change one of the hoses, but the engine was too hot to fix it. He had to wait for it to cool down. When I heard him say *hoses*, I remembered the night before when I couldn't go back to sleep because of a bad dream. Ba thought I was cold and told me to go underneath the deck of the boat to stay warm. It was too dark and low that I had to crawl in to find a comfortable spot to lie down. I remembered bumping into something hot. I did not think anything of it since I was tired and just wanted to lie down and sleep. It must have been me who loosened the hose.

As we were sitting on the beach, praying that Chu Tien would get it fixed soon, we felt a strong gust of wind blowing toward us, and the sky darkened as opaque clouds covered it. We looked around and saw men gathering their belongings, quickly putting the dried fish in the baskets, and running. They pointed to the sky, screaming in a language we could not comprehend. Understanding their panic, we ran with them to hide from the upcoming storm.

"Let's follow these people! I think they are heading to their hiding places!" the captain shouted. "You all join them first. I'll go get Tien and will catch up with you all."

Like an army that obeyed their commander's order in a decisive moment, we followed these men, hoping they would take us to a safe place. While we were running, one of the men we met on the shore turned and tried to say something. He kept pointing at a building in front of us. We sensed that he wanted us to go there for shelter. The captain and Chu Tien were quick. They caught up with us and we all ran toward the building. There we saw those policemen waving their hands to tell us to come in. It was a police station and as we walked in, they had us sit in the hallway. After waiting for us to settle in, they brought out hot congee for everyone.

It was getting dark, but the wind and rain were still quite strong outside. There was no way for us to get back on the boat and be in the ocean under this weather condition. The policemen seemed to know what was on our minds, and using their hand gestures again, they invited us to stay for the night. Without any hesitation, we gratefully took the offer. That night, twenty-five of us were in one open space, sleeping peacefully despite the rain and wind.

Early in the morning of the fourteenth day, Chu Tien, the captain, and a few of our men headed out to the boat to continue fixing the engine while the rest of us stayed back with the policemen. We felt grateful they were never any harm to us. They gave us dried food, water, and a few more containers of fuel. Everyone left the police station and got back to the boat to continue our journey. Later that day, I heard from Chu Tien that the hoses were disconnected. He had to reconnect the whole thing, which was why it took him a long time. He couldn't figure out what was the cause for it to detach like that. I was afraid to say anything because I didn't want to create another commotion. However, I told myself that I would never go down the deck again regardless of the reasons.

4 The Barge

After leaving what we called "The Policemen Shore," I noticed a change of atmosphere in the boat; the screaming and yelling ceased. Even the captain regained his positive outlook knowing that the engine was completely fixed. It must've been a big relief for him knowing it would no longer be a hindrance to our journey. It looked to be a good sign that we were heading in the right direction since no arguments occurred. We saw hope in front of us.

However, in the afternoon when the sun's rays hit us directly, everyone was motionless on the deck of the boat. Some were lying with their legs hanging over the edge letting them drag along the water. I was beaten and had to rest my head on Ba's lap while he was leaning against the side of the boat wearily. Everyone was lifeless and ready to surrender to this ghastly journey.

Suddenly we heard a loud engine roar. I opened my eyes and saw a fast movement from a distance. It was nothing I had seen before and was quite different from the boats that we had encountered during this journey so far. The boat was enclosed and traveled on metal rails on both sides of it. Later, I learned it was a hydrofoil, a boat that carried passengers from Macau to Hong Kong. As we were consumed watching a few of the hydrofoils, someone pointed to the land. It was different from what he had seen during this journey. The structure of homes was much bigger. We didn't know which part of China we were near; however, something bigger caught our eyes.

"Look! A ship. A big ship!" we all screamed.

"I think we are in safe waters now!" the captain cheerfully announced.

Everyone stood, raised our hands, and screeched for help as loud as we could. I had never screamed louder than that. My lungs were about to jump out of that little chest of mine. All the men took off their shirts and waved them in the air. We screamed and beseeched loudly, hoping to receive another miracle.

As we saw the ship approach us, we got down on our knees and prayed to Buddha that this would be the ship that we had been waiting for, the one that would rescue us. When the ship got closer to us, it seemed they knew we were the boat people who were waiting to be rescued. They nodded their heads and signaled us to turn off the engine. As soon as they pulled their ship next to us, one of them threw a rope ladder down to the side of their ship. Tears ran down our faces, but this time they were tears of joy. We could not believe we were finally rescued after thinking that "hope" was out of our reach.

They showed us signs that they were Macau Coast guard and motioned for the women and children to grab onto the ladder to climb up. One by one, we lined up and clutched the dangling rope to get onto their ship. Dehydration and starvation made everyone's legs wobble as we tried to move up the steps on the ladder. I watched them struggle and prayed for all of us not to slip and fall into the ocean.

"Be careful. Hold on tight to the rope, and I'll see you up there soon," Ba told me when it was my turn.

"Yes, Ba." I nodded my head as I tried to be brave.

I grabbed onto the ladder and slowly pulled myself up each step. I could feel the struggle of those who had gone before me. The rope felt unstable as it was swaying each time I attempted to step up. I took a quick glimpse at Ba as he was watching me from the bottom. That sight from above was petrifying as the vertical distance between Ba and me got farther. Feeling afraid of slipping and falling, I gripped tightly onto the ladder, clinching five fingers at a time with each step that I took. When I almost got to the top, a coast guard reached out his hand, and I immediately grabbed onto him as he pulled me onboard. I looked down again to see the relief on Ba's face. After all the women and children got on the ship, two of the coast guards, one at the front and one at the back, threw two thick ropes down to our boat. They signaled Ba and the men to tie them onto the front and back of the boat. However, they did not signal for any of the men to climb up the ladder.

Within a moment, the coast guard ship revved up the engine, and they carried our boat along on the side of their ship. I could hear some women screaming their husbands' names while their kids were profusely calling for their fathers. I was just as startled as why the men were not on the ship with us. Why didn't they let Ba come up? Where would they take Ba? Would they capture Ba and sell him to the pirates? So many questions were going through my head, but the brain of a seven-year-old just couldn't come up with any answers, which confused me more. Thoughts of being separated from Ba scared me even more than the time I almost drowned back home. I couldn't be with Ma already and I didn't want to be apart from Ba too.

After an hour that felt like forever, the coast guards escorted us to a barge in the middle of the ocean. They docked their ship to the barge and finally signaled for Ba with the rest of the men to climb up the ladder. The reason that the coast guards wanted to keep the men in our boat was that they wanted to be cautious in case we tried to seize their ship.

I ran towards Ba with all my might and gave him a big hug the minute he got off the ladder. I held him so tight and didn't want to let go; I was afraid he might be taken away from me again. I told myself that I would stick to him like glue from now on, no matter what. All the women and children were crying and hugging their husbands and fathers. I could see an enormous relief on Ba's face and all the men's faces as they finally got to be with their loved ones again. It was a joyful reunion for all of us.

As we were lining up to disembark onto the barge, I saw hundreds of Vietnamese of all ages, from children younger than me to adults of Ong Noi's age. I wondered if this was it, the end of our journey. I hoped it was because I never wanted to step back onto that little boat again. As we were standing on the barge waiting for the instructions, someone screamed to look at our boat. Everyone turned around and saw our little boat being raised by a crane and then crushed in a bin on the barge. We sadly stood there watching our boat get dismantled. Although there were times that we all got sick and tired of being stuck on that boat and couldn't wait to get off, we felt a part of our possession being taken away. I would never forget the fourteen-day journey on that boat, facing many ordeals and keeping us afloat on the South China Sea. It was an incredible journey, and we were extremely lucky to stay alive.

On the barge, large tents were set up from one end to the other. Ba and I were assigned to the same tent with the captain. As the three of us entered the tent, I noticed it was one big open space, similar to the size of our room in the village, which could snugly fit ten people. A few people were lying in the tent with fatigued looks on their faces, while some greeted us and told us to find any spot we liked. It didn't seem much to choose from. All three of us sat in the middle of the tent, but it didn't take long before we were all lying down with our eyes closed, drifting asleep.

At mid-morning, there was a smaller ship compared to the Macau coast guards that came to drop off food for us. Everyone on the barge lined up and wondered what they were feeding us. When I approached the server, he handed me a bowl of rice and a can of sardines. I received my portion and followed Ba and the captain back to the tent. Just when everyone gathered behind on the cemented floor of the barge, we gobbled the rice and sardines within minutes. The taste of the marinated sardines reminded me of Ma's signature dish. I didn't know if I was hungry or because I got to try something new for the first time.

I looked out of the tent and saw people being loaded onto the boat that just dropped off the food. We didn't know where these people were brought to since we couldn't understand what they said. Still, we wanted to be on that boat because the barge wasn't what we had in mind for what we set out to find.

After seven days of living on the barge, finally, all the people from our boat along with some others got picked up. We were excited yet anxious about what our next destination might be. One thing was for sure—we were getting closer to our goal. The boat ride was about fifteen minutes long. From a distance, I noticed tall buildings next to each other, and I wondered if this was where they would have stayed. When the boat arrived, we were told we were in

Hong Kong. From the early 1980s to the mid-1990s, the Hong Kong government accommodated the influx of Vietnamese boat people.

We got off the boat and were taken to a tall building by bus. For the first time in my life, I set foot in a building. Up until this point, I'd only experienced life in the countryside, walking barefoot in the sand and dirt, showering with water from a well, and living in a small house with no separate rooms. Standing in front of this building made me feel so small. I wondered how a building could be this tall. It was only three stories high, but when I first laid eyes on it, it looked like a skyscraper. This building took my breath away, and I could not wait to go inside and explore its massiveness.

The interpreters greeted us at the door and asked us to follow them. One of the interpreters handed Ba a few forms and asked him to fill out as much as he could remember. These forms would be what we needed to apply for asylum later on. After completing the forms, we were told to stay in this building for the next couple of days to learn English and wait for them to process the paperwork. Before allowing all of us into our assigned rooms, we were lined up to be sprayed with chemicals. They wanted to make sure we wouldn't bring any kind of diseases into their country. Then, we were given new clothes and sent to our assigned rooms. The room had four bunk beds. Ba and I were on one side, and another two men on our boat were across from us. We were happy with the arrangement since we all knew each other. That night, before we went to bed, Ba and the two men were chanting, calling the Buddha's name in gratitude for guarding us during our journey and bringing us to a safe place.

The next morning, I felt someone moving my body as I was in a deep sleep. With my eyes half-opened, I saw Ba patting my shoulder and saying, "Wake up, Con. You have to go to school."

"This is not Vietnam and I don't know the language, Ba," I whined.

"That's why you need to go so they can teach you English," Ba replied.

I knew when it came to studying, I couldn't argue or change Ba's mind. I got off the bed feeling unhappy, but I was raised never to disobey my parents. At that moment, I tried to be positive and thought of how amazing it would be if I could speak another language. I put on the new clothes that were given to us and followed Ba to school. We walked along the block in silence as my eyes were wandering tirelessly; I was still astonished by these building structures. Ba dropped me off and said that he would be heading to the nearby immigration office. He also said that he would be sending a telegraph to let Ong Noi and Ma know that we made it to Hong Kong. Instantly after hearing that, I immediately changed my mood. I wanted to let Ma know that I was there and safe.

I walked into the class and met my teacher at the door. She was American, in her thirties, with blonde hair and blue eyes. I looked at her wondering how was it that she was so different from me. Not only the differences in the colors of her hair, eyes, and skin but also the structure of her face. Her nose was much thinner and pointy, and her eyes were caved into the sockets. With curiosity still running in my head, she said hello in Vietnamese. The students she had been teaching were Vietnamese boat people, so they taught her a little of the language. She asked for my name and showed me my seat. There were about twenty kids of different ages, and also some adults in the class as well. I was happy to see the kids on my boat there too. She started the first lesson by teaching us how to greet and introduce ourselves.

"Good morning. My name is Linh," I said, following her instructions. It sounded funny hearing it as all the students were giggling while repeating the sentence. However, the longer we practiced, the more we took learning the new language seriously.

Lunch break was around noon. The class followed her to another area which was a couple of rooms down the hall. There was rice with chicken and soymilk on the side. Growing up in the countryside, I'd never had a chance to drink any form of milk besides my mother's when she was nursing me. I didn't know what it was but seeing other kids drinking it, I didn't mind having some. The soy milk came in a small carton. I squeezed one end on top of the carton to open it and folded at the corner to create a spout. I took the first sip of the soy milk and to my amazement, the thick sweet milk took over the entirety of my tongue as I slowly swallowed it. It was something that I had never tasted before. I continued to suck on my tongue to relieve the sweetness that was still on the surface of the tongue and in my mouth. The smell and taste of that soy milk still linger in my mouth after all this time. I asked the lady who handed me my lunch if I could have another carton of soymilk. I wanted to give it to Ba so he could try it too. She nodded her head and gave me one.

School ended after the lunch break. Ba was waiting for me outside of the classroom as we were wrapping up to end our first class. As we were walking home, I excitedly raved about school and the soy milk. I managed to fit the carton into my pocket and pulled it out to show him. I could see the smile on his face as he wondered if the soy milk was as good as I described it. As soon as we entered our room, I opened the soymilk for Ba to try. As I expected, his eyes brightened with surprise. He took another sip and told me to finish the rest since he could see my eyes were also gazing at the milk carton.

I continued to learn English and brought the soymilk home to share with Ba every day. After class, there wasn't much for us to do besides stay in our rooms. On the morning of the third day, we were informed by the interpreters that our paperwork had been cleared. We would be moving to our next destination. All the people on our boat were happy thinking that our journey on the open sea to search for freedom arrived. We finally found what we had been looking for. I couldn't wait to start our new life with "freedom" which Ba and everyone were willing to risk their lives searching for.

5 Hong Kong Refugee Camp

With my face up against the glass window, different shades of green taking the form of trees captivated my eyes. It was a bright day, with the sun highlighting the most beautiful parts of Hong Kong. On April 28th, 1982, we arrived at the Argyle Center refugee camp. When we got off the bus, I noticed thousands of other Vietnamese adults, children, and even babies. Were these people here for "freedom" too? When Ba was explaining to me about "freedom," he seemed happy about it, determined to obtain it, however, the people around me looked lifeless and hopeless. The atmosphere of the refugee camp was also vastly different from the views of before. All I could see were six long shelters with blue tin roofs and small windows on both sides. The entire area was built on dry dirt. I could see how the environment affected the moods of everyone here. We were ordered to get in line and enter the main building, which looked like all the other shelters but was instead used for the immigration office, school, cafeteria, and clinic. There, they checked our paperwork and gave each person two pairs of pants, shirts, and towels, then assigned us to one of the shelters. Once again, we were in the same shelter with the captain.

Inside the shelter was one open space, with bunk beds alongside the walls, leaving the middle area as a walkway. We got assigned beds on the left side of the windows, while the captain was next to us. I slept on the top and Ba was on the bottom. Outside of the shelter were a couple of public shared bathrooms. The showers and stalls were right next to each other, so whenever I used the bathroom, at least ten other people were in there with me. The bathroom was where we also washed our clothes, but there was usually no soap. We washed our two pairs of clothing and let them hang over our beds to dry.

Each morning, around 10:00 AM, all the children gathered and walked to the main building for school. An English teacher was assigned to teach us how to speak and pronounce the language, but at times, our accents were so rooted in us that it was too difficult. Although I had learned the word "morning" at school before arriving at the refugee camp, I still had a hard time getting the "or" sound together. I practiced curling my tongue for that ability.

Our class usually lasted for two hours and then lunch would begin in the cafeteria, open to everyone. The food was the same every day: white rice with stir-fried bean sprouts. However, at least it was much better than the hard-rolled rice on the boat, so not one soul complained about it. Some would bring it back to the shelter, while others got together and sat on the dried dirt, enjoying their meal and conversations.

The best part of our meal was when they gave us a can of condensed milk filled with sugary goodness. Ba and I would take turns sucking on the thickened milk from the can. It could last for days as we stored it by our bunk beds.

After lunch, the kids were allowed to play. We gathered outside of the main building, sitting, talking, and running around on the dried dirt. I taught the other kids the game "Cong Ngua (Horse Ride)," a game that I used to play at school in Vietnam. One team member gets on the back of one of the other team members in a horse-riding position. The team on the top would throw a ball to the other. If the ball drops, then we have to switch positions and carry the other team in a horse-riding position. While playing the game, somehow, it felt as though I never left Vietnam.

After break time, we got back to class and studied some more. Being kids, we were excited at the end of the day, since we would continue to hang out by our shelters and play some more.

When I got back from playing, Ba would tell me to head to the public bathroom to shower before going to the cafeteria for dinner. While walking to the main building, Ba asked, "How was your day, Con?"

"It was hard to learn English, but I had lots of fun playing with my new friends," I answered.

I told him about how I taught the kids Cong Ngua. I could see the smile on his face knowing that I was making new friends and getting along with other kids at the camp.

"It will get better with English, but I am glad that you are having fun with your friends," Ba said.

"How about you, Ba? How was your day?" I asked

"Same for me. I learned English and also met new friends," Ba said.

The campsite was separated from the outside by chain-linked fences that were over six feet tall. We were forbidden to go beyond the fences or there would be consequences. The security guards constantly monitored the site, catching those who tried to break the rules. However, after eating the same food every day, it became distasteful. We also got fed up staying within the wired fences. We had escaped our country to find freedom, and yet, we were now confined within a different space—a refugee camp.

Word had traveled that we could find work outside of the camp by working for the locals at the market. We could make money to buy food and other personal items. People started to climb over the fences and were creative and stealthy enough to get through the security guards. They would come back with food and personal items to share amongst themselves. Delighted to receive something new for their taste buds, the escapees could care less about being caught. They were excited even if they were only able to bring back just a pack of cigarettes.

One day, Ba told me, "Linh, hang out with your friends after class today. I will be back in the afternoon."

"Where are you going?" I asked.

"I am going outside with my friends to find work and will get you something good to eat," Ba whispered. I couldn't concentrate in school that morning. I kept thinking of my dad climbing over the fence and what would happen if he was caught. It scared me thinking of him getting in trouble with the security guards. Out of habit, I called on Buddha's name to help keep my dad safe wherever he was.

After school, I didn't want to be with other kids. Instead, I walked up to the fence, looking outside, hoping to see a sign of Ba, but he was nowhere to be seen. Later that night, Ba came back with his friends who had joined him to explore the outside beyond the refugee camp. They brought back a few boxes of cigarettes and some other foods.

I was happy to see Ba come back safe and sound. I didn't bother to see what food Ba brought back. All I wanted was to hold his hands, afraid that he would leave me again. We were sitting outside in front of our shelter, sharing the food that Ba and his friends brought back, when one man said, "There is work out there. You work and they'd pay you."

"Do they pay well?" another man asked.

"Enough to have a few packs of cigarettes."

For these men, cigarettes were much better than sucking on condensed milk cans. Cigarettes somehow made them feel less lonely and eased their worries about this foreign land. To them, sitting together and sharing stories about their lives while smoking cigarettes made the time go by faster.

That night, I asked to sleep with Ba on his bed because I wanted to be next to him. While lying beside him, I could feel his uneasiness. I didn't know what was going on in his mind.

"Ba, is this the freedom you were looking for?" I had been wanting to ask Ba ever since we got here because I didn't think life here was any better than in Vietnam. But there, at least I had Ma, my siblings, Ong Noi, and Ba Noi. I felt lonely and missed them every day.

Ba looked shocked to hear my question. He held me closer and said, "It will get better soon, Con."

Even though he answered me, I felt like he was reassuring himself. And although it was dark and I could not see, I knew he was suppressing his tears. I heard his sniffling and felt his tears wetting the pillow we shared. He was always a reserved person, but that was the first moment I witnessed a strong emotion coming out of him.

Ba and the men continued to sneak out for work. The rumor of making money outside of the camp was spread among shelters and that alerted the guards. The camp officials imposed a strict rule prohibiting anyone to climb the fence and leave the site for any purpose. They installed barbed wire on top of the fences, which was very sharp and would pierce even the thickest skin. Those who were caught were beaten by the guards with a baton, right in front of everyone. I was scared to death after witnessing a public beating and made Ba promise not to go outside for work again. After seeing the look on my face and the consequences that the men who climbed over the fence faced, Ba stopped.

Ba and I made many friends during our stay at the camp. The stories that we exchanged during meals and before bed about our lives back in Vietnam and the boat journeys, created a strong bond among us. After all, we were all victims of the communist regime.

After the fall of Saigon in 1975, lives changed completely for the worse. The communists took over Southern Vietnam by taking away the people's freedom, currency, and liberty. All families lost everything regardless of being rich or poor. No one would be able to challenge the communist government. If anyone refused to give up their wealth, they would be sent to the "New Economic Zones Program," which was implemented by the communist government, forcing men from their homes to relocate to uninhabited, mountainous, forested areas, and expecting them to plow the land to turn it into an agricultural zone. In addition, the communist government prohibited anyone to pursue a higher education except those in their parties. Therefore, Ba was stripped from his education to be a doctor and lost his dream. There was no hope for our family to be better off.

Everyone at the refugee camp shared the same situation as our life's possessions were taken from us. We had no choice but to leave our motherland to search for a better life, wherever that would be. We didn't care about the risks that may lie ahead. The stories we shared brought joy and tears as we took turns detailing some of the obstacles that were faced at sea. However, these stories reminded me not to lose hope and continue with our journey to find the freedom that we set out to seek.

The next two months at the Argyle Center were merely a matter of interviewing and waiting for the U.S. Immigration Office to let us know when we could leave for America. Ba took the interviewing seriously. Every day, I would hear him mumble his answers to the questions he thought they might ask at the interview. He didn't want to be unprepared, which might delay the approval process.

I learned later from Ba that those who had a clear record of employment with the government of South Vietnam would be qualified to immigrate to the U.S.A in general. In our case, since Ba showed them all the documents with pictures and official stamps thereupon, the U.S. consulate in Hong Kong accepted us right away.

After back-and-forth interviewing, Ba finally came back to give me the news.

"Are we going to America?" I asked excitedly.

"Yes, but we need to stay in the Philippines first," Ba answered.

I had never heard of the Philippines, but I was just as excited as Ba to know that we were leaving the refugee camp and getting closer to freedom.

Ba shared the good news with everyone at the Argyle camp. There were bittersweet tears and hugs once again. One of the ladies who was on the boat with us came up to me and said, "Be a good boy for your dad." I nodded my head as a promise to them as well as to myself.

I overheard some of the ladies murmuring to each other, "I feel bad that Thuy has to take care of Linh."

I looked over at Ba while he was talking to his friends. I knew it had been tough for him ever since he took me on this journey. I wanted to hug him and tell him how much I appreciated him.

As the day got closer for us to leave, I started to miss all my friends. I thought about the Philippines and imagined how lonely I would be. I wondered if there would be any Vietnamese people in the Philippines.

One of my friends, Quoc, who was around my age, suggested a brilliant idea, saying, "Why don't you tell your father to wait for us? It would be fun if we all can go together."

That was a great idea. That way, I wouldn't be so lonely over in the Philippines. Problem solved. "Yes, let me ask my dad later," I said.

"Just make believe that you are sick, then you don't have to go," Chien, another one of my friends, said.

As much as I wanted to be with my friends, the thought of lying to my dad made me feel extremely guilty. After all, I did promise to be a good boy. I told Chien and Quoc that I would ask

Ba, but faking to be sick was not an option. I wouldn't want Ba to worry because of my selfishness.

The night, during dinner, I asked Ba, "Can we wait a little longer and go with our friends to the Philippines?"

"It is not up to us. The Immigration Service said we have to go." Ba smiled while acknowledging my request. He patted my head knowing how much I clicked with the kids at the camp.

Later on, I learned that the Immigration Service decided who would go depending on the answers given during the interview. Ba must have been consistent with his answers, so we got to go first. The nights of him mumbling words were to help us get to this moment. He was always prepared.

That night, I couldn't help but feel restless. I kept thinking about life in the Philippines. I was excited, but I was also very conflicted. Going to the Philippines was one step closer to freedom, yet one step farther from Ma and my siblings. I wondered how they were back at home. I wondered if they missed us and if I would be able to see them again. I called for Ma and my siblings in my mind as tears ran down my face.

I missed Ong Noi too. I missed how he spoiled me every time I asked for a horse ride. He would let me climb on his sixty-year-old back and carry me around the house during late afternoons when the temperature got cooler. Ong Noi never complained about me being heavy or told me to get down so he could take a break. I missed walking with him along the beach to cut some cactus leaves so Ma could make cactus soup for dinner, which was another signature dish of hers. I missed home and everything there. Reminiscing about the past felt exactly like a dream. As I dozed off, I hoped to continue this dream that I could only hold onto for a couple of hours until I awoke again to the cold reality.

The next morning, Ba and I got up early to get ready for our departure. We packed our stuff: two pairs of pants, shirts, and a towel, which were given to us during our first day at the camp.

Our friends gathered near the bus parking area as we said goodbye. We promised to see each other again but didn't know how or when that would be. As the bus was leaving the camp, I saw Quoc and Chien crying and waving at me. I felt a strange knot in my stomach as I just lost two good friends, not knowing when I would see them again.

When we got to the airport, I thought I was in another world. Feeling like a country bumpkin, I looked curiously and saw hundreds of people swarming the gigantic halls pushing large luggage, as the sound of the intercom filled my ears. My eyes darted to the big vehicles placed outside the airport and I asked my father, "Ba, what are these things with wings?"

"They're called airplanes," Ba said.

We walked inside the airplane, and I felt so small. It was much bigger on the inside. There were many seats, and I wondered how it was possible to have many people up in the air. Ba showed the airplane tickets to the flight attendant, and she walked us to our seats. We walked down the very long aisle until Ba stopped and sat at the seat closest to the window. I was very curious to see the view outside, so I asked him if I could take his seat. Ba smiled. He nodded and told me to slide over.

After a very long wait, the airplane started to move to the runway and suddenly accelerated. I was nervous as I processed the fact that this big machine making a rumbling noise was really going to take off. I grabbed onto Ba's arm, felt a lightness of weight, and finally the plane was off the ground. My heart was beating fast as I wondered how this plane was capable of flying. Out of anxiety, I could barely open my mouth to ask my father if we were okay. I closed my eyes, braced onto his forearm with both hands, and prayed to Buddha to keep us safe.

A few minutes later, the plane ascended into the sky. I opened my eyes to look out the window to see the bright blue sky and fluffy white clouds. I couldn't believe it with my own eyes as I remembered when we prayed to Quan The Am Buddha during the time we were at sea, and she brought the rain to us. I felt as though, once again, she was there with her arms gracefully wrapped around the airplane, helping us stay afloat. With my mind now at ease, I knew that she would take us to our next destination safely. I was able to drift into a peaceful sleep and dream of my new life in the Philippines.

6 Bataan, Philippines

Ba and I landed at Manila Airport, Philippines, on June 12, 1982. We, along with other Vietnamese refugees, were picked up by the Philippines Immigration Services. The bus ride from the airport to our new refugee camp had different scenery to offer than in Hong Kong. The homes looked dilapidated similar to our village in Vietnam—no tall buildings, just simple single homes along the streets. It looked quite mundane in contrast to the vibrant city of Hong Kong.

After two hours of driving, we arrived at Bataan Refugee Camp Center (BRCC). We were greeted by an immigration officer as we got off the bus. They checked our documents and assigned us to our new living space. Instead of the open-space shelters that we shared with hundreds of people at the Argyle camp, there were rows of small huts with brick walls and tin roofs that would be shared among four people.

We walked to our assigned hut and saw two men about Ba's age approaching us.

"Welcome. I am Minh and he is Dao," one of the men said.

"I am Thuy, and this is my son, Linh."

"They told us that both of you were coming so that place over there is for you and your son." Minh pointed to the bed on the left side of the hut.

The hut was about twenty feet long and ten feet wide. There were two small beds with wooden platforms on the right that belonged to Minh and Dao. The bigger bed on the left and the long bench next to it for sitting would be ours.

After settling into our hut, Minh took us outside for a tour of the area. There were a couple of public bathrooms behind our hut. Minh pointed us to the male's bathroom, which was farther away from the females. The bathroom had one side for showering and the other side had a primitive canal with no flushing.

There was also a fire pit for cooking in front of the hut. Similar to the Argyle Refugee Camp, we picked up our food at a designated area near our hut. Since it was raw, we got to be our own chefs. Since pots and pans were already given to Minh and Dao when they first arrived, we cooked together during lunch and dinner.

Ba and I quickly adapted to the new life in Bataan after being told that we would be here for the next five months. For us refugees, before getting settled in a country that would grant us asylum, we needed to learn English and its culture while in the Philippines. This would help us adjust once we arrived at the resettlement.

Our daily routines here were not much different than in the Argyle Refugee camp. In the morning, Ba and I would go to school to learn English, but in separate locations. The school was more formal than the Argyle camp. Classes were divided between age groups rather than a large mixed group of kids of all ages as in Argyle. My teacher was an American lady. She was genuinely nice and patient with us. She kept on repeating words and phrases to us until we would get at least close to what she was teaching. There were times when the students would get rowdy, but she maintained her composure and only told us to calm down. Unlike schooling in Vietnam, when the students did not pay attention, the teacher would have the students stand in front of the classroom to then get spanked, as an example for everyone to see. I was glad that this teacher didn't punish us the same way. Learning English from her reminded me of the two months at Argyle. I still had trouble pronouncing the words and the sounds seemed different and funny to my ears.

Lunch was served at around noon. I was hoping there would be soymilk since the taste still lingered in my mouth, but sadly there was none. After finishing lunch, we got a short break for recess until class started again. The second portion of the class was doing math. This was my favorite part of going to school since I'd always enjoyed doing it. Back in Vietnam, Ong Noi always prepared me well when it came to math. He would make me recite the multiplication tables repeatedly until I memorized them completely. He wanted to prepare me well. Thanks to his preparation, I always got the questions correct. My teacher gave me two thumbs up, complimenting how fast I solved these math questions. I wished Ong Noi was there so that I could brag about how good I was with math. I bet he would have been proud of me.

School ended at 2:30 PM for the kids and adults. I walked home with other kids who lived near my hut, while Ba and the adults would go to another site for volunteer work, such as cleaning the community and the schools. They would come back around 5 PM to pick up food and prepare for dinner.

After dinner would be our study time. Ba and I went over some of the things that we had learned from school. I told him about my problems with English, especially pronouncing the words and understanding the English grammar. I opened my book and showed him some of the verb tenses that I didn't understand. Ba saw the frustrations on my face and said, "I have the same problem as you, too." Ba laughed.

"Why are there so many rules in English?" I asked.

"Well, we just have to keep on learning. Practice will make it better, Con," he answered.

The school gave everyone, kids and adults, the same vocabulary book. It had pictures of all subjects with English text next to it for easy understanding. Ba told me to try and study one page per day so that I could enhance my vocabulary. Despite the difficulty of learning English, I listened to Ba and made an effort to learn one page per day and practiced my grammar. I told myself I had to be able to speak English when I left for America.

Sleeping at night in Bataan was my least favorite part of the day. Since the weather was always hot there, we needed to leave the windows open, but that was also an invitation for mosquitoes and flies. Even though we slept with a net surrounding the bed, it couldn't stop the mosquitoes from biting us. Besides the annoying pests, the breeze that cooled us often brought an unpleasant smell from the public bathroom behind our hut. The extreme odor felt like a smack to the face, waking us up, and causing another sleepless night. These annoyances became my pet peeves when I was surrounded by mosquitoes.

Ba and I made more new friends, and they were nice like those in Argyle. Every time they cooked something, they would invite us over to share with them. I guess people felt sorry for us when they saw a single parent with a young child. One of our new friends, Chu (a *respectful way to call a male who is your parent's age in Vietnamese*) Cho, lived across from us with his entire family: his wife, Co (a *respectful way to call a female who is your parent's age in Vietnamese)* Tram, Ha, his daughter who was the same age as me, and Bi, his son who was a couple of years younger than me. Co Tram was known for cooking, and one of her special dishes was fish stew. This dish reminded me of Ma's signature dish. I got along with Ha and Bi. We walked to school every morning, and Ha was in the same class as me. I spent most of my time playing with them after school and on weekends.

My favorite part of the day was playing with Ha, Bi, and other kids after school. Since the rules in the Philippines were not as strict as in Argyle, there were no enclosed fences, and we were able to roam around the area. One day, we felt adventurous and decided to go beyond the woods and explore what was out there. Excitingly, we discovered a lake near a hill. The other kids were excited and took turns jumping into the lake for a refreshing swim. I was tempted to join, but Ong Noi's warning about getting close to the water and the image of me almost drowning in the ocean in Vietnam, re-emerged in my head. It stopped me from taking another step closer to the lake. I was afraid of drowning more than the embarrassment of not knowing how to swim.

As I was standing there watching everyone swim, one of the boys shouted, "What are you waiting for? Get in here!"

"I don't know how to swim," I yelled back.

"It's not hard, jump in and I will show you."

"I am fine here. I'll watch you guys."

I stood under a tree while watching them all swim freely and easily. I was wondering if I could do the same thing someday. At that moment I made a promise to myself that I would teach myself how to swim one day. Years later, I taught myself how to swim one night, alone in a pool for three hours.

One afternoon, Ba and Chu Cho brought home a few bottles of a black drink. They were raving about how great this drink tasted. We couldn't wait to sip it. As much as they were describing it to me, I just couldn't imagine what it tasted like. I would rather have it on my tongue and experience the sensation myself. Chu Cho gave me a bottle to share with his kids. Ha, Bi, a few kids, and I sat staring at the bottle. We played rock, paper, and scissors to see which one of us would take the first sip. I won, so I got to try it first. I took a small sip, afraid it might taste strange, but when I felt the very first drop of the black water on my tongue, the sensation was sweet and refreshing, although I had to get used to the burning sensation.

"Ba, what is this?" I ask my father.

"Coca-Cola," he said.

This cola was quite different, yet enjoyable at the same time. I thought the condensed milk at Argyle was the best thing I ever tasted, but the Coca-Cola outweighed it by a landslide. I wanted to take another sip, but I had to pass it along to the other kids. As the bottle rotated around to each kid, I wondered if it'd ever make it back to me. I watched each kid gulp down their sip and the Coca-Cola in the bottle got less and less. By the time the bottle got back to me, it was empty. I turned the bottle upside down and smacked it, trying to drain any last drops out. Sadly, the last drop was long gone.

After we all had our share of the Coca-Cola, we couldn't stop talking about the gas that would come right up our noses and burn—a weird, tingly feeling. None of us knew how to open our mouths and let the gas come out, we just burped with our mouths closed, leaving us with an uncomfortable sensation.

The lingering taste of the Coca-Cola was addictive; however, we couldn't afford to have it all the time. It was only occasionally when some parents would bring a bottle or two home from the volunteer work they did.

One day after school, while waiting for our parents to come back from volunteer work, one of the boys asked to play *Oc Tan*. It was a fun game that every kid who grew up in Vietnam knew how to play. It was similar to American baseball. Instead of using a bat to hit a ball, we used a wooden broomstick, cut into two pieces, one about six inches and the other about fifteen inches long. One team member holds both sticks in the same hand, tossing the shorter stick in the air, and then hitting it with the longer stick. The opposing team had to catch that shorter stick before it landed. If it didn't get caught, then the other team got points. The only problem was that the shorter stick was dangerous to catch if it was hit hard. If the stick was caught incorrectly, the fingers could get broken or the forehead could be left with a bruise.

That day, Bi got hit with the shorter stick on his forehead. It happened so quickly, and all we heard was a scream. When he removed his hand from his forehead, we saw a big protrusion. He cried profusely and called for his mom. We stopped the game and walked him back to his hut. Co Tram rushed from the hut, panicked and concerned about Bi's injury. She held him tightly while calming his pain. She didn't ask any of us what had happened as though she already knew. She gently walked him inside and sat him down while massaging his bump with salt and water. It was a remedy that we used to subside bruises. When Bi was at ease, she continued to caress him so that he could sleep. As I watched her motherly love, it reminded me of when my eyes got burned from the chili peppers. Ma would tell me to rub my eyes on her hair until the burning went away. She would then turn around and give me a big hug just like how Co Tram held Bi tightly in her arms. At that moment, I realized again how much I missed Ma, her love, and the care I once had.

That late afternoon while having dinner with Ba, I sat quietly. Ba wondered if I was sick. I told him that I was fine. I looked over at Co Tram's hut and saw that Bi recovered from the injury. She continued to hold him while the entire family enjoyed their dinner. I could hear their laughter as one happy family. The more I looked, the more I wanted my entire family there with me, having a meal that I wholeheartedly missed.

That night, I couldn't sleep. It was not from the annoying mosquitoes nor the sewage odor coming from the public bathroom, but rather, I was irked with random thoughts in my head. I turned to face Ba, who I knew was still awake.

"Ba, why didn't you bring our family with us like Chu Cho's?"

He opened his eyes and stared at the ceiling for a while. He let out a deep sigh. "Let's go back to sleep. You have school tomorrow."

I wanted to ask why he left everyone behind and only brought me. I had so many whys in my head and craved an answer from him, but the expression on his face stopped me from further asking him those questions. We both turned to opposite sides of the bed and drifted away into our thoughts. It was another sleepless night for both of us as we tossed and turned the entire night.

The next day after dinner, Ba suggested we go to the beach since it was a weekend. Ba was always busy with either studying or participating in volunteer work. We had never gone anywhere even on the weekends. I was surprised by his idea but going to the beach sounded so enticing… more fun than staying at the hut, so I nodded my head and agreed to it.

The beach was not far away from the Bataan Refugee Camp. We got there around noon and found a shady spot to have the food that Ba brought along. While eating, Ba was asking random questions about school and some of my friends. After we finished eating, he reached into a bag and took out bamboo sticks, strings, and papers.

"Let's make a kite!" It was the first time we ever got to spend time together like that.

I was excited when Ba suggested we make a kite together. It reminded me of the times when Ong Noi and I used to make a kite on windy days and flew it along the beach. Ong Noi taught me how to use bamboo sticks, paper, and rice to glue them together. We made it into the shape of a fish with a long tail. It was almost breathtaking to see the tail waving so gently in the wind. Seeing all the stuff that Ba brought along, I knew Ong Noi must have taught him how to make a kite too. Ba and I made a kite similar to the one Ong Noi made: a fish with a long tail. When we were done, Ba told me to fly the kite as he sat and watched. I ran along the beach, holding the strings while the kite took off. As the kite rose higher in the air, I watched as the fish came alive, breaking through the wind and swimming along the blue sky. I turned to look at Ba and saw the resemblance of Ong Noi watching me.

We had a fun time at the beach. Even though Ba didn't say much, he showed his care through small actions. He knew how lonely I had been without Ma and my siblings. He knew how much I missed them and wanted them there. He tried to fill in their places as much as he could. I immediately gave my father a hug to show my gratitude. I held onto my father tightly, but I held onto that memory even tighter. I still treasure that moment until this day.

Five months went by, and the day that we had been waiting for finally arrived.

"We are going to America!" Ba shouted as he entered the door.

As soon as the words left his lips, I jumped with joy and gave him a big hug. His dream to leave Vietnam to find freedom had become mine too. I felt blessed at that moment to know that we would be able to start a new life in America. I couldn't contain my excitement as I would also get to leave the musty hut, annoying mosquitoes, and sewage odor.

We were set to leave the Philippines in a week. Ba told me to keep my body in the best shape and to be healthy. We wanted to avoid being sick or injured, otherwise, it would delay our departure. I took his words seriously, and for that whole week, I refused to play *Oc Tan* whenever my friends asked me to play. I didn't want a bruise to be the thing that held me back from getting out of there. I sat and watched them play while I dreamt of a life in America.

The night before our departure, our new friends came with food and drinks to say farewell to us. They wished us all the best in the new land that we risked our lives for. It was always a sad thing to say goodbye like that since we didn't know when, where, or if we would ever see each other again. We shared our last meal and drank Coca-Cola with them until midnight. By then, I was a professional at controlling the gas from burning my nostrils.

After everyone left that night, Ba took me in his arms and said, "We are finally at the end of our journey now."

"Is it going to be better in America, Ba?" I asked.

"Yes. It's going to be much better." Ba smiled.

7 New York City

On November 28, 1982, over seven months since we left Vietnam, Ba and I were ready to board the airplane that would take us to the land of freedom—America. The flight was long and had some rough turbulence that neither of us experienced before. Although the flight attendants served food and drinks every few hours, my stomach was not able to contain what I had eaten or drank. I went through bags of vomit, one after another. I felt the pain rushing through my chest as I was forced to regurgitate the undigested food. The dizziness took a toll on me. As much as Ba was trying to comfort me, I kept telling myself that I could control the vomiting. I had survived the rocking of the boat on the treacherous sea and the loneliness during the refugee camps. This was just another obstacle that I would have to conquer before Ba and I could reach our destination.

After almost sixteen hours, we finally landed at John F. Kennedy airport in New York City. Ba turned to me and whispered, "This is it, our new home, Con."

"Are we going to have a home, Ba?" I asked.

"Yes, we can have anything here."

I couldn't wait to get off the airplane and see our new home. I looked outside the window and was amazed by what I saw. The night in America was vastly different from the night in Vietnam and at the refugee camps. I was astonished to look at the glowing lights coming from buildings and streets. The city was covered with lights shining from every direction. I was in a moment of awe and felt blessed that I no longer had to live in a shelter or a hut.

We were the last ones to leave the airplane. As we walked toward the flight attendants, I could see the nervousness in Ba's eyes, but to my surprise, Ba spoke English to them, asking for directions. After a short conversation, Ba grabbed my hand and knew where to go. I was impressed by his English skills, but also his courage, speaking to an American. He didn't waste the time he spent learning English at the refugee camps. He made me believe in what he always said to me, "Practice makes better."

We got off the airplane carrying a small bag with clothing that was given to us at the refugee camps and an IOM (International Organization for Migration) bag that had our documents for entering the United States. I held Ba's hand and followed his lead. JFK was a huge, confusing airport with many signs. However, Ba managed to find his way around and reached the exit gate by following the flight attendant's instructions. While walking with Ba, I saw a lot of people with blonde hair and blue eyes, just like in the vocabulary book we'd been given in the Philippines. I saw a variety of people, some with darker skin and different shades of hair. It was peculiar as I had never seen people like that before. I thought everyone in America looked the same as everyone in Vietnam looked the same.

As we almost arrived at the exit gate, we started to worry. Ba was at a standstill and didn't know where to go. The direction that was given to him was that someone from HIAS (Hebrew Immigrant Aid Society) would come and greet us at the exit gate once they saw us with the IOM bag. Ba and I walked slowly back and forth near the gate, hoping to be spotted. Suddenly, I saw an Asian woman in her forties heading toward us. She approached and greeted us in Vietnamese. "You must be Thuy and this is Linh."

"Yes, yes! That's us," Ba excitedly responded.

At that moment, hearing someone speaking our language and looking like us was a relief. We met someone who understood us.

"Hello, my name is Kim. I am from HIAS and welcome to New York City," she said with a smile.

After a short greeting, we followed Co Kim and walked out of the airport. She told us we needed to take a taxi to get to the hotel, where we would be staying for the night. I didn't understand what she meant by a hotel. I thought it would be another refugee camp that we needed to stay at before another transfer.

The taxi pulled towards us, and we got in the car. There were only the three of us and the taxi driver—not like the bus where we had to sit with other refugees going towards the refugee camps. During the ride, Co Kim asked Ba questions regarding the documents. As for me, I was still mesmerized by the tall buildings, bright lights, and many cars driving alongside each other. I was amazed by New York City and surprised to see people walking on the streets during the nighttime. I wondered if our home there would be as tall and as beautiful as these buildings.

The taxi stopped in front of a gigantic building. We got off, and Co Kim said, "Welcome to Manhattan, the Big Apple! This is where you will be staying for the night." She pointed to the building in front of us.

I raised my head, turned my neck, and kept rolling my eyes back to see the tall building. It seemed to take forever for my eyes to see the top, as though I was trying to reach the stars in the sky. We followed Co Kim inside the hotel. It was much brighter than outside in the streets with many humongous lights dangling from the ceiling. The floor was padded with a clean, elegant, and soft material that I was reluctant to step on. I didn't want to dirty it with my shoes. Everything around me was beyond my expectations. I couldn't stop admiring in awe.

Co Kim took us to our room, handed us a ten-dollar bill and said, "You both sleep here tonight. Use this money and get some food. I will be back in the morning to pick you up."

Ba looked confused holding the American bill she gave us and asked, "Where do we go collect food using this?"

"Oh, you don't collect food here. Use this money and buy food at the restaurant," she replied.

"I see. Thank you!" Ba nodded his head.

"Tour around the place if you want. You are in Manhattan after all," she said with a big smile on her way out.

After Co Kim left the room, I walked slowly towards the bed and pressed onto the mattress. It was soft and springy. How could a bed be this soft, I wondered. In Vietnam and at the refugee camps, we slept on a hard-wooden surface platform and felt grateful already. I slowly climbed on top of the mattress and laid down. It felt like feathers and was amazingly comfortable.

"Ba, this bed is so soft. Come and try it!" I said.

"Wow, it is soft." Dad smiled. Then he continued, "We don't have to worry about mosquito bites tonight!"

"And the sewage odor," I added.

Ba and I both laughed. We lay on the bed, closed our eyes, and let our bodies enjoy the softness of the bed. It had been a long day for us since we left the Philippines. Sitting and walking were all we did until we arrived here. We were exhausted and needed the rest. While relaxing on this feathery bed, Ma and my siblings appeared in my head. I wished they were there to enjoy this bed with Ba and me. I thought of Ong Noi too. I thought about how this bed would help him with his back pain. He always had a hard time getting out of bed every morning.

The rumbling sound from my belly brought us back to reality. I was hungry since there was nothing left in my stomach after all that vomiting. Ba looked at me and smiled as he understood what that rumbling sound meant. He got up from the bed, grabbed the picture- vocabulary book from the Philippines, and opened it to the section that taught how to order food. He looked at it for a couple of seconds and said, "I think I know how to buy food now."

We left the room and carried the book with us. We walked with our eyes constantly glancing from side to side, looking for a *food* sign. It was late at night, but the streets were crowded with people rushing and bumping into each other. The constant honking from cars was loud. I wondered how anyone who lived there could sleep at night. As we kept walking, bright lights were shining from every store on every block. I looked forward and backward and didn't see an end to the stores. New York City was different from the places I had been to.

Finally, we saw a store with a picture of a sandwich that looked like the ones in Ba's vocabulary book. We knew for sure we could get food there. Ba and I went inside, got in line, and Ba was put to the test of speaking English once again. He kept mumbling to himself about how to order our food. I watched him practice the lines repeatedly before it was our turn to order.

"May I please have two Big Mac," Ba said when it was our turn, while also pointing to the picture on the menu.

The lady at the cash register seemed to understand Ba well. She placed the order, then asked, "What do you like to drink?"

I eyed the Coca-Cola picture on the menu. Without any hesitation, I said, "Co Ca Co La." The lady gave me a strange look as though I was asking for something that didn't belong on the menu. She asked me one more time and I responded the same way. I could see the frustration on her face. I turned to Ba for his help, but there wasn't much help from him either, since "Co Ca Co La" was how he pronounced it too. We paused for a few seconds, pointing to the picture, and saying the word again. She turned to look at the picture, smiled at us, and said, "You mean Coke? You want a Coke?"

"Yes. Coke," Ba said, relieved she finally understood us.

I was confused as to why it was Coca-Cola in the Philippines, but it was Coke in America. Whatever the reasons were, I was happy I got to drink Coca-Cola again.

We got our food, sat down at a table, and had our first meal in America. We ordered two Big Macs. It had two slices of bread with meat and lettuce in the middle. We kept looking at it and didn't know how to start. Bread was something we hadn't eaten before. Rice, vegetables, and fish were mainly what we ate in Vietnam, as well as in Hong Kong and the Philippines. We looked around and saw a man sitting in the corner, holding a sandwich like ours with both hands and eating it. We stared at him for a few seconds, then picked up our sandwiches and ate just like he did. Luckily, he wasn't paying attention to us staring at him.

My first bite of the Big Mac tasted very different from the fish and the cactus that I had back home. The meat and the sauce in between the bread gave it a creamy taste. I found it to be quite appetizing. I finished the entire sandwich quickly since I was so hungry.

After we finished our food, Ba and I toured around New York City, just as Co Kim suggested. We wanted to see what else was there in America. We walked by many stores and restaurants and couldn't stop ourselves with the "ohs" and "wows" every time something new caught our eyes. Ba and I looked like two country bumpkins roaming the streets.

As we passed by humongous buildings, I wondered how it felt to be up there. Would I be able to touch the clouds? Would I be lucky enough to see Buddha floating just like when I was inside the airplane up in the sky? I was hoping to get a chance to be up there and experience it myself.

It was late November, and the weather was cold in New York City. I began to shiver after a long walk. Ba had to rub my shoulders to keep me warm since all I had on was a shirt and pants—the only clothes we got from the refugee camps. Ba didn't want me to get sick from walking in the cold, so we headed back to the hotel.

When we were in our room, Ba asked, "Did you have fun seeing America?"

"Yes, Ba. It was nice and different," I said. "I love the food and the toys hanging in the stores."

"Hopefully, I can find work soon so I can buy you more food and those toys," Ba said with a smile. "Co Kim will take us to our new home tomorrow," Ba continued.

"I can't wait to see our new home. I just hope it will be as nice as this hotel!"

8 Welcome to the Bronx

The next morning, Co Kim came to the hotel and picked us up. She asked if we had a chance to tour around the city and if we were able to buy food. I excitedly told her about our encounter at the restaurant and how we stared at the gentleman and copied the way he was eating the sandwich. I also told her about the awkward moment when we tried to order the Coca-Cola.

"How come she didn't know what Coca-Cola was?" I asked.

"Oh, they call it Coke here, not Coca-Cola. I am sure you will get used to it," she replied. "But good job trying to speak English."

As we were leaving the hotel, Co Kim told us that we wouldn't be taking the taxi today because she wanted to show us how to use the subway, another type of transportation in New York City. It was convenient and cheap, and since we didn't have a car, it would be perfect for us. Ba and I were unsure of what the subway was, but we figured we might as well get used to it.

The subway station was a couple of blocks away from the hotel. When we got to Grand Central-42nd Street station, Co Kim pointed to the direction below ground with the stairs heading down towards a tunnel. From a distance, it was dark and dingy. I saw cigarette butts and black sticky gum all over the steps. We walked down a few steps and a gust carrying an uninvited smell of urine met us at the tip of our noses. At that moment, a memory brought me right back home to Vietnam. In the village, we didn't have a bathroom in the house. People would take care of their business anywhere outside behind the bushes or in unnoticeable places by others. On windy days, that foul odor would travel in the air and viciously hit anyone in its path. That day, we stood on the path of that same foul odor. Ba and I were confused that an odor like that would be in a big city where bathrooms were available everywhere.

"Get used to this. It's New York City." Co Kim chuckled, noticing our expressions.

We got to the end of the stairs and walked toward a booth. Co Kim spoke to a man inside of the enclosed booth, and I saw him exchange her money with bronze rounded metals. She handed them to Ba and me, then told us it was a token for the subway. We placed the token into the slot at the turnstile and spun ourselves to the other side of the platform. She took out a pamphlet from her bag and handed it to Ba. It was the map of the Subway. She showed us which train line we were about to take to our new home. The map looked like a maze, with many different train lines and colors. Ba looked overwhelmed and kept on asking her questions about different stops and changing lines. Co Kim told us that we could go anywhere in New York City if we used this map as a guide.

After we finished looking at the map, we walked farther out to the platform to wait for the train. I looked below the platform to see rails clamped onto the thick black wood with large nails. I turned my head to both sides of the platform, looking beyond the tunnel to see nothing but a pitch-dark path. Suddenly, I felt a light breeze on my face and body, a screeching noise escalating. Co Kim warned me that the train was approaching. I stepped back farther toward the wall and away from the rails as I felt the rumbling, grinding noise, and a stronger gust of wind. A bright light shined through the tunnel as I braced myself to expect something gigantic. A large number four sign appeared at the corner of the train. I looked at the train passing by, section by section, until it fully stopped.

The train door opened, and we followed Co Kim inside. People were sitting or standing and scattered throughout the train. We found empty seats and sat down. I watched the people around me and saw some sleeping, eating, or leaning against the door. I was afraid they might fall out of the train when the door opened. I continued to observe the train and saw all kinds of writings and doodles everywhere on the train.

"Why are there so many writings on the train?" I curiously asked.

"That is called graffiti. You will see it everywhere in New York City," she replied. "People like to write and draw stuff like that around here."

The train ride was loud as I could hear and feel the metal wheels clashing onto the rails. As the train turned, it rocked me back and forth, forcing me to hold tighter onto Ba. After a few stops, more people got on and the train quickly became overcrowded with people standing next to each other. It was so crammed that people would bump into each other when the train picked up speed or stopped. However, people didn't seem to mind. I guess they were used to it. For almost thirty minutes, we were riding in the dark tunnel. At times, the lights would flicker, turning off and on. When it was off, the darkness reminded me of the times we were floating at night in the middle of the ocean.

"We are going to your home now. Are you excited?" Co Kim asked me.

"Yes, Co Kim. I can't wait," I excitedly replied.

"Is this another refugee camp like the ones in Hong Kong and the Philippines?" Ba hesitantly asked.

"No, this is an apartment, and you will have your own space," Co Kim explained.

Even after the explanation from Co Kim, Ba and I couldn't imagine what an apartment was. As for me, I envisioned our new home would be the same as the hotel that we stayed in, with beautiful ceiling lights, soft padded floors, and a feathery bed. I would love to sleep on that bed every night in our new home.

Finally, we arrived at our stop, Fordham Road. We got off the train and walked along the platform to the stairs. This stop was different from the Grand Central station. Instead of being underground, the station was above ground. We walked down two flights of stairs to the street. It was different from Manhattan; there was less traffic, and the buildings were not as high. However, on every block, there were a lot of people walking and many stores just like in Manhattan. Then I saw the same restaurant sign that Ba and

I had dinner at last night. I pointed to the restaurant and asked Co Kim how to pronounce the name.

"McDonald's," she said slowly for me to hear. Our first meal in America was fast food at McDonald's.

We walked for another ten blocks. I saw a big park with lots of trees and a huge playground. A few kids were playing with an orange ball, bouncing on the ground, and trying to throw it into a metal round rim attached to a pole. On the back of the round rim was a metal board. They were laughing and cheering for each other. As we got closer to the park, I turned and asked Co Kim what they were playing. She told me it was basketball. I never heard of that game before. Growing up in the countryside, we were poor. We came up with our own games with whatever we could find around the house. This basketball game was unique to my eyes since I grew up in a village with a house built on top of dirt. There was no concrete for us to bounce a ball or a metal rim on a pole. There were so many new things in America that a country boy like me needed to learn.

Coincidentally at that moment, the sound of a familiar language brought joy to my ears. I turned and there he was, a boy, who was about my age, with black hair and tan, olive skin. But there wasn't only him—I saw a couple more of them chasing after him. Excitement filled my body, as I was thrilled to know that there were Vietnamese kids around there. I hadn't seen any Vietnamese besides Co Kim ever since I got there. I was a little sad thinking that I would have a tough time making friends since my English was limited. I was hoping to meet other Vietnamese kids like at the refugee camps. It was a dream come true when I saw these kids.

"Do you see that building across this park?" Co Kim pointed at one of the tall buildings.

"That one in front of us?" Ba asked.

"Yes, that's your home," she said.

I was ecstatic to hear that our new home was across the park. I could hang out with kids who looked like me and spoke the same language. I couldn't wait to befriend them.

We walked toward two buildings that were connected. Co Kim motioned us to the right side where our home was. We walked up the stairs and opened the door to the building. The floor was tile and dirty. There were also a few broken glass windows. There was an elevator that seemed old and had a small window on its door. This building had six floors and ours was on the first. We walked past the elevator to the third door down the hall and there was our apartment, our new home.

Co Kim knocked on the door and after less than a minute, a man opened the door. He was about Ba's age and with a smile on his face, he said, "Hi Kim. How are you?" The man warmly greeted.

"I am good. How are you? How is everything at the apartment so far?" Co Kim asked.

"Everything is good. We got used to it now," he replied.

"I am bringing you a new roommate," she introduced us.

"Hello, my name is Chau." He turned to Ba and extended his hand for a handshake.

"Hello, my name is Thuy. This is my son, Linh," Ba replied while shaking his hand.

"Welcome to America!" He looked at me.

"Thank you, Chu Chau," I addressed him formally as Chu.

We entered the house and walked toward the living room. Another man walked towards us from the kitchen and greeted us. His name was Tri. He looked much younger than Ba and Chu Chau, maybe in his twenties. After a short conversation with our roommates, Co Kim gave Ba a bag and asked to speak with him privately. I stayed in the living room and talked to Chu Chau and Anh *(a formal way to address a male who is about 10 years older)* Tri.

"How do you like America so far?" Anh Tri asked.

"It's different from Vietnam. So many new things here," I answered.

"Don't worry, you will get used to it," he said.

"Did you take the subway here? How did you like it?" Chu Chau asked.

"Yes I did, but it was very loud and crowded."

"That's how people use transportation in New York City," Chu Chau said.

"Do I have to take the subway to school?" I asked.

"No, your school is nearby so you can walk there."

I got comfortable talking to Chu Chau and Anh Tri. They seemed friendly. I was happy that our new roommates were Vietnamese and very nice people. After a short while, Ba and Co Kim walked into the living room. Co Kim asked Chu Chau and Anh

Tri about their jobs and if they had gotten used to their work yet. She walked around the house, making sure everything was in good working order. She told us to let her know if we found anything wrong at the apartment.

Just as Co Kim was about to leave, she bent down to my height, patted my head, and said, "Enjoy your new home, and be a good son for your father." She told me exactly what the ladies at the refugee camps told me. I wondered why they all kept saying that to me. I guess they wanted me to be on my best behavior so that Ba could focus on settling in sooner. I obediently nodded my head.

We all said goodbye to her as she headed for the door. Anh Tri got two glasses of water from the kitchen sink and offered them to us. We sat on the living room floor and got to know more about each other. As the conversation went on, we found out that Chu Chau and Anh Tri were also boat people. They didn't know each other until they met in the apartment. Chu Chau arrived there a few months ago and Anh Tri joined him a few days later. Ba told them about our journey and was glad we shared the apartment with them.

"Are you hungry yet?" Chu Chau asked me.

"Yes, Chu Chau," I timidly answered. I didn't want to concern them with my hunger, but I couldn't help but admit it.

"Let's have some instant noodles for lunch," he said. "Tri makes good instant noodles."

Anh Tri nodded his head with a confident grin and got up. We followed him to the kitchen. While Anh Tri was taking out the pots and getting ready to cook the noodles, Chu Chau was taking some of the ingredients from the refrigerator, while Ba was helping him prepare the finishing touches. As I was watching them, I could see the camaraderie even though we just met each other within the hour. When the noodles were done on the stove, I could smell the aroma of the seasoning that they added to the pot. It was simply scallions and cilantro added to the boiled noodles with a bag of ingredients that came with it. I couldn't wait to taste a meal made by these three men. We carried four bowls of hot, steamy noodles to the living room, sat down on the floor again, and shared our first meal. While Ba and the other two exchanged stories about Vietnam, I was busy slurping every strand of noodles. I didn't forget about the broth either and drank to the last drop. Just when I finished, I could see how happy they were while having this simple lunch. They were deep in their conversations as though they were once best friends. I felt the joy to be with them in my new home—my new family in America.

After we finished eating, Chu Chau pointed to the room straight ahead and offered it to Ba and me.

"Oh no, we can sleep anywhere," Ba said.

"No. You both take the room. Tri and I are two single guys. We can sleep in the living room," Chu Chau insisted.

"Thank you very much," Ba gratefully responded.

Chu Chau patted Ba on the shoulder and told him not to hesitate to take the bedroom. He told us that we should consider each other as a family from now on since fate had brought us together. Ba and I were truly blessed to meet good people throughout our journey: the captain of the boat, Chu Cho's family in the Philippines, Co Kim, Chu Chau, and Anh Tri in America. They made us feel that we should never lose hope regardless of the circumstances. There were always helping hands when we needed them.

Dad and I went into the bedroom, and I was surprised to see nothing in there but a blanket and two pillows. They were the same type of blankets and pillows we had sat on in the living room. After walking around the entire apartment, I realized there was no furniture in the entire apartment, just bare hardwood floors throughout every room.

Our new home wasn't what I had envisioned. No beautiful lights hung from the ceiling, no soft padded floors, no big, feathery bed. However, I wasn't disappointed. I felt grateful to have something that we could call home. Our home. Even though we still had to share with others, at least we knew they were good people—people we could trust and count on. We were blessed to have our room with locked doors and closed windows. I would no longer have to deal with the annoying mosquitoes and sewage odor.

That night, Ba and I couldn't sleep. We talked to each other for hours. Ba was more anxious than I was. We finally made it to the land of freedom, but he was concerned with the unknown that we might face ahead. I didn't know how to make Ba feel any better as we were lying on the hardwood floor. The only thing that I could do during that moment was again praying to the Buddha that we could have more strength to overcome whatever we might endure.

9 Treasure Hunting

Co Kim had given Ba some money before she left the other day. However, Ba didn't know how to use it. The money had different colors and writing on them.

Ba asked Chu Chau if he knew the differences and how to use them. Chu Chau explained that the green bill was regular money, and we could use it to buy anything. The other types of money with different colors were food stamps, and we could only use them to buy food

"Where can we go to buy food here?" Ba asked.

"Let's go food shopping today, and I will show you the neighborhood too," Chu Chau suggested.

"Sounds good! Dinner is on me tonight," Ba said thankfully.

Ba wanted to do something special to thank Chu Chau and Anh Tri for giving up the bedroom and splitting the rent among only three adults. However, with the little money that he had, Ba thought that a home-cooked meal would be more affordable.

The supermarket wasn't that far away from our apartment. It took about ten minutes to walk there. Inside, there were aisles of food, and I remembered thinking that there was no way anyone would be hungry in America. Behind the food aisle was a section of household items… pots, pans, and other items that I was clueless about their functions. Chu Chau said that we didn't have to buy any of these items since they had bought them when they moved into the apartment.

We continued along the meat section, and I was shocked to see a variety of meats packaged neatly in foam packages. I had never seen so many different types of meats that were carefully sliced, cleaned, and displayed elegantly on a cold air-blowing apparatus. Back in Vietnam, the meat market was in the open with some of the meat hung for display, while the larger pieces of meat were placed on the stalls with nothing wrapped to prevent the meat from being contaminated by flies and dirt. We were happy to even have meat. We were poor, and food safety was never a concern. This was the reason behind many people experiencing bloating and later realizing that tapeworms were living in their intestines. Unfortunately, I was one of them. A few months before Ba and I left Vietnam, I was feeling symptoms of having tapeworms in my body as my stomach was bulging. Ba gave me the medicine and within hours, I could feel something unusual and ticklish in my anus. I reached behind to feel what it was and pulled out a long white tapeworm about eight inches long. It was the weirdest feeling that I never wanted to experience again.

Ba gathered a few trays of chicken legs since it was the cheapest in the meat section. We headed to the produce section, and I was taken aback by all the varieties of fruits and vegetables that were different from our garden in Vietnam. Anh Tri said he was hesitant to try them and had a hard time remembering all the names. We ended up buying the vegetables that we recognized: scallions and cilantro, the herbs that we grew in our garden.

We passed by the seafood section, but everything was expensive. We settled with canned fish. We loaded cans of tuna, sardines, mackerel, and whatever else that had a picture of a fish.

After getting all the food that we needed, we headed toward the cash register and remembered what Chu Chau said. Ba handed the cashier the food stamps to pay for the food and the money to pay for a pack of cigarettes.

Later that afternoon, I was helping Ba prepare dinner for the four of us—simple dishes of chicken with cilantro and scallions, mackerel stew covered with cilantro to bring out the aroma, and fried eggs with onions. We didn't have Ma's special ingredients. Instead, Ba modified it by just using salt and sugar. I brought all the food to the same spot where we ate the noodles and spread them along the hardwood floor. I was surprised that Ba's cooking was not bad at all, and that I enjoyed it.

During dinner, we reminisced about our families and the beautiful memories we had in Vietnam. Chu Chau mentioned his wife and two kids living in the countryside. They were poor, and he couldn't afford to bring them along. He had to make the difficult choice of leaving them behind. I could hear the trembling in his voice and see his tears as he chewed and told the story. Anh Tri also shared with us how he had to leave his parents and younger siblings behind. He made a promise to his family that once he was able to make money, he would send it back to help his family. When it was Ba's turn to tell his story, I attentively listened when he mentioned how we struggled to survive in the village. I cried after hearing all their stories. It reminded me of Ma and my siblings. I wondered if any of us would ever see our families again.

That night when we were in our bedroom, Ba told me he needed to find a job soon so that he could save up some money and send it back home to Ma. He even asked me if I missed them. For the last seven months with Ba, he didn't mention why we left our family behind, but that night, I finally understood his reasons. It was similar to Chu Chau's and Anh Tri's. He had to risk his life to find better opportunities so that he could provide a better life for our family. It was an ordeal that almost every family had to sacrifice—one had to leave while others stayed behind. I felt the loneliness in Chu Chau and Anh Tri's words as they expressed their emotions. I felt fortunate that Ba brought me along in this journey – at least I could share the hardship that he had to face and keep him company during unbearable times. I turned to Ba, squeezed him tightly, and screamed, "I love you!" in my head.

The next day in the late afternoon, Co Kim came back to the apartment to check on us. Ba and I were the only ones at home. Chu Chau and Anh Tri had left for work. Co Kim gave Ba information to find work and additional information to continue learning English. Most importantly, she came for me. She gave Ba information about the elementary school that I would be enrolled in. While they were talking, I asked Ba if I could go to the park. I wanted to look for those Vietnamese kids; I wanted to play with them. Ba nodded his head, told me to be careful, and come back early.

I walked to the park and saw kids playing marbles on the dirt next to the basketball court. It reminded me of the times when my friends and I played in front of my house on the sandy ground. I was known for shooting marbles in my village. I won almost every time. When I got closer to the crowd, I saw the two Vietnamese kids from the other day. I approached them, hoping they might ask me to join if they saw me. However, they were too busy focusing on their game and didn't pay attention to my existence, even though I was standing right next to them, clapping and cheering for them. I was shy and reluctant to introduce myself as I stood and watched them play. However, I was content being outside of the apartment and seeing these Vietnamese kids again. I told myself to be brave and asked to play with them next time.

After watching them play for a while, I decided to explore the park. I walked to the end of the park and discovered a big Catholic Church across the street, Father Zeisure's Place. That street later became my usual route as I would always head to the Catholic Church right after school or when my father wasn't home, because they always gave free food to children of low-income families.

While I was touring the park, I heard screaming from those kids. I turned around and saw them congregate at the basketball court. I got interested and moved closer. There were more kids on the court. I was surprised to see a team of Vietnamese kids playing against a team of American kids. They bounced the ball back and forth around each other and shot through the rim. It looked interesting. I wanted to ask if I could try, but my shyness took over and stopped me. Instead, I became a supporting fan, cheering silently from the outside. I found it interesting the Vietnamese kids were wearing beaten-down flip-flops while the American kids had on sturdy sneakers. I watched the Vietnamese kids running and smacking their flip-flops onto the ground while being able to twist and turn with the ball. There was a point where one of the kids removed his flip-flops and played barefoot. I looked down at the sneakers I was wearing that were given to me in the Philippines from Chu Cho. I wanted to lend the sneakers to the boy playing barefoot, but I continued to be timid and remained silent.

It was getting dark, and I knew it was time to head home or Ba would be worried. On the way back, there was a group of people playing loud music in a language I couldn't understand, but I knew it wasn't English. I minded my own business and kept on walking. Out of nowhere, two of them crept up on me and screamed something that sounded like "ching chong" and "hiyah." I was scared because I had no idea what they were saying or asking of me. They followed me and repeatedly said those words. I ignored them and continued to walk, hoping they would stop and leave me alone. Luckily, after a little while, they stopped and walked back to their group. Either they didn't see the fear on my face, or they got bored. I ran straight home without looking back.

When I got home, I met Anh Tri at the door. I asked him if he knew the people who were playing the loud music. Anh Tri told me they were a group of Hispanics. That group would always stand at that spot and liked to tease whoever walked by them. I told him what they did to me, and Anh Tri was angry because they did the same thing to him. He praised me for ignoring and walking away.

We walked into the kitchen and saw Ba preparing dinner. Ba asked me if I had fun and made new friends at the park. I told Ba the truth about me being the audience instead of playing with them. Ba rubbed my head and told me not to be afraid and to just ask them nicely next time. Since we were on the subject, I asked Ba if he could buy me some marbles. I thought it would somehow cure my shyness, then I could finally muster up the courage to play with them. Ba paused for a second and gave me a strange look as to how or where he would be getting the marbles for me without making money. He quickly changed the subject and told me to get ready for dinner as Chu Chau would be home soon. As he was about to walk away, he turned to me and said that we would talk about the marbles later. I didn't know if Ba was seriously going to buy them for me or not, but I was happy to hear him say we could talk about it later.

Anh Tri and I were setting up the bowls and chopsticks on the floor when Chu Chau entered the apartment and Ba told him to get ready for dinner. We were having fried eggs, canned fish with salt and chili peppers, and rice… our usual meal every night. We ate these dishes so much that they became my signature dishes. Every time Ba cooked them, he would make me watch and practice. Each time Ba cooked anything, he would say, "This is how you do it, and don't forget, because someday you will have to cook for yourself." It was as though Ba knew he would be busy with work in the future. He wanted me to be self-sustained whenever he wasn't home.

During dinner, Chau asked Ba, "Do you want to go treasure hunting with me and Tri after dinner?"

"Treasure hunt?" Ba curiously asked.

"It's a saying for when we go look around the dumpster outside the apartment." Chu Chau laughed.

"Why are we looking around the dumpster?"

"Sometimes people throw stuff in the dumpster that we can reuse," Chu Chau explained.

"I see. Then let's finish eating and we can go," Ba excitedly answered.

"Can I go too, Ba? I can help to look," I volunteered.

We finished dinner and headed outside for our very first adventure. That night, we roamed the streets of Father Zeisure's Place. We walked up and down all the streets searching for anything that could be salvaged. It seemed that both Chu Chau and Anh Tri had walked around this block many times looking for stuff. Chu Chau knew where to go and even told Ba which part of the dumpsters normally have the most treasure.

People brought their trash out twice a week and left it on the dumpster site for the garbage truck to pick up. We just needed to carefully look and find anything practical that we could use. We walked for an hour and couldn't find anything useful. There were a lot of broken chairs and items that were unusable or things we didn't know how to use. Anh Tri suggested we go to the back of the dumpster on the ground floor of our building. We headed back to our building and stepped onto a metal staircase down to the dumpster. We got closer to the dumpster area and a whiff of trash unexpectedly greeted us. There was a big pile of trash. I looked up and saw our apartment. I realized we were only one floor above the dumpster. No wonder on certain days, I would hear something being slammed outside of our windows. Now I knew these were furniture pieces that people threw away.

As we kept on searching, I spotted something from afar, lying underneath the garbage bags. I ran over and saw a mattress and a small couch.

"I found it!" I shouted.

"What did you find?" Anh Tri asked.

"A mattress and a couch."

They rushed over to see what I had found. We were happy that we found something that we needed for the apartment. Since the dumpster was behind the building, carrying these treasures home wasn't much of a hassle, but we had to make two trips since I was too small to help carry them.

Ba, Chu Chau, and Anh Tri carried the mattress home, while I stayed behind to guard the couch. I remembered when we carried the couch back there were a few people who kept looking at us. I couldn't tell the reason behind them staring at us. Maybe they felt pity that we had to bring home what was someone else's trash as our new treasure. Although it looked embarrassing, it was a fortunate experience for us, as we could make effective use of items that weren't even half damaged.

We didn't feel shameful for having people looking at us and managed to carry the mattress and the couch home before the trash pick-up truck came by the next morning. After deep cleaning with wet towels and scrubbing the dirt off, we made both pieces look new. Out of kindness again, Chu Chau was thoughtful and told Ba to keep the mattress in our room and leave the couch in the living room for everyone. Ba and I were very grateful. We planned to come back for more treasure hunting and hoped to find another mattress for them.

Although the bed wasn't as soft as the one at the hotel in Manhattan, I enjoyed sleeping on it because it meant more to me than what money could buy. The treasure hunting with Chu Chau and Tri that night would forever be a memory I could never forget as it was a learning lesson in life.

10 Time for School

After a week in New York City, I was enrolled in school. Ba and I woke up early that morning to get ready. He handed me an outfit and a second-hand backpack that was given by Co Kim. I felt nervous as I was slowly combing my hair and getting dressed. I didn't know what to expect and wondered if it would be the same as in the Philippines. I had so many thoughts running through my mind and felt low energy that morning. Ba saw my anxiousness, rubbed my head, and told me that everything would be all right. While he prepared eggs for me to eat, I opened the backpack. There were a few pencils, a blank notebook, and a note. On the note, it said, *"Here are the pencils and a notebook for you to start school in America. Be the best student you always have been. Remember to believe in yourself. Love, Ba."* I took the note and slid it into the side pocket of the notebook. While Ba placed the eggs on the floor, I stood up and hugged him. I told him that I would try my best at school as he wanted me to.

    Ba and I walked for thirty minutes along the Major Deegan Interstate Highway 87. I could hear the cars driving past us at a very fast speed, behind the trees and bushes, which separated the sidewalks we were on from the highway. We got to the front of the school, which was gated with vertical black metal rods all around. At that moment, I thought of the Argyle Refugee Camp in Hong Kong. I was puzzled as to why the school needed to be surrounded by a metal fence. "Are we no longer refugees?" I wondered. We continued to walk along the fence toward the corner of the block and saw a sign, P.S. 122.

"I think this is it. Your school. Are you ready?" Ba asked.

"Yes, Ba." I looked at him, still a bit nervous.

"You can do this," he said as he rubbed my shoulder.

He opened the door, and I followed him up the stairs. We walked to the main office and a lady approached us. She led us to the administration office. Ba showed them the documents of my school application. After they finished reviewing my application, I was told that I would be placed in second grade.

Ba turned to me and knelt at my eye level. He softly told me to remember our conversation from this morning. The thought of him leaving me alone in the very big building intimidated me enough to push me over the edge of tears. I quickly wiped the first drop and told him I would be a good boy. I didn't want Ba to be bothered while looking for a job after dropping me off since he had some referrals from Co Kim. I hugged Ba as he was about to leave, but also reminded him to pick me up after school since the walk was long and difficult to navigate. Ba promised to be waiting for me the minute I was done with school.

The school secretary took my hand and walked me down the long hallway. Unlike the school back in the Philippines, this one was cleaner and more spacious. Seeing all the rooms filled with children made me wonder how many students this building held. We finally got to my classroom, and she gave me a little nudge of encouragement. She opened the door, and a teacher came to greet both of us.

"Good morning. My name is Mrs. Powell. What's your name?"

"Good morning. My name is Linh." My Vietnamese accent was still prominent.

Mrs. Powell escorted me to an empty seat, and I looked around to see if there were any Vietnamese kids in my class. I kept looking, but unfortunately, I was the only one. I realized that I was no longer in the Philippines with my refugee friends. I was in America with kids who shared nothing in common with me. I felt lost as an outsider, and I didn't belong.

My heart pounded harder and harder as I tried my best to understand what Mrs. Powell was saying. I tried to remember the words I learned back at school in the Philippines, but all I heard were noises that went through one ear and out the other. Everyone in the class seemed to have no problem understanding her. They were raising their hands, answering questions, and even giggling among themselves. I became dizzy with anxiety kicking in my gut.

The school regulations in America were different compared to the schools in Vietnam. Students in Vietnam had to always obey the teachers and weren't allowed to speak during class. The punishment for those who didn't follow the rules was to be spanked in front of the class. I must admit that I had been spanked a few times since I couldn't keep quiet. However, it was different at P.S. 122. Some students were talking back to Mrs. Powell, and it sounded confrontational, while others were making noises and laughing while she was teaching. All she did was raise her index finger and whisper, "Shh," and everyone quieted down. I liked the school regulations there. At least I wouldn't be embarrassed about being spanked if I couldn't keep quiet.

Around noon, Mrs. Powell lined us up with boys on one side and girls on the other. To keep us in sync, she made the boys and girls hold each other's hands, but I didn't understand what she was saying. Suddenly, I felt my hand being grabbed by someone. I turned sideways to see a girl holding my hand and smiling at me. I was confused and shocked that she held onto my hand. She said something that I couldn't understand, but as I looked in front and back of me, everyone was holding each other's hands. I figured it was what Mrs. Powell wanted us to do.

I had held Ma, Ba Noi, and my sisters' hands, but never any other girl's hand. Without knowing the reason, I didn't want to let go of her hand. As I continued to walk along the hallway, holding her hand, I felt more relaxed and less nervous. I warmed up to the class, although if I was asked to speak at any moment, I wouldn't know what to say.

I got in line at the cafeteria just like everyone else. I wondered what would be served for lunch. Would it be stir-fried bean sprouts with rice and soy milk like in Hong Kong? Or the Big Mac with Coca-Cola that Ba and I had as our first meal in America? I kept thinking about the food as we got closer to the food stand. To my surprise, I saw different types of food in various metal pots. The boy in front of me was selecting what he wanted. It was different from Hong Kong and the Philippines where everyone was given the same food. The lady standing behind the stand asked me what I wanted. I was clueless looking at the vast selection of unfamiliar foods. I felt stumped and pointed to the same food that the boy in front of me selected.

My first lunch at P.S.122 was pizza, canned peaches, and chocolate milk. I carried my lunch and followed the other students to a table. I sat down with a tray of food but didn't know how or where to start. I paused to look around just like our first meal at McDonald's in Manhattan. I watched the boy who got the same lunch. He was holding the pizza with two hands and quickly bit off the corners. I picked up my pizza and did the same thing. I noticed the way they ate in America was very different from Vietnam. They used their hands more while we mostly used our chopsticks.

After I finished the pizza, I figured it was time to use the plastic spoon for the canned peaches. I scooped a spoon of the peaches, and the taste was very different from any other fruits I had eaten before. The syrup that the peaches were submerged in gave it an interesting but pleasant taste. It was overly sweet, but I enjoyed it. I finished the entire serving and didn't leave any drop of syrup behind. The chocolate milk was the last thing for me to try. I was surprised that it was sweeter than the soy milk from Hong Kong and wasn't as gassy as the Coca-Cola in the Philippines. It became my favorite drink.

When we finished lunch, the entire group of kids left the table, and we walked out to the playing field. It was a big open concrete space with basketball courts and swings. The kids seemed to know each other and ran to their positions. They already knew who the teams were when they assembled on the basketball courts. The girls and boys took turns on the swings and pushed each other higher and higher. I stood there, exposed to the sun, and leaned on the wall of the cafeteria. I watched them having fun, but I didn't know how to engage. I saw the boys and girls playing tag. I knew that I could run as fast and tag someone, but once again I was reluctant to ask, or even knew what to say. I was afraid to say the wrong words and to be made fun of. With that thought, I stood there feeling isolated and lonely as I had ever been. It was difficult to make friends with anyone due to my barrier of inadequate English and uncontrollable shyness.

Playtime was over after thirty minutes. Mrs. Powell came out to the playground and asked us to stand back in the same formation to head back to the classroom. I turned to the girl who held my hand earlier, but this time, I took the courage and reached to grab her hand. We walked back to class. I was one step closer to being comfortable around other kids, and one step closer to making new friends. I was proud of myself for taking the initial step.

We got back to the classroom and saw another teacher sitting in one of the seats. She stood up and introduced herself as Mrs. McKeever. She was in her forties with short hair and was about five feet tall. Her warm and inviting smile made me feel welcomed.

Mrs. Powell told me to follow her. I was confused, but I didn't want to disobey my teacher, so I followed Mrs. McKeever. We sat at the back of the room. She asked me a few questions, but I couldn't understand until she asked where I was from. I immediately answered her. I had learned this question in the Philippines besides "Good Morning" and "My name is." All those days practicing English with Ba had paid off. I later learned that Mrs. McKeever taught ESL (English as a Second Language). She taught and helped kids like me to learn better English.

"I am from Vietnam," I said enthusiastically with a thick Vietnamese accent.

Mrs. McKeever gave me a big smile and gestured both thumbs up. I felt proud of myself at that moment and internally celebrated my first short conversation. She continued with a book that she had in her hand. The book was similar to the dictionary book that was given to Ba and me before we left the Philippines. She read the words next to each picture and asked me to repeat along. I read with her for about half of a page until she looked up and praised my effort. I wanted to continue and finish the entire page. I didn't want to stop. The more I read with her, the more she made me feel like I could learn this new language. More importantly, I gained a moment of confidence for the first time.

After our session, Mrs. McKeever told me we would meet again for tomorrow's lesson. I was disappointed to finish so soon. I wanted to learn more from her. As I sat in my seat, I saw Mrs. Powell write a math problem on the blackboard. I was excited to see something familiar that I could understand. Right when she finished writing the math question, I intuitively knew the answer. The days Ong Noi hammered the multiplication tables into my head were worthwhile. However, I was apprehensive to raise my hand and give an answer. Instead, I wrote on a piece of paper, pretending to answer the question out loud.

"Linh, what is eight times three?" Mrs. Powell suddenly asked.

I was not expecting her to pick me. I had no choice but to answer. I couldn't rely on the paper anymore. With my thick accent, I stood up and answered, "Twenty-four."

"Very good!" Mrs. Powell said.

I sat back in my chair with relief, as if I had accomplished something in a class I barely understood until then. I felt satisfaction from answering and hearing my own words. After all, I wasn't as bad as I thought I would be. She understood me! I was eager for more math questions, but I was more excited to speak English again. As Mrs. Powell continued to write more math questions on the blackboard, I continued to jot the answers on the paper, but I simultaneously and fervently raised my hand to give the answers verbally. She recognized my hand but instead called on another boy who sat next to me. He was caught off-guard and stumbled with his voice. He glanced over at my paper and raised his eyes towards me. I nodded my head to assure him that he could use my answer. He stood up and responded to Mrs. Powell.

He turned to me and gratefully acknowledged my help. For the rest of the class, he and I took turns answering Mrs. Powell's math questions. I stopped writing my answers on the paper and passionately raised my hands for every question without hesitation. The boy gave me high-fives each time I got them right. That was how James and I became friends on my first day at P.S. 122. He became my math buddy ever since.

The first day of school went by quickly. Everyone was packing up their backpacks and getting ready to leave. As we were lining up to walk to the main door for dismissal, I was worried if Ba remembered to pick me up or not. As soon as I approached the main door, Ba was standing at the gate waiting for me. I ran toward him and hugged him.

Ba held my hand and walked along the same path that we took that morning. He asked me how my first day was at school. I eagerly told him about my success in math when I participated and wasn't afraid to raise my hand to answer. I told him about James and how we became friends, but I was exuberant when I told Ba about meeting Mrs. McKeever. I described to him how she patiently helped me with English. I even told Ba about the girl who I held hands with. Ba burst out laughing and made me feel a little embarrassed. When I told Ba that I wanted to overcome my shyness and feel like I fit in, he eventually stopped laughing and fondly looked at me. I knew he was proud of me for adjusting to the new life there and didn't let my inability of speaking English hold me back. Ba also had good news that he wanted to share with me.

"I also went to apply for school today," Ba said.

"You went to learn English like in the Philippines?"

"Yes, but not only to learn English. I just enrolled in the GED program."

"What is GED?"

"It's a program that I need to finish before qualifying for college."

I didn't know what college was, but I knew it was always his dream to get a college degree since he always mentioned it. Ba came here when he was thirty-two, but regardless of his age, he didn't allow it to stop him from pursuing his dream. In Vietnam, Ba had been at the top of his class in medical school. I remember Ong Noi would always say, "Make sure to be like your dad when you grow up. He is a scholar." Ong Noi went on and bragged about Ba's achievements during school. I knew he was proud of his son and so was I. Co Kim suggested that Ba should go back to school and finish his education so we could live our American dream. She introduced the GED program to Ba and helped him to enroll in it. I was elated to see Ba on the path to his dream.

A week later, Ba got accepted to the Bronx Community College for his GED and got a job as a bus boy at a pizza parlor near our apartment. Each morning, Ba walked me to school and then walked to work. Since Ba had to go to school right after work, I had to learn to walk home by myself. I even cooked dinner for everyone since Chu Chau and Anh Tri got second jobs. I guess Ba saw that coming, hence why he taught me how to cook so I could take care of myself during times like that. I would go home, do my homework, prepare dinner, and wait for everyone to come home and eat together. However, our family dinners became less and less frequent, since everyone became busier. Chu Chau and Anh Tri got home late from their second jobs. As for Ba, he had late classes almost every night. By the time he arrived home, I was already in bed.

Ba and I spent less time together as his school and work occupied most of his schedule. I grew to dislike the weekdays as most of the time I would finish chores and had nothing else to do. I would sit alone in the apartment with no toys to play with. Since the days were getting darker sooner, and colder, there weren't any kids at the park for me to play with. I couldn't wait for the weekend to arrive soon enough. At least everyone would be home. We would cook and eat just like our first time together while sharing funny stories that we encountered during the weekdays.

Even on weekends, Ba would review with me what I had learned from school. He wanted to make sure that I understood everything and wasn't behind. We sat on the floor, studying together, using the dictionary that Chu Chau suggested he buy. Determined to get better in English, Ba diligently made me study with him. And thanks to that little push from Ba, we both could see improvements after a few weeks. Even though we couldn't say perfect sentences, we were at least able to communicate with everyone.

As time went by, the adults got busier, especially Ba, since he was always up late doing his homework. There were times when I woke up in the middle of the night and saw him sitting on the floor in the corner of the room studying. I never knew how much sleep he had gotten, but I would always hear him in the kitchen before I woke up. Ba would be making fried eggs and bread for me while I brushed my teeth and got ready for school. Most mornings, he didn't have time to sit and eat with me. With his usual reminder, Ba told me to concentrate in school and then headed for work. I could see how dedicated he was to obtain his GED to make more money to support us. I knew it wasn't easy for him to work full-time and attend school, but one thing I have learned from him is his devotion to getting an education. To ease some of Ba's responsibilities, there were evenings after I got home from school when I would cook the rice and make fish stew for everyone before they got home from work. While waiting for them, I didn't forget one of Ba's tasks he assigned to me. I continued to read the vocabulary book and tried to memorize as much as I could. I did pages of math problems that he had written for me every night before his studies. I always remembered his words, "Practice makes better." There were times I got lazy and frustrated for not understanding what I read. I relinquished to constantly looking up words in the dictionary and putting everything aside. When Ba asked me to recite what I had read, I honestly admitted to him that I surrendered to the daunting task. I could feel his anger in his silence. He gathered his composure and had me sit down. In his monotonic expression, Ba once again gave me his "little talk." He reminded me of our struggle to find freedom through pain and suffering and how we finally made it to America. He reminded me not to waste the opportunity that was given to us and to at least try our best to strive for a better life. It was always the reiterations of his words that made me feel guilty each time I wasn't working as hard as he was. I should have had it ingrained in my head by now, but I was glad to stand in front of him and receive his words of wisdom. His "little talk" helped me to become who I am today.

11 The TV

It was late December 1982, and the temperature was dropping. I experienced nothing that cold before. Growing up in Vietnam, I was exposed to tropical weather all year round. If it was cold, at least it was bearable with just a sweater. I was used to wiping my sweat from the blazing heat, but now I was constantly finding myself sniffing and wiping my snot while shivering from the harshness of the frigid air. Ba and I had been wearing the same clothes given to us in the Philippines and some donated by Co Kim's friends. However, none of them were thick enough to keep us warm. We needed thicker clothing.

Co Kim told us about a thrift store near the subway station which was thirty minutes of walking distance from the apartment. She mentioned the store sold second-hand clothing and we could get a good bargain. We were excited since that was what we could afford. We wanted to go to the store right away, but since everyone was busy working, we postponed it until the weekend.

On Sunday, Ba, Chu Chau, Anh Tri, and I woke up early. Each of us wore at least three layers of under-shirts with a sweater to prepare for the long walk. We made quick instant noodles and gulped them down in less than ten minutes. We wanted to be at the store early since we talked about it the night before. The minute we got out of the building, we were greeted by the cruel winter wind. We looked at each other wondering if we had worn enough clothing to fight through this bitter, chilly air. Chu Chau, with his optimism and determination, told us to cross our arms together to keep warm. As we walked, we talked to keep ourselves distracted from the cold. I could see the steams of breath leaving our mouths each time we spoke. I felt sorry for Anh Tri as he was frustrated with the steam constantly fogging up his glasses, partially blinding him. Halfway through the walk, we ran out of things to say. The constant, unbeatable wind was seeping through the thin layers of our clothes that we thought could sustain us from the piercing weather. This time, Ba initiated and told us to run. We ran and jogged until we made it to the store.

Anh Tri held the door open while all of us walked in. I was amazed to see so many items on display. I thought Co Kim said the store only carried clothing, but I saw furniture and other household items as well. Everything at the store was unbelievably cheap and affordable. We walked along different aisles to see what we could buy. However, we agreed not to buy any household items or furniture, since we could always test our luck at the dumpster. We took turns trying on a few jackets and coats. After an hour of looking and trying on clothes, we were lucky to get coats, gloves, scarves, and hats for all of us. We got out of the store and immediately put on everything that we just bought.

Our way back was less extraneous and unbearable. We took our time strolling through the streets instead of running while shivering. Finally, we could walk with warmth and enjoy the cold, which we never thought we could do. Anh Tri wished for snow so that we could go skiing while wearing his new coat. I was clueless as to what he was saying. I had never heard of skiing or snow growing up in the countryside of Vietnam. Curiously, I asked him. He told me that he'd only heard from others and saw pictures of it, but never saw it in person. The more he talked about it, the more I wanted to experience it for myself. Snow became the only subject we talked about until we got back to our apartment.

The next day, during the walk to school with Ba, he told me he was able to pick me up after dismissal since he didn't have class after work. I was happy because I didn't like walking home alone on a cold day, and besides, it had been a while since I walked home with Ba. When we got to my school, he hugged me and left for work.

Things had gotten better for me at school due to Mrs. McKeever's help. She taught me many new things, from speaking to writing. My English got better, and I understood Mrs. Powell. I participated often and tried to overcome my shyness. James introduced me to some of his friends, and I felt less lonely during lunch and recess. The more I felt acclimated to the class, the more I found learning to be interesting.

My other favorite class besides math was ESL (English as a Second Language) with Mrs. McKeever. Two more new kids joined my class in the back of the room. One boy was from Cambodia and the other boy was from Eritrea. They were both immigrants like me and needed help learning English. We spent an hour every day studying with Mrs. McKeever. As always, with a smile, Mrs. McKeever patiently repeated herself over and over again until we could say the words correctly. I never once saw the frustration on her face regardless of how clueless we were. "It's OK, you can do it" was what she would say to us each time we made a mistake. These simple words from her were like the note that Ba gave me on my first day of school. They were a great comfort that helped me to stop feeling like I was incapable. They gave me the strength to try everything to the best of my ability until I could excel. I took these words to heart as a reminder that I should never give up, always be persistent, and that I could achieve anything.

At dismissal, Ba was waiting for me by the main entrance. On the way home, I told Ba about the two new boys who just joined my ESL class, and how I felt more at ease for not being the only one who needed help with English. At the moment of the conversation, I felt droplets of white particles on my face. I reached to pick them off, but instead, the particles melted on the tip of my finger. I turned to Ba and saw the same white particles on top of his fluffy black hair. We both turned our necks backward and looked straight up to the sky. A constant flurry of these white particles graciously trickled from the sky. At first, I wondered if the rain in America was different from the rain in Vietnam. I looked at Ba for an answer, but instead saw a look of confusion on his face as he was trying to figure out what these things were as well. He paused for a while, then told me this must have been what they called snow.

I was ecstatic to see the snow that Anh Tri mentioned. I couldn't wait to run home and tell him about my first encounter with it. I was mesmerized as the snow came down. I opened my hand to catch as much snow as I could, but as soon as it touched my hand, it would melt within seconds. I opened my mouth to taste it. I wanted to see if it had any flavor, but it was no different from droplets of icy water. The ground started to build a thin layer of white snow. As I walked, I left imprints with my shoes. It reminded me of the times when my siblings and I would walk on the wet sandy beach comparing our footprints. I wished they were there to compare footprints again on the glistening snow.

As the snow fell harder and covered the entire ground around me, I wondered about how much more it could snow. What if the snow did not stop and bury us all? I frantically turned to look for Ba but didn't see him. Panicking, I kept on looking, and there he was, half a block behind me. I was so immersed in playing with the snow that I unknowingly ran far away from him.

"Are we going to be buried under this snow, Ba?" I asked as I ran back to him.

"No, we won't. It's not that much." Ba laughed as he wiped the snow off my head.

I felt reassured as Ba was saying that the snow wouldn't hurt us. I held onto his hand instead of wandering along the sidewalk by myself. We continued to walk toward the apartment as the snow kept on drizzling.

When we got back to the apartment, Ba dried my hair and told me to get ready to cook dinner. I helped him but continued to be distracted by the snow. I kept on looking out the window to make sure there was still snow. I couldn't wait for Anh Tri to come home so I could share my experience. At dusk, Chu Chau and Anh Tri got back from work. I immediately asked them if they had seen the snow. Anh Tri said they could only catch the snow for a little while before it turned into rain.

I was kind of disappointed that it stopped snowing. I was hoping to go outside with Anh Tri, letting the snow pile on our heads, and wondering how it would feel. In Vietnam, each time there was rain, the kids would run outside, stomp on puddles of water, and get soaked before heading back in. We would wait for moments like that to have a refreshing shower from nature.

We all helped to carry dishes of food that Ba cooked out to the living room. During dinner, Chu Chau thanked Ba for making the food while he and Anh Tri were at work. He described his lunch time as being quick-paced and lonely. Because of his limited English, he was a recluse at work. Having dinner with all of us while speaking our native tongue, he felt much more comfortable. As I listened to them elucidating how the language barrier was a problem, I saw the joy in these men as they couldn't wait to get home for Ba's dinner.

"Do you guys want to go treasure hunting again?" Chau asked. "People are putting their stuff in the dumpster today."

"Yes, we can go. I hope we can find more mattresses today," Ba said.

We put the dishes in the sink and then left for another round of treasure hunting. This time, we didn't go far. Instead of walking up and down the block, we went straight to the dumpster behind the building. Anh Tri spotted a small television exposed under some cardboard. We rushed to the television, pulled the cardboard away, and were excited to see no broken screen. Without hesitation, Anh Tri lifted the twelve-inch TV, and we quickly headed back home. We were elated to have found a TV. There were numerous times that we walked by electronic stores and saw many displays of TVs that we knew we could never afford. Our desire had come true.

When we got back to the apartment, we wiped our new prized possession with water, and then realized it was missing a knob that was supposed to be held on a small stick for changing the channels. Anh Tri plugged in the TV and we saw something, but it was blurry. Chu Chau played with the two metal rods on top of the TV and explained to us this was how his boss at work fixed his TV. By moving these rods, which were called antennas, the picture got clearer. After he maneuvered the antennas for a few minutes, we could see clearer pictures on the screen. Jumping with excitement, I realized that I didn't have to stare at the walls anymore. Anh Tri left to go to the kitchen and came back with a pair of pliers. We were curious as to what he was about to do. He grabbed the little stick with the pliers, twisted left and right, and each time a different channel appeared. I volunteered to stand by the TV and switched the channels for them. I was their remote control for the entire night.

That was the first night we heard voices besides ours. Although we couldn't understand most of the things that were said, we were enthused by what we saw. As I randomly flipped through the channels, Anh Tri stopped me when he saw two men battling in a ring. I walked farther away to get a better glimpse and curiously watched these men fight. We were amazed at how two men furiously beating and throwing each other were still able to survive without injuries. We were glued to the TV until it was over.

The next day after school, it was different on the way home. Instead of taking my time walking, I felt a rush of eagerness to watch something new on the TV. I decided to run. At times I slowed down for air, but I wasted no time. When I got to the apartment, I felt the urge to turn on the TV right away, but I remembered the chores Ba had left for me. I did my homework, cooked the rice, and made the usual dishes, all within two hours. Then I grabbed the pair of pliers and was thrilled to see what would be showing on the TV.

As I flipped through the channels, a big yellow bird caught my eye. It wasn't an ordinary bird; it was a talking bird that was taller than the humans it was talking to. As I continued to watch, other colorful animals conversed with humans. The more I watched, the more I felt it was made for me. They were teaching me how to speak English slowly and I followed along. Despite struggling at times due to my thick Vietnamese accent, I kept on saying the words out loud. I repeated Big Bird, Elmo, and Cookie Monster's names each time they appeared on the screen. For every commercial break, I heard, "*Sesame Street* will be right back." When *Sesame Street* was over, I saw a man walk into his home, remove his jacket, and replace it with a red sweater. He sang a song, *Won't You Be My Neighbor?* I was captivated as he sang while changing into his loafers. I spent the next thirty minutes watching him and wished that I could be his neighbor.

Sesame Street and *Mr. Rogers* became my two favorite shows after school. I diligently watched them every day and told Ba that these shows were supplementing my studies. I didn't want Ba to think I was spending too much time watching TV. I followed what Mr. Rogers said, being good neighbors and greeting people who I saw several times at the building. I recited words that I had learned from Sesame Street to James and his friends at school. I saw that my English was getting better as I bravely spoke without worrying about pronunciation. I tried to suppress all the scary thoughts that someone might laugh at me for saying something wrong. Big Bird was always compassionate each time he spoke to others. I just imagined that whoever I spoke to was as forgiving as Big Bird.

Besides learning English from TV, Mrs. McKeever introduced me to books that I could use to improve my reading. She took me to the school library and helped me check out a few books. Most of the books were easy to understand since they had more pictures than words. The pictures were so colorful that at times I found myself engrossed in the images rather than the words. I would create a scene for myself. Among these books, *Curious George* was my favorite. The colors were vivid, and I could picture myself as the little monkey wanting to explore anything new. The man in the yellow hat was always there taking care of George, reminding me of Ba.

One night during dinner in the middle of January 1983, we were glad that we watched the news. We had never watched the news before, but that evening while flipping through the channels, we saw the weatherman forecasting snow for the next several days. I was excited and told Anh Tri that we were finally going to be able to play in the snow. He was elated as well and couldn't wait to see it. By the next morning, while getting ready for school, I looked out of the window and saw snow accumulating on the walkway. I remembered what Ba said about the snow and that it was harmless. That morning, I walked alone while following other kids walking with their parents in front of me. The snow was coming down harder and faster as the trees were now engulfed with snow. Some of the kids in front of me dropped their backpacks, compressed a handful of snow in their hands, and threw it at each other. They laughed as they played, and I thought about how fun it would be to throw snowballs at Anh Tri. When I arrived in front of the school, I saw a couple of janitors shoveling the snow, placing it off to the side of the sidewalk. They cleared a pathway, and I could understand why. I slid on the slippery, icy snow right before I got to school.

When it was about time to leave at dismissal, I saw parents standing outside waiting for their kids as I walked along the hallway toward the main entrance door. I knew that Ba wouldn't be able to pick me up that day, but surprisingly I saw him waiting outside with Anh Tri. I ran toward them and was met with another surprise. The snow that had fallen that morning was now above my ankles. I approached Ba. "Why are you and Anh Tri here today?"

"I heard during work that it will be snowing hard today so I wanted to come and pick you up," Ba said.

"I got home early today too and saw your dad, so I wanted to go with him," Anh Tri added.

"This morning, I saw kids making snowballs and throwing them at each other," I excitedly told Anh Tri.

While the janitors were shoveling snow, I bent down and piled as much snow as I could in my hands. I threw the snowball and hit Anh Tri on his chest. He rolled up one for himself and happily returned the favor. We three walked home, and while Ba didn't want to participate, Anh Tri and I had a great time chasing each other and having a snowball fight.

After the third day of constant snow, it was no longer fun. The snow finally stopped, but the temperature dropped and the snow turned to ice. Walking to school became worrisome as I tried to find a dry spot to prevent slipping and falling. Throwing snowballs wasn't fun either, since it was hard and felt like throwing a rock. After this first encounter with the snow, I told Anh Tri that I preferred showering in the rain.

For the next two months, I didn't like to be outside that much, except for going to school and food shopping with Ba. The harsh winter was too much for me to bear. I wasn't used to the chilly wind and chapped lips. I chose to be inside the apartment to watch *Sesame Street* and *Mr. Rogers* and improve my English.

As the cold weather ceased and the spring of 1983 came, I wanted to show Mrs. McKeever what I had learned from watching TV and reading books. I wanted to show her the things that she taught me as well. I wanted her to be proud of me and acknowledge her efforts in teaching me. I told her about an entire scene that I had watched on *Sesame Street*. I knew that it would be a challenge for me to articulate in detail what I saw, but at the same time, I was determined to accept the challenge. She attentively listened to me with her eyes focused on mine while her smile gave me the comfort to continue. I stumbled on my words at times, but she remained patient during my struggles. At the end of my delivery, she clapped her hands profusely, praised my effort, and reminded me again to believe in myself.

After my delivery, Mrs. McKeever tasked me to draw a scene of my hometown in Vietnam. I was delighted and grabbed the pencils and crayons in front of me. I folded the drawing paper in half, and on one side I sketched a drawing of Vietnam while on the other side I wrote America. I drew a picture of our home in Vietnam. Next to it, I drew a boy on a water buffalo to represent how kids helped their parents to plow the land. I showed how I ran on the beach with the kite that Ong Noi made for me, but I also didn't forget to draw Ba and me on the boat to America while Ma and my siblings were wondering. I didn't know that this drawing would later become something valuable to me for many years later. Mrs. McKeever had always been a kind soul and I was extremely lucky to have her as a teacher. I will always be grateful for her support. We keep in touch to this day.

12 My Friends

Summer was approaching and it was near the end of second grade. I felt more comfortable talking to other students in the class. I no longer feared choosing what I wanted in the cafeteria line. I knew what I wanted to eat and how to eat it. At recess, I chased down James and his friends while playing tag. When we played basketball, I got to practice dribbling the ball. I wasn't good at it but was hoping to improve someday. Although my English wasn't as good as others, I was able to raise my hand and answer some of the questions Mrs. Powell asked.

Ba was also near the end of his semester. There were nights that he stayed up late to finish his studies. However, I never heard him complain of being tired or feeling overwhelmed with both work and studying. I saw him use the dictionary so often that the corners of the book started to wear down. I wished that Ba had a desk and a chair to sit on. Those nights sitting on the floor and hunching over to write, I could see he struggled to get up at times. I hoped that one day we could find him a table.

Chu Chau and Anh Tri were getting home later than usual. I remembered they mentioned working at another place where they got paid more. The only problem was that the new job was in a different borough, Brooklyn, which took them almost an hour by subway going in a single direction.

On the last day of second grade, Mrs. Powell told us to clean out our desks. Six months had passed by quickly. I was surprised to see so many papers I had accumulated in my desk. I looked at some of my assignments and saw improvements in my English. However, I was sad to say my goodbyes to Mrs. McKeever. Although she told me we would meet again after the summer break, I felt uneasy and afraid. I didn't want to fall behind once I started third grade.

The summer of 1983 was rough for me. Chu Chau and Anh Tri had to move to Brooklyn so that they could be closer to their new work. It was sad to see them leave, but Ba and I understood it was a good opportunity for them. We were sad to say farewell. I thought by now Ba and I would be used to saying goodbye since we had departed from our friends from Hong Kong and the Philippines. However, this time was different. We had spent many memories walking through dumpsters and having cheerful nights sitting on the floor. Our bond in friendship had escalated to seeing them as family members. We were grateful for their kindness during the past six months.

The apartment felt empty since it was only Ba and me. It felt strange cutting back the portions when I prepared dinner. It became a habit that I would pour four cups of rice into the pot. Every time I had to remove the extra two cups and put them back in the rice bag, I thought of Chu Chau and Anh Tri. I wondered if they were doing well at the new place. Whenever I watched TV and saw wrestling, I missed the screaming and yelling from Anh Tri. He was so much into the fight, especially when he saw one guy slam the other. Everything at home reminded me of them. I didn't realize they had taken a place in my heart. It felt like I just said goodbye to my family again.

The days seemed longer because I didn't have to go to school. After Ba left in the morning for work, I continued with my daily routine of finishing up the homework that Ba left for me. I read books that I checked out from the public library. My reading improved since I read a lot during the winter and spring. I started to prefer books with more words than pictures. As much as I loved reading, I would always revert to watching *Sesame Street* and *Mr. Rogers*. One night, after dinner, I was flipping through the channels and stumbled upon a black car driving by itself and talking to Michael Knight. I was immediately glued to the TV and was astonished that there was such a thing as a talking car. The car's name was KITT (Knight Industries Two Thousand) and the more I watched, the more I wished I could have something like that. After that night, *Knight Rider* became a show that I never missed.

Since the weather had gotten warmer, I went back to the park hoping to see those Vietnamese kids. It had been a long time since I spoke any Vietnamese to anyone my age. When I got to the park, I spotted the same boy who I saw on my first day coming to the area. I decided to approach him and his friends.

"Hello, can I join you guys?" I bravely asked him.

"Sure, do you know how to shoot marbles?" he replied nicely.

"Yes, I do."

"Here is a marble if you don't have one," he said. "What's your name? My name is Bang."

"Thank you for the marble. You can call me Linh."

Bang introduced me to his friends, Tam, Dan, and Hien. We were all about the same age, except for Hien. He was at least five years older than me. However, Hien seemed very nice and was like a big brother that day. We squatted on the ground to shoot marbles. I was happy to speak Vietnamese again as I didn't have to struggle with translating my thoughts into English. It felt like I was back in Vietnam playing with my friends. The five of us played and laughed as though we were best friends. I had never laughed that much in a long time playing with kids my age even though my skill wasn't as good as when I was in Vietnam. Since I hadn't played in a long time, I finished last in most of the games, but luckily, they weren't bored of me and let me try again. We played for almost two hours until we had to go home for dinner. Bang told the group to meet again the next day at 3 PM.

During my walk home, I felt ecstatic that I made new friends but mostly was proud of myself for overcoming my shyness. I couldn't wait to tell Ba about the day's experience, especially letting him know that I got out of my comfort zone and made new friends. I was sure he would be happy for me. I got home, still feeling euphoric, and while making dinner, I started to sing Mr. Rogers' song, *Won't You Be My Neighbor?* I saved Ba's dinner in the refrigerator since he was getting home later than usual. He had been taking more classes in the summer so that he could finish his GED to start college in the fall. I sat with my dinner and couldn't wait to watch *Knight Rider*.

Surprisingly, Ba came home early that night since one of his classes was canceled. Excitedly, I turned to Ba and pointed to KITT. He was also amazed and wished that one day he could own a car, let alone a talking car. I told him about my new friends and how I got to shoot marbles again.

"It sounds like you had fun today!" Ba said.

"Yes. These kids were nice, especially Bang. He lent me one of his marbles," I said.

"Oh. I am sorry. I forgot to buy you the marbles that you asked for last time. Use this to buy them tomorrow so you can play with your friends." He handed me ten cents.

I was delighted and overjoyed to hear Ba say those words. I planned to ask him to buy me marbles but was hesitant since I knew how hard he had been working. I didn't want him to think that I wasted his hard-earned money. But since he was willing to give me the ten cents to buy marbles and have fun with my friends, I gave him a bunch of hugs and kisses. It might not be worth much to someone, but for me, that amount was the world.

The next day, the moment the stationary store opened, I ran across the park, crossed the main street (Fordham Road), and got to the store. I quickly ran to the aisle and found a bag of marbles, which was the cheapest bag of five marbles costing ten cents. I gave the money to the cashier and ran home, then took a blanket to the living room and laid it flat. With the five marbles that I had, I started to practice my shooting skills. I wanted to sharpen my skills to impress my friends. One by one, I increased the distance as my accuracy got better. After a few hours, I got the hang of it and couldn't wait to play with them. At 3 PM, I ran to the park, and there they were. I showed them my new marbles and we quickly started the game. After a couple of shots, they seemed surprised that my skill improved overnight. I didn't tell them about my practice on the blanket. I won some of the games but refused to take their marbles since they didn't take any from me. Usually, the winner would take the marbles from the loser depending on the wager.

For the next couple of weeks, we regularly played marbles. However, there were older groups of teenagers playing near us. They were betting a large number of marbles in their game. There were times that Hien would join them, and we all stood there cheering for him. As I watched them play, and when Hien lost bags of marbles, I counted the marbles that I had in my pocket and thought there was no way I could bet that much. Bang joined in the games at times, and he didn't have much success either. I was reluctant to follow suit. I didn't want to lose my marbles and have to ask Ba for money to buy them again, but when there were times when Hien and Bang won, they would graciously give me some.

Bang and I became close as I got to know him more. He was a year older. He lived with his mother and a younger sister who was two years younger than me. I had never heard him talk about his father. His apartment was a few blocks away from the park, but we didn't go to the same school due to different zoning. After a few weeks of playing marbles, he invited me to his apartment. I met his mother, Di (*a formal address for older female adults*) Lai, and his younger sister, Lien. His mother was about Ba's age. She was talkative but genuinely nice. She always welcomed me and offered me food whenever I came over. On the other hand, Lien was quiet and shy. The first time I was at their apartment, Di Lai asked me about my family. I told her that I was there with my dad and that my entire family was still back in Vietnam. She continued to ask if I'd missed my mother. I wondered why she would ask such a question, but maybe because after telling her about how Ba and I lived together, she might have felt empathetic towards me. I answered her anyway and told her that I missed my family every day.

I never invited Bang to my place even though I wanted to. I was honest and told him about the TV that we found at the dumpster and how it would take a while to fix the antenna for a clear picture. I didn't have anything fancy in the apartment and no place to sit but the floor. On top of that, I didn't have extra food to offer him. I felt embarrassed to invite him over. Bang seemed to understand my difficulties and never asked to visit.

One day, while waiting for Bang at the park, I roamed around and saw something with wheels near a pile of trash bags. I ran over and saw a red tricycle. It wasn't a typical tricycle with three wheels. This one had a big wheel at the front, two smaller ones at the back, the seat was near the bottom by the smaller wheels, and the entire tricycle frame was made of plastic. However, the back of the seat was broken, but I couldn't care less. I hurriedly carried the tricycle back to the apartment and couldn't wait for Bang. I was hoping that if he didn't see me, he'd go to my apartment to find me. I placed the tricycle into the bathtub, filled the water halfway, and wiped it down. After fifteen minutes of cleaning, there were more sparkles in my eyes than in the shiny paint illuminating from the tricycle. The tricycle was ready for a test drive. I excitedly brought it to the park to show Bang, but he was nowhere to be seen. Running out of patience, I biked from one end of the park to another, while my toes were pressing onto my flip-flops and maneuvering the pedals. I felt a sense of joy as the wind was blowing on my face. At that moment, I thought of KITT. I imagined that I was Michael Knight talking to my red KITT, my very first favorite bike. I continued to bike and didn't want to stop until I saw Bang walking toward the basketball court.

"Where did you get that new bike?" Bang screamed.

"I found it in the dumpster over there," I pointed to the dumpster. "Brought it home and cleaned it. It looks new, doesn't it?" I proudly continued.

"Can I try it?" Bang asked.

"Of course! Here!" I replied.

I stood there watching Bang steering my KITT. He was increasing the speed, steering side to side, going on the grass, and heading back out to the concrete ground. As much as I was happy to share it with him, I was hoping that KITT was strong enough to handle such a rough test drive. Hien, Tam, and Dan approached and wondered where Bang got the tricycle. I told them that I found it. When Bang pulled up to us, everyone was fighting to go next. For the next thirty minutes, my KITT served everyone around the park. After everyone had fun with KITT, we decided to play marbles. I didn't want to take a chance of leaving KITT to the side. I feared that someone might take it or ask to borrow it. I told them to play first while I took KITT back to the apartment.

That night, Ba came home to see a red tricycle next to the kitchen. He asked me if I borrowed it from one of my friends. I told him how I found it at one of the dumpsters near the park and brought it home to clean it.

"How did you carry it home?" Ba seemed concerned.

"I just carried it for two blocks. Not heavy at all, Ba," I excitedly said.

Ba paused for a while, and with a sad face, he headed to the kitchen as he asked if I had dinner yet. I followed and helped him prepare dinner for both of us.

"Are you sad that you had to find toys at the dumpster?" Ba sadly asked.

"No, I am not, Ba. The bike looks new. I love it!" I said.

"I promise to get you a new bike when I get a pay raise," Ba said with a cracking voice.

"You don't have to. I am happy with this one." I leaned in to hug Ba.

Ba held me fondly as he appreciated my understanding of our situation. However, I still saw the sadness in his eyes. As we sat down to eat, I tried to make him feel better by telling him how all my friends loved my new bike. They all wanted to take turns riding around the park. I even told him how I named the bike KITT just like in *Knight Rider*.

During the last month of the summer, I brought KITT to the park almost every day, in the mornings and afternoons. After Ba left for work, I would have a quick breakfast and then take KITT to the park. I rode around for at least five laps before going back home to finish the math assignments that Ba always left for me. In the afternoon, my friends were waiting for me at the marble-shooting site and were ready to ask for a ride. One day, I noticed a metal rod connecting the two wheels had broken off causing one of the wheels to fall off. I asked Ba to help me fix it, but he didn't know how to weld the metal rod together. I was disappointed, but no one could help me get it repaired. There was no other choice but to let KITT go. It was extremely sad for me to bring KITT and place it in the same dumpster where I had found it in. The moment that I turned away from KITT, I felt a heaviness in my heart. I couldn't help but tighten my face as the tears welled up in my eyes. I walked away with tears streaming down my cheeks knowing that would be the last time I saw KITT.

13 Third Grade Awakening

I said goodbye to KITT as I said goodbye to summer. I was ready to go back to school as a proud third grader. It had also been a monumental effort for Ba as he completed his GED and got accepted to the Bronx Community College. Those late nights that he spent studying on the hardwood floor paid off. The night while lying in bed, before both of us started our next educational path, Ba encouraged me to do well that year. He had set examples throughout the last ten months as we resided in New York City. I didn't have to imagine what he had done, but I witnessed what he went through—from working in the mornings to attending school at night and still being able to accomplish his goals.

As I got dressed in the morning for school, those words that Ba told me the night before had been ingrained in my head. I felt a burst of confidence and determination to do well that year because I wanted Ba to be proud of me as much as I was proud of him. As Ba was preparing breakfast for us, I saw the excitement on his face as he couldn't wait to start college.

I was a little sad since Ba couldn't take me to school on the first day, but by now I had gotten used to walking alone. Some parents walked their kids, and I would follow along in their path. When I got to school, I was excited to see James. I never knew where he lived, otherwise, I would ask him to join Bang and my friends for a game of marbles. We greeted each other and excitedly walked to our new classroom. During our last day of second grade, we compared each other's report cards which indicated we both would be in the same class. While walking to the class, I had a few marbles in my pocket. I took them out and with my broken English, I told James how I played and met new friends at the park. When we got to the classroom, our new teacher, Mrs. Tepperman, greeted us at the door. We told her our names as she checked off the list and assigned us our seats. This time, James and I weren't next to each other, but close enough so we could share our math answers.

Mrs. Tepperman was much older than Mrs. Powell. She was in her fifties, with short curly hair, and glasses hanging on the tip of her nose, below her eyes. Her demeanor was intimidating as she only nodded her head in confirmation rather than using spoken words. I was full of enthusiasm to start third grade, but facing Mrs. Tepperman's cold aura took my excitement away like a deflated balloon. After everyone settled into their seats, she immediately apprised us to raise our hands if we had any questions. When she spoke, I promptly had flashbacks of my teachers in Vietnam. They were exactly like her, except with long black hair and always walking around with a stick. I looked around to see the trepidation on these students' faces. We all sat quietly with our hands folded and placed on top of our desks as we silently listened to her instructions. However, the silence didn't last long. Some of the kids started to talk when Mrs. Tepperman was writing on the blackboard. Immediately, she turned around and didn't hesitate to scream at us. She was terrifying, to put it simply.

After a few days in Mrs. Tepperman's class, I found she was more difficult than I had imagined. It wasn't easy to get her permission for a bathroom break. She would firmly say "no" most of the times that we asked, especially during her lessons. We all tried to adjust to her strict rules by not drinking too much water during school. However, at times it was arduous holding a full bladder until recess or lunchtime.

It was during lunch that I first felt a stomach ache. I skipped the beginning of recess and ran to the bathroom while James and my friends played on the field. When I got back to class, I still felt unsettled in my stomach. Near dismissal, I felt the pain creep up on my insides again, forcing me to tightly grasp my stomach, trembling and holding back my cold sweat. I managed to sit through class until my bowels couldn't hold it any longer. I nervously raised my hand, expecting that Mrs. Tepperman would deny my request. However, I needed to take that chance.

"Mrs. Tepperman, may I go to the bathroom?" I beseeched.

"No! It's almost time to go home," she firmly replied.

I wasn't disheartened to hear her response, but it frustrated me she couldn't see the dire image of a desperate nine-year-old needing to expend his relief painted on my face. I sat with my legs crossed, holding my stomach, and squeezed my behind. I prayed that class would be over soon so that I could rush home. The minute that Mrs. Tepperman allowed us to leave, I ran for the door and out of the school. I tried to walk as fast as I could while controlling my bowels, but I failed halfway through my walk. I slowly walked as I defecated in my pants. I was filled with anger and embarrassment. I didn't want to get too close to the people in front of me, but not too slow that the people behind me would catch up. I continued to walk, but I didn't want to shed a tear, since I had promised Ba I would be strong and determined. When I got back to the apartment, shame took over me as my behind was still uncomfortably holding in the mess of a defeated nine-year-old. Although I wanted to cry and blame Mrs. Tepperman for my accident, I knew Ba would want me to do otherwise, so I removed my clothes and turned on the water in the bathtub. I grabbed the detergent bottle and poured it just how Ba would. As the stains disappeared, so did my resentment towards Mrs. Tepperman.

That afternoon, I prepared dinner but wasn't in the mood to watch any TV. That was the first time in my life I came home feeling embarrassed that I soiled my pants. I sat on the couch in silence waiting for Ba to come home. When he entered the room, he sensed something had happened to me. He looked at the window and saw it was opened with my clothing hanging on the fire escape rail. He sat next to me and with a crack in my voice, I held in my tears to tell him what had happened. Ba placed his hands on my shoulders and commended me for being mature. He said that I shouldn't feel bad, and it could have happened to anyone. As he talked to me, I felt much better and the shame slowly went away.

I was so absorbed with my incident that I forgot to ask how his day was at school. I quickly changed my mood and asked how it went. As we were eating, Ba kept on telling us how his college was hugely different from getting a GED. He was all over the campus, walking from one building to another for his classes. I couldn't visualize what Ba was talking about, since the only class I had to change was going from my class to the lunchroom. It sounded like he had multiple buildings that he had to get used to. Ba talked about how his classes were mainly students at least ten years younger than him, but there were a few in there who were also immigrants like us from different countries. As he kept on telling me about his day, I could see the enthusiasm he had during his first week in school. I was glad that at least one of us had a good day. By nighttime, Ba went to the fire escape and brought back my clothing. He was impressed that I did an excellent job cleaning them. Before we went to bed, he reminded me again to stay strong and not let what happened today bother me.

The next day back in school, I hoped no one noticed my awkwardness the day before as I dashed for the exit door. Walking from the main entrance to my classroom, I nervously looked around the hallway and hoped no one would approach me to ask questions. I reminded myself of Ba's words, forgetting what had happened, as I kept on walking. When I got to the door, I timidly looked at Mrs. Tepperman and greeted her. I went straight to my desk and sat down quietly waiting for the first assignment to begin.

Mrs. Tepperman told us to take out our reading comprehension assignment. She sat in front of the class and read passages as we were silently reading along. After reading the passages, there were multiple questions for us to answer. She called on a student to answer the first question, and he answered it correctly. She called on the second one, and she got it right as well. She turned to give me eye contact and called on me.

"Linh, read question number three!" she said with a stern face.

I stood up and read it out loud. "The boy ____ the stick."

There were four multiple choices for me to choose from to fill in the blank. I stared at them and had no idea what they even meant. I had never seen any of these words before, plus I didn't understand what the passage she read was about. I stood there as she waited to hear from me. I could feel the trembling in my legs as I had to guess to give her an answer. I raised my head and looked at her, hoping she could give me words of encouragement like Mrs.

McKeever. Instead, she gave me a straight, unmerciful face, expecting a response soon. I felt the tingling throughout my body as my heart beat faster, and I broke out in a sweat. Somehow, my eyes were fixated on the letter C.

"C," I nervously said.

"Why did you pick C?" she asked with a smirk creeping between her lips.

"C, I think," I said again as my voice cracked.

"C is swallowed. Why would the boy swallow a stick?" She chuckled.

The entire class laughed. I was so ashamed that I just wanted to run out of the class and hide. All my confidence and determination that I would do better that school year went down the drain. I froze, standing there as my legs were glued to the ground. I had my eyes fixated on the floor, afraid the kids would make fun of me if I looked at them. I felt like time had stopped to let me face this humiliation from everyone's laughter. I wanted to cry but didn't want to give them more reason to look down on me. That moment seemed endless. The laughter ended as Mrs. Tepperman continued to the next student. However, I still heard continuing soft laughter as some students mocked my answer. For the entire morning, I was glad that she didn't call on me for another question. I couldn't stand to bear any more embarrassment.

During the walk to lunch, I quietly followed at the end of the line, hoping that no one would see or hear me. More than ever, I wished my existence was invisible. I got my lunch and walked toward the class table, but I was reluctant to sit near them. I didn't want anyone to laugh at me again. I wished James was there so I could sit with him and feel less isolated. I knew James would be a good friend as he always had been. He would say words to comfort me. Unfortunately, he was absent that day. I spotted a table, which was occupied by a few kids. I sat at the very end and ate my lunch. Although I tried not to make myself noticeable, I could still hear the laughter of other kids. Some of them were pointing at me and gave me a new name: "The swallow stick boy." As much as I tried to ignore them, I was tearing up inside. I held it in and refused to let any tear drop from my eyes, as I remembered how Ba taught me to be brave and not be bothered by others who had nothing nice to say.

Recess was no better than lunch. I continued to hide from being seen. I saw James' friends playing at our usual spot, but I couldn't bring myself to go over to play with them, afraid they might hear other kids calling my new name. I walked to the wall where I used to stand on my first day of school. I wanted to go home and be safe with Ba.

We got back to class, and I couldn't wait for school to be over. The minute I heard the last bell, I darted out as fast as I could. I got home, locked myself in the room, and waited for Ba to come home. I wondered why so many terrible things happened during that school year. Was I not good enough for third grade? Should I quit school and study at home by watching *Sesame Street* and reading books from the library? So many thoughts were pounding in my head, and I doubted myself. Finally, I burst into tears. I felt bad for letting Ba down. I wanted to make him feel proud, but I just wasn't good enough.

Ba came home before dinner since he had an early class. I rushed out of the room, ran to Ba, and held him tightly. With tears pouring down my cheeks, I told him what happened. Ba led me to the couch, and with his usual reassurance, he comforted me.

"It's OK if you don't know the answer. This is why you go to school to learn," Ba consoled me.

"But everyone laughed at me," I cried.

"They can laugh all they want. We can't control it. But most importantly, you should not look down on yourself." Ba patted my head.

I paused for a while and nervously asked Ba, even though I already knew his answer, "Is it OK if I stay home and study by reading books and *Sesame Street*?"

"No, it's not OK, Con. You need to go back to school. Both you and I need to go to school so we can improve ourselves," Ba fondly said.

Ba changed the subject by asking me about math. It immediately changed my mood, and I told him that I understood everything. I told Ba that those math problems he gave me over the summer to practice made it much easier in third grade. I saw a smile on his face as he rubbed my head. I could see his intention for making me regain my courage and confidence back. He told me not to let a small mistake hold me down. We both got off the couch; I headed to the bathroom to wash my face while Ba went to the kitchen to prepare dinner.

While waiting for Ba to cook dinner, I turned on the TV, and *Sesame Street* was playing. I saw Big Bird talking to a little boy, "Bad days happen to everyone, but when one happens to you, just keep doing your best and never let a bad day make you feel bad about yourself." Tears ran down the little boy's cheek, and I found myself in tears as well. I felt as if Big Bird was talking to me. Those words were exactly what I needed to hear. Big Bird just lifted my spirit and made me feel that everything would be okay. I wiped my tears and wanted to hug him just like the little boy did.

The next day I went to school, I tried to put everything behind me, and continued to do my best. However, as I walked into the classroom, I heard some kids giggling and whispering, "The swallow stick boy is here!" Mrs. Tepperman continued with another assignment, but this time she didn't call on me. I sat there quietly and was afraid to participate in anything. By mid-morning, I had to attend ESL with Mrs. McKeever. I walked to her office, and she noticed my dispirited mood. She asked if I was feeling okay. I told her everything that happened yesterday from the embarrassment and the loneliness after lunch. I tried to speak slowly and hoped she understood me.

After I finished, she looked at me and said, "It's okay. Everyone makes mistakes. That is how we learn." She continued to hold my hand and with a smile, she said, "I believe in you!" For the first time, someone besides Ba believed in me. I looked down at the table and was about to tear up. It wasn't because I was sad, but hearing those words meant so much to me. At that moment, I felt the motherly love that I had been longing for. I felt as if Ma was sitting there and saying those words to me. I guess Mrs. McKeever had become a motherly figure to me. I reached out to hug her as I wholeheartedly thanked her for all the help and encouragement she had given me.

Three months went by, and my first report card was given to me to bring home for Ba. I could see a dull look on his face as he went through the grades. Almost every subject was needing improvements except for math and behavior. Everything pertaining to English was below average. After reading the comments from Mrs. Tepperman, Ba sat down and wrote a long comment back to her on the parents' rebuttal box. I didn't know what he wrote, but I was thankful that he did. The day after Mrs. Tepperman received Ba's note, her demeanor completely changed. She stopped yelling and screaming. She became nicer and I could finally see somewhat of a smile on her face. She even permitted us to use the bathroom whenever we needed it. But most of all, she paid more attention when I needed help with whatever subjects I was behind on.

    Third grade was a game changer for me. With the help of Mrs. McKeever and Mrs. Tepperman, I excelled and improved in all subjects. I could see a big smile on Ba's face every time he read my report card. School became fun and interesting. Mrs. Tepperman was no longer the mean teacher I thought she was. I had a lot of fun studying in her class and was thankful for all her help.

14 The Change

It had been a couple of months since Ba enrolled at the Bronx Community College for his associate's degree. Ba applied for financial aid, but he still needed money to pay for books and other expenses. Since Chu Chau and Anh Tri moved out, Ba had to pay the entire rent himself, which forced him to work more hours. On top of that, occasionally I would see Ba spending more nights studying as if his college coursework was getting harder. His schedule became so busy. Between work and school, he didn't even have time for a proper meal. Munching on dried noodles and drinking tea became his everyday meal while stayed up late to finish his schoolwork. As a result of eating unhealthy food at irregular times, Ba developed a stomach ulcer. His stomach flared up every few weeks. Each time the pain got worse. Ba would scream and tuck a pillow underneath his stomach while rolling on the floor grunting. I tried to rub his lower back hoping it would help relieve the pain, but it didn't. There was nothing I could do to ease his pain. I could only stand there, cry, and wait until his pain subsided.

After seeing the doctor about his ulcer condition, the doctor suggested that Ba take Mylanta, an acid reflux medication, to reduce the acidity in his stomach. I could see that Ba kept a bottle of Mylanta in the refrigerator all the time. It helped him from time to time during a flare-up. The thing I admired most about Ba was his mentality. His determination always amazed me. As soon as he felt a little better physically, he would get right back to his studies. He would curve his back with a pillow pressed against his stomach, grimace in pain, and look at an open book in front of him. Ba never wasted any chance to study. He kept telling me over and over again that we came to America for a better life, and that the only way to get that was through education. Ba had set his goal for his college degree and was adamant to get it.

    One night, I was asleep while Ba was studying. He woke me up suddenly in the middle of the night and told me to put on a jacket so that we could rush out of the apartment. I was still trying to understand what was going on. I heard someone banging on our apartment door. Ba ran to open the door and from the corner of my eye, I saw a firefighter. Hurriedly, I put on my jacket as I could tell something was serious and we needed to move quickly. We ran out of the apartment and exited the building to see so many people standing across the street in the middle of the night. Some had blankets wrapped around their bodies. Firefighters rushed through the building, carrying hoses, and profusely banging on doors. I stood there watching smoke exhaust through the windows from an apartment on the top floor. The smell of the cloudy smoke reminded me of our village in Vietnam when someone's kitchen was in flames. In fear, I held Ba's hand tighter. I didn't want to see the entire building burn down so we wouldn't have a place to live. After an hour of standing outside watching firefighters scuttling through the building, we were allowed to enter our apartment.

    After that incident, Ba became extremely cautious. He kept reminding me to turn off the stove when not in use and to always check it regardless. However, I could feel the trepidation in his voice as he constantly told me to be wary when cooking. Luckily for us, during the fire incident, we got to meet some of our neighbors while waiting outside in the cold. Among them was a Vietnamese couple who were a few years older than Ba: Chu Hung and Co Lan. They lived on the 2nd floor in our building with their two sons, Vinh and Huy, who were older than me and attended junior high school. As they got to know our situation, they offered to take care of me after school until Ba got home. Co Lan was a stay-at-home mom, while Chu Hung worked in a factory in lower Manhattan. Ba offered to pay for keeping me at their place, but they refused to accept. We were grateful for their kindness. Once again, we were thankful to meet people with good hearts.

Every day, I would go straight to Co Lan's house after school, have dinner with her family, and wait until Ba came home to pick me up. Vinh and Huy were very disciplined and focused on their studying. After getting home from school, they would sit and study until dinner. They rarely watched TV or went outside to play with other kids. Homework seemed like the only thing that interested them. After they were done with one subject, they would move on to the next. Their English was really good. I took advantage of that and asked them to help me with my writing and reading. They were glad to be my tutor. Seeing how dedicated they were to their academics, I became influenced to study just as hard as them.

After a few weeks of staying at Co Lan's place, I missed hanging out with Bang. I asked Ba if I could go to Bang's house to play with him sometimes. Since Chu Hung and Co Lan didn't take money from us, Ba felt bad to have me there every day, so he let me go to Bang's house on the days that Bang's mom was off from work. Bang's mom knew our situation too, so she didn't mind having me stay at her place until Ba came home from school. Besides shooting marbles and watching movies at Bang's place, he and I sometimes went to St. Nicholas Catholic Church across the park for free food. The church gave out free sandwiches to everyone who came to attend their service, regardless of their beliefs or religion. Bang and I would go there after school, clasp our hands, and pray with them, then pick up our sandwiches afterward. Bang never got anything from the Church. He said he didn't like American food and that his mom always prepared good food at home for him and his sister, so he just went with me for fun.

I alternated between Co Lan's apartment and Bang's place for almost two months until I had to say goodbye to Chu Hung and Co Lan's family. They moved to Boston to be closer to Co Lan's sisters. It was sad to say our farewells since I got along well with Vinh and Huy and learned a lot from them. I lost my babysitter as well as my English tutors. Once again, Ba and I had to adjust our schedule, since he was still reluctant to have me home alone after the fire incident. He came up with the idea of bringing me to school with him in the evening. We would walk from the apartment to the Bronx Community College along the path to Bang's building. I was excited and nervous at the same time. I wanted to see what it felt like to be surrounded by college students. When I entered one of Ba's classes, I could see the curiosity on everyone's faces, including the teacher. Ba introduced me to his class as his son. I sat at the back with Ba while the teacher taught. I didn't know what was being taught, and it was a good thing that I brought along my homework to finish. Surprisingly, with the amount of time I had to do homework in Ba's classes, I felt I had learned more. Spending my days at the elementary school and then fixating myself in Ba's class forced me to study more.

Our weekend wasn't as hectic as the weekday, but we still made sure the apartment was cleaned before we started our day. Ba had this ritual that he didn't allow me to wake up after 8 AM on weekends. It didn't matter which day of the week it was, he would make sure I got up and either studied or cleaned the apartment. This was the kind of discipline that he imposed on me during my childhood. There were times I was tired, but I got used to being conditioned to wake up early. After finishing what needed to be done in the mornings on the weekends, we either strolled along the streets to see things displayed at the stores or walked to Bang's apartment. Ba met a new friend, Chu Tuan, who was five years younger. While I would be at Bang's apartment, Ba went to Chu Tuan's apartment, which was across from Bang's building on Andrews Street.

Ba and Chu Tuan became good friends as they matched in personalities. Chu Tuan and his younger two brothers, who were in their mid-twenties, were also boat people. Chu Tuan left his wife and son behind with his parents while planning to leave the country with his brothers. They arrived in New York City a year before us and, with the same sponsor, they were placed in a building near our neighborhood. All three brothers worked as dishwashers in Chinatown. Chu Tuan always talked about his son, who was a few years younger than me, and how he wished his son was there. As we got to know him and other Vietnamese people in the area, we realized we had similar stories of leaving Vietnam to find a better life. It was rare to see an entire family immigrate to America. Those who had made it were trying to make money and hoping to send home some goods to support the families left behind.

Many families were broken up, as stepping foot onto the boats to leave Vietnam was a risk of death, whether it be at the hands of pirates or the unpredictable sea. I had heard Ba's conversations with his friends there and at the refugee camp about kids being kidnapped and women being raped by pirates. These stories were horrendous. In addition to the pirates, there were many Vietnamese lives taken by the South China Sea during merciless storms and waves. Ultimately, the husband usually was the one to take those risks since the stakes were too high to bring an entire family. I had never asked Ba why he took me on this journey instead of the others. Maybe it was because I was the oldest son. Regardless of the reason, I was thankful that Ba took me along. At least I could share this hardship with him. I was grateful that we had made it here and had the opportunity to make our dream come true.

The winter of 1983 was the first time I experienced Christmas. I heard about it a couple of months after we came to America the previous year, but I didn't know what it was about since we never heard of it, let alone celebrate it, in my hometown. I was excited to hear from the church that gifts would be distributed on Christmas Day. Ever since I lost KITT, I wanted another car toy. While walking with Ba along Fordham Road, I saw a flashy one at one of the toy stores, but it was too expensive. I knew we couldn't afford to buy it, so I prayed that I would get one as a gift from the church. Ba and Chu Tuan were off from work that night and they wanted to experience Christmas as well, so they took me there.

At the church, we met more Vietnamese people, mostly single men like Ba and Chu Tuan. We found our seats in the third row, sat down, and listened to the priest preaching. Everybody at the church clapped their hands and sang along with those on stage. Although we could not understand what they were saying, the singing performance was rather good. After the mass was over, they told all the kids to get in line and walk up to the stage for their gifts. I quickly ran to the line and impatiently waited for my turn. I had been waiting for this the whole night. I was hoping that I would get another KITT, or at least a toy car where I could play in my living room. I got to the stage and was greeted by a lady who handed me a small shoe-size box gift wrapped with a red bow. I nodded with a joyful smile and couldn't wait to open the gift once I got back to my seat. Next to us was one of the boys who I regularly saw during late afternoon free meals. I overheard his parents say to open it at home. Although I was shaking the box to get an idea of what was inside, I wanted to do the same as that boy. I wanted to see the surprise when we got home.

Upon entering our apartment, I ran to the living room and got ready to unwrap the mysterious gift. Hesitating to open it, I wondered if it would be something I wouldn't want. I took a deep breath and slowly tugged at the wrapping paper. As I unwrapped it, I was speechless with widened eyes and a dropped jaw. It wasn't the dark blue car with flames that I wanted. It was not a car, but a doll—a doll in a shimmery pink dress. I sat there motionless looking at the doll as I didn't know what to do with it. All the excitement that I had been waiting for was gone. Full of disappointment, I stood up and headed to the bedroom. Ba saw the whole thing as he watched me from the couch. He walked over, picked up the doll, and held my hand.

"Don't be sad, Con. It was a gift for you from their good heart, and that's what counts," Ba softly said.

"But it's a doll, Ba. I don't play with dolls," I complained.

"How about we put it here for display? It's not nice to throw it away." Ba placed it on a small table near the couch.

I stood there confused as to why the church gave me a doll and why Ba wanted to keep it. I took a deep breath as I tried to accept the disappointing turn of events. However, that doll was displayed on that table in our living room for a long time.

As the winter came, Ba and I hustled with our hectic schedules between home and school every day. There were days that I wished to stay home and not walk to school with Ba due to the heavy snow. I didn't find joy or excitement under the snow anymore. After many falls on the ice and so many walks through the bitter cold, I'd rather stay at home and wrap myself in a blanket. I had no choice but to bundle myself up and walk with Ba. The weekends became the only thing that I looked forward to. I only needed to walk for two blocks to Bang's house and we would hang out for almost the whole day. Ba walked with me to Bang's house, then went to Chu Tuan's place to meet up with his friends. Lately, Chu Tuan's place became a gathering point for the adults. I saw more Vietnamese men and women gathered there. They would sit and talk about their stories of coming here over sips of beer. That was how our second winter in New York City went.

One Saturday afternoon, as usual, Ba was doing his homework and also checking on mine, making sure I completed everything. Normally, as soon as he was done, we would be out the door to enjoy our little time left on the weekend with our friends. But that day, he asked me about school, about my English with Mrs. McKeever, and if I got used to being around other kids. He kept asking almost the same questions, and I felt he was a little nervous as he was trying to have a conversation with me. However, I didn't think much of it, answering him quickly so I could leave to go play with Bang. He told me his mom just got him a new video game and couldn't wait to play with me. As I was trying to put my books back in my backpack, Ba held my hands, looked at me, and paused for a second as his eyes started to tear up.

"There is something I want to tell you," he said, his eyes looking towards the floor.

I started to get nervous seeing his reaction. Ba wasn't someone who would show his feelings, especially with teary eyes. I sensed that whatever he was about to tell me must have been especially important. I put down my backpack, turned to him, and waited anxiously. Ba still sat quietly with his head down, and this made me feel even more uneasy. Tears started to fall down my face as I had a feeling that this might not be good news.

"I met someone, and I want you to meet her." Ba forced words out of his mouth. I could hear the strain in his voice.

I was confused. I didn't understand what he meant. He met new friends like Co Lai and Co Lan, our neighbors. Why was he so serious and wanted to tell me about it? Suddenly I realized that it wasn't what I thought. I was shocked as I turned to him and bawled.

"What about Ma?"

"I will always love your mom and your siblings," he cried. "But it has been very hard for us lately. I've been busy with school and work, and I make you suffer."

"I'm okay, Ba. I'm not suffering. I'm happy with you!" I wiped my tears as I tried to convince Ba.

Ba held me close to his chest. Both of us let the tears that we'd been holding in until that moment escape our eyes. We sat there and cried until our eyes dried up. Ba told me that it had been tough not only for me but also for him. He was constantly on the clock trying to provide for us and achieve his goal while taking care of me at the same time. He felt exhausted and didn't know when he would collapse. He needed a helping hand to take care of me when he wasn't around. But mostly, he needed the care and comfort from someone too. The day Ba and I got on that boat and left our home was the day Ba had to accept the fate that he might not see his wife again.

After hearing the news from Ba, I wasn't in any mood to go play with Bang anymore. I went to the bedroom and covered myself under a blanket. It was a lot for me to take in and I didn't know where or how to start. I thought about Ma and all my siblings in Vietnam as I cried. I didn't know how it got to that point. I noticed that we hadn't received any mail from Ma lately, and I didn't see Ba write any letters to them either. However, I thought maybe Ba was busy due to school and work. This whole thing wouldn't have happened if I had paid more attention and reminded Ba to write them more often. I couldn't help but blame myself for that. I wished for a miracle that they could be there at that moment so we could be a family again and Ba wouldn't have to be involved with someone else. I called out for Ma and all my siblings. I missed them so much. More than ever, I wanted a hug from Ma telling me this was only a dream, that everything would disappear when I woke up and our family would never change. I tried to crack the head of a nine-year-old so I could come up with something to help keep my family together. Sadly, nothing came to mind because I didn't even know if there was a chance for us to be together again. Helplessly, I cried and fell asleep as I dreamt of being reunited with Ma and all my siblings.

The next morning, Ba made breakfast for both of us. Usually, we would take turns talking until we were done with our food. I would tell Ba about the fun things that I did with Bang or my friends at school. Ba, on the other hand, was always about school—how I did in school, and that I should always focus on school. I never minded listening to him because I knew he wanted the best for me, and besides, I felt happy knowing that Ba was always there for me regardless of his busy schedule. However, that morning there was a long silence; I even heard the sound of us chewing our food.

"Are you mad at me?" Ba broke the silence and asked.

Without saying a word and with my eyes still on my bowl of food, I shook my head.

"I'm sorry to put you through this. I know you need time to take in and understand." Ba paused for a while and continued, "When you are ready, I want you to meet her and her children. I think you will like them."

Ba's words hit me again. She had kids too? Ba wanted me to have another family? The family I wished to be with now seemed to fade away and this unexpected family was about to take its place soon. Just like our boat that was drifting away from the shore that morning, I was drifting farther away from Ma and my siblings. Suddenly, I felt the anger build up. I was mad at Ba for meeting this woman. I wanted to scream at him, wondering why he was doing this to Ma. I looked up and was about to let my vexation take over, but I saw tears falling down Ba's face as he sat quietly looking out the window. All my exasperation subsided. I couldn't be mad at him anymore. It had been really hard for him. He never had a day off ever since we came to America. Whether working, studying, or taking care of me, he was constantly busy fulfilling his role as a father. He couldn't even rest when he was sick. I saw what he had to go through when his stomach ulcer attacked. He had been taking care of me, but there was no one to take care of him. I felt bad for even being mad at him. I loved him so much. I walked over and hugged him. Again, we held each other and cried.

One week later, Ba took me to his friend's apartment. I had so many thoughts in my mind on the walk to her place. I wondered if she would like me or even if her kids would like me. I thought about Ma and my siblings, and how they would react if they knew I was on my way to meet this family. My mind was filled with so many questions that I had no answers. I kept walking with my head looking down until Ba told me that we were there. Surprisingly, they only lived a couple of blocks away from us. We entered the building and Ba knocked on the apartment door. A woman opened it and greeted us. She was about Ba's age and had long hair and a very warm smile.

"Hello, this must be Linh," the woman excitedly cheered.

"This is Di Yen," Ba introduced her.

I folded my arms in front of my chest and bowed my head as in traditional Vietnamese culture to greet an adult with respect.

"Chao Di," I said in Vietnamese.

"Please come in." She stood aside and gestured the way for us to walk in.

We followed her inside the apartment. It was bigger than ours and had more furniture too. Di Yen decorated her apartment nicely and kept it clean. We walked into the living room and saw her two sons standing as they were expecting to meet us. They were older than me and looked very friendly as well.

"These are my sons, Dung and Bao," Di Yen said.

"Chao Chu, and hello Linh," they both said their greetings to us with an affable smile.

"Chao Dung and Bao," Ba smiled and replied to them.

"Chao Anh Dung, Anh Bao," I politely replied as well.

After our greetings, Anh Dung and Anh Bao took me to their room to show me around while Ba talked to Di Yen in the living room. I didn't know whether it was because I had never had an older brother before or they were very welcoming and genuine, but I felt comfortable around them. We talked and I felt more relaxed as the conversation went on. We got along well. Anh Dung was eight years older than me and was a sophomore in high school. Anh Bao was four years older than me and was in sixth grade. I told them my age and about school. I was surprised we had a lot of things in common. We all liked *Knight Rider* and that the park was our favorite hangout spot. Mostly, we all liked to drink Coca-Cola.

Di Yen came to the room and asked us to come out for lunch. We walked out to the living room, and there I saw a table full of food. Suddenly, I remembered our everyday meals of just canned fish and rice. We sat down and started eating. Di Yen sat next to me. She kept asking me if I liked the food, constantly putting more food in my bowl. I knew she was trying to get to know me as well as make me feel comfortable. I could feel her authenticity by the way she treated me. We ate and talked throughout the meal. I had to admit, it felt like a family having a meal together, which I had been longing for a long time. But instead with Ma and my siblings, I shared a meal with the people soon to be my new family.

For the next few months, Di Yen's apartment became our second home. Besides spending time at her place on the weekends, I also went there after school since she worked from home, doing sewing work for a factory. I was happy I didn't have to walk to school with Ba at night anymore. Di Yen cooked and took care of me until Ba came back. Ba also had dinner there before we went home. Finally, Ba could have a proper meal and didn't have to munch on dried noodles anymore. His stomach ulcer hadn't been acting up lately, so no more Mylanta or tucking a pillow on his stomach while grunting on the floor. I was glad that finally there was someone to take care of Ba. As I got to know Di Yen, I saw she was really nice. She never asked me about Ma or my siblings as she tried to respect my feelings. She never tried to take Ma's place either. She just wanted us to be a family. I felt bad sometimes that I held myself back from being close to her because I felt as if I was betraying Ma, or I just needed someone to blame even though I knew it wasn't her intention. However, it didn't stop her from treating me like one of her sons.

As for Anh Dung and Anh Bao, I felt more comfortable being close to them. Maybe because I didn't think that they stole Ba away from Ma. They really cared for me like big brothers, and that made me feel safe around them. It was nice to know there was someone who would be there for me besides Ba. Every day, I would finish my homework and go with them to the park for a game of basketball with their friends. I also introduced Bang, Tam, Dan, and Hien to them. We all became good friends and got together almost every day to play basketball against some Hispanic boys who lived in the area. We would bet a few dollars on each game so we could buy ice cream afterward. The Vietnamese kids were still wearing slippers or playing barefoot, while kids of other ethnicities had proper sneakers. Only one difference: I joined the team and became one of them. No more standing on the side, watching and cheering for them as a supporting fan.

Six months later, Ba asked me if I was open to the idea of moving in with Di Yen. I wasn't sure how to feel, as my head was telling me I was abandoning my real family, but my heart convinced me that I could enjoy life with this newfound comfort. Ultimately, it was up to Ba to decide. Wherever he went, I followed. The week after that, we didn't go to Di Yen's place. Ba was anguished to decide between the two families. There was a time when I woke up in the middle of the night and saw Ba sitting in the dark looking outside in a daze. I knew he was going through what I had been feeling. Moving in with Di Yen would further distance us from Ma and my family. The beginning of a new family would be the end of another. However, in the end, Ba told me to pack our belongings, a few pairs of clothes, and our books, and get ready to leave our apartment.

15 Living Together

During the summer of 1984, Ba and I moved in with Di Yen and her two sons. It didn't take long for everyone to adjust to the change since Ba and I was there often before we moved in. We also didn't have much stuff to bring with us, besides our clothes, leaving only the sleeping situation needing to be rearranged. Since it was a two-bedroom apartment, Ba stayed in Di Yen's room, and I shared a room with Anh Dung and Anh Bao. Their bedroom was large enough to fit three twin-size beds. Ba and Di Yen bought me a twin-size bed at the thrift store. I told Ba that we could save some money, and I walked back to the dumpster for a chance of finding another one. But instead, he assured me that they had enough money to buy me a bed.

The first night sleeping in a new room in my bed was nice, but the whole idea of living together with Di Yen's family still made me feel uneasy. Although it wasn't my decision, I couldn't help but feel the guilt that I somehow betrayed Ma and my siblings. I wondered if Ba broke the news to Ma and how she took it. I was too young to figure that out, but I was sure it wasn't something that Ma would want to hear from Ba. That thought persistently bothered me.

Nevertheless, I had to admit that I mostly enjoyed the new change. Ba and I no longer had to resort to eating dry noodles when there was nothing to cook. Di Yen had lived in Saigon, in Southern Vietnam, and she cooked dishes that I had never seen before. Not only was her cooking tasty, but I tried some vegetables I never had before. I cleaned my plate every time and wouldn't hesitate to ask for seconds. Knowing that I enjoyed her food always put a smile on her face. I could also tell Ba felt at ease seeing that I was well cared for.

Everyone seemed acclimated to living with each other quickly. That summer was certainly better compared to the previous year. After our farewell with Chu Chau and Anh Tri, there were numerous times that I felt lonely in the apartment. However, that all changed with five people in the apartment. There were always interactions between us or someone watching TV. Since none of us kids went to school during the summer break, we were either constantly horse-playing at the apartment or walking to the park to play marbles. The summer break created a bond between us that we were more than just stepbrothers. They were always there for me and made sure I stayed away from trouble. I reminisced about the good memories with them as I said goodbye to the summer.

At the beginning of fall in 1984, I started fourth grade, while Anh Bao was in seventh grade and Anh Dung was in high school. All three of us were in different schools since we were in grades that were not close enough to be in the same school. Each morning we went our separate ways; all of us still had to walk to school. I didn't get to watch much *Sesame Street or Mr. Rogers* while living with them. After school, Anh Bao and I would do our homework together in the living room, and he didn't want to get distracted by the TV. The many times we spent trying to pronounce English words were distracting enough. We kept saying words over and over again until we thought we got them right. However, I was glad to go through the struggles with Anh Bao as we found it amusing, mimicking each other's mistakes. English was always a problem for us, but math was fairly simple. While passionate about my math homework, I would glance over at Anh Bao's papers and try to solve his math problems which were a lot more advanced than mine. He wasn't annoyed with me looking over his shoulder or bothering him with my many questions. He would always joke around telling me to learn it so I could do it for him instead.

Anh Dung, on the other hand, hung out with his friends more. He often brought his friends home to study together with the door closed. At times, he would come out to tell both of us to lower our voices and stop giggling. I didn't seem to understand the seriousness when they studied, but each time when I saw Ba spending countless nights studying, I figured that the higher the grade level, the more the complexities. Anh Bao and I would finish our homework and then head to the park instead of staying in the apartment.

A few months after school started, one weekend, Ba and Di Yen came home with four large garbage bags. We thought they found some good deals at the thrift store, and we were excited to see what was inside. I had grown a few inches over the months and wouldn't mind some new outfits. However, when Ba opened the bags, we all were too stunned to speak. The bags were filled with fabric only, not clothes. Seeing our disappointment, Ba cleared his voice and tried to explain the situation to us.

"We are going to get some extra money by doing work from home," Ba said.

"What is it that we have to do?" Anh Dung broke the awkward silence and asked.

"We are going to make hair clips," Ba replied with enthusiasm. "It's simple. Your mother and I saw the process at our friend's house, and we think this might be a reliable source of income," Ba continued.

Ba picked up the fabric from the bag and tried to demonstrate the process to us. He cut the thread off the fabric, which was around eight inches long, to disconnect it from a long stretch of at least one hundred feet long. He creased the piece of the fabric that he just cut off into three folds and took a piece of scotch tape to wrap around the middle to keep the pattern in place. Then he took a metal clip from another bag, put hot glue on the back side of the clip, and glued it to the middle part of the fabric.

"We stop at this step. The next step will be finished at my friend's place. It's easy, isn't it?" Ba said.

The three of us were hesitant as the task seemed very tedious; however, we knew how important money was for us. We all sat down in the living room, and Ba assigned each of us different tasks. It started with me, cutting the threads, and separating the pieces. Ba kept reminding me that the threads should be removed completely, otherwise during the final inspection by the company, they would reject the product and we would have to fix it. The next step was to be done by Ba and Di Yen, creasing the fabric, and taping it in the middle. Then the final step was to be done by Anh Dung and Anh Bao, gluing the clip onto the fabric.

Although we would rather be outside playing, Ba was right about how easy the job was. It soon became our bonding time, as we would talk and laugh while working. One of the things we talked about was what we would use the money for. Di Yen and Ba didn't mention one particular thing, they just wanted to gain more money to support everyone. For us boys, we wanted to get a Video Cassette Recorder (VCR).

We had been asking to buy a VCR for a long time to watch Vietnamese music and Chinese series. Back in the eighties, the Chinese drama series were very popular in the Vietnamese community. These Chinese series were dubbed in Vietnamese and rented out to the boat people like us. Almost every Vietnamese household watched it. Every time we visited Di Yen's friend, Co Tien, the one that introduced us to hair clip making, she had a VCR to play Vietnamese music and the Chinese series we highly anticipated. Anh Bao and I were attracted to the Chinese, Hong Kong TVB drama series. I remembered we were glued to the television watching those series while the adults played cards or talked in the kitchen. There were times that Anh Bao and I didn't even want to go home until we finished an episode. As we were begging Ba and Di Yen for a VCR, they just smiled and nodded.

Powering through to complete our work as fast as we could to advance to the weekend, we ignored the constant growling from our stomachs. However, the emptiness beat us to it. With numb legs and sore eyes, we gave in and got up to get something to eat for dinner. I looked over at the garbage bags, hoping there wouldn't be much left. Sadly, we couldn't even finish half of one bag. That was when I realized that this job was harder than it looked. The full process was daunting after getting dozens of those hair clips done. I thought we could get it done quickly, but we ended up spending the entire weekend trying to finish more than five hundred pieces of the hair clips. On a Monday evening, Ba and Di Yen put all the finished products back into the black garbage bags and into a cart to bring back to Co Tien. We three boys were relieved that we finally got the job done and didn't have to look at those hair clips again. It was such a dreadful weekend that we never wanted to experience it again.

Unfortunately, it was too soon for us to think it was all over. A couple of hours later, Ba and Di Yen came home looking the same as when they left, still pushing the cart full of black garbage bags, but with a bigger smile on their faces. Although we saw their excitement, the garbage bags spoke louder. Anh Dung and Anh Bao turned to me and gave me a look as if I had messed up my part, meaning that we had to do it all over again. Immediately, I tried to go over the entire process in my head as to how I did it.

"It wasn't me! I double-checked each piece that I cut!" I defended myself.

"Couldn't be us, because we double-checked our part too," Anh Dung and Anh Bao both claimed.

We turned to Ba and Di Yen. They were still smiling and looking at each other. We didn't understand how they could be so happy knowing that we had to spend more time fixing those hair clips.

"None of you made a mistake. You all worked hard, and we made fifty dollars from those hair clips," Di Yen proudly said as she raised the fifty-dollar bill to show us.

"This is why we brought home some more so we could get another fifty dollars," Ba chimed in as he pointed to more garbage bags.

We were conflicted as we were happy to earn a good amount of money, but the idea of repeating the hair clip-making process seemed daunting. I thought that making hair clips was a one-time job, but Ba and Di Yen just announced that they planned to do it regularly. They said it was a reliable source of income, and most importantly, it allowed us to work from home, which was perfect for our situation. Therefore, they needed our help whenever we were free, which meant after school and on the weekends. The faster we got the work done, the faster we could earn more money.

Our new routine for the following weeks was school, homework, and then the ever-so-painful hair clips. There was no break in between each load. We weren't even able to be relieved with the last hair clip, because there were hundreds more after Ba and Di Yen returned from their friend's house. It was a never-ending process. I hated it increasingly each day. Every time I held the scissors to cut the threads, I wondered what would happen if I cut the fabric into multiple pieces. Maybe the company would stop giving us work and we would be free. I let go of a big sigh as I knew we would lose our source of income if that happened. Back to reality, I continued to cut the threads as my mind wandered off thinking of when I could see Bang and play marbles with him again. I was sure Anh Dung and Anh Bao felt the same way. However, they were excused to spend more time on their homework since theirs was much harder than mine. They only helped whenever they had extra time.

It was non-stop work for weeks. As much as I despised the tasks, when I saw the smile on Ba and Di Yen's faces after getting paid, I was happy and proud of myself for at least doing my part. Although they made us work, they rewarded us generously with tasty food from the money we made. Everyone was satisfied with the delicious meals that Di Yen made for us.

One day after bringing home bags of fabrics, as usual, Di Yen gathered us in the living room as she had something to announce. We were wondering what the news could be this time. Looking at the expression on her face, it didn't look like we would stop working any time soon. We sat down but didn't expect to hear any good news from her.

"Let's go buy a VCR!" She cheered.

"For real?" Anh Bao and I jumped up.

"Yes, we saved enough money now and you all deserve it."

We were happy, especially Anh Bao and me. Our wish had been granted and finally, we could enjoy Chinese dramas in the comfort of our own home. At that moment, we didn't mind making more of those hair clips, since they helped make our dream come true.

Di Yen and Anh Dung took the subway to Chinatown to buy the VCR. Ba, Anh Bao, and I stayed home to work on the new load that was brought home earlier. Anh Bao and I couldn't stop talking about those series and which one we should watch first. We went on and on one after another. Ba, on the other hand, wasn't into those dramas. He always said it was a waste of time spending hours watching them. He'd rather study. However, seeing how excited we were, Ba told us that we could go to Co Tien's to borrow VCR tapes so we could watch. I gave Ba a big hug to show him our appreciation. Anh Bao and I ran to Co Tien's apartment. She was happy to lend us some of her collection. We thanked her and hurried home, hoping Di Yen and Anh Dung would be home with the VCR. We ran to both of them at the door and were happy to see Anh Dung was carrying the VCR box. The first thing we did when we got home was hook up the VCR to the TV. For the rest of the day, we made hair clips while watching our favorite dramas.

The majority of the series we watched were mostly martial arts and stories of heroes back in the early 1900s. After watching these series, I fell in love with martial arts. I would run around the apartment trying to copy some of the moves pretending I was the hero fighting the bad guys. My passion for martial arts began then. Something about it kept drawing me back, and I could never give up on it. Thanks to Chinese dramas, we were able to glue ourselves on the living room floor and finish making those hair clips. It helped keep us entertained throughout the dreadful and boring time stuck at home.

16 Birth

It had been a year since we moved in with Di Yen. Not much had changed as we continued to make hair clips to earn extra income. We boys still disliked the task as it was tedious. Ba was still busy juggling school and work, but Di Yen faced a new chapter of her life: motherhood. Although Di Yen was genuinely nice to me and genuinely took care of Ba and me, seeing Ba and Di Yen build a life together made me sad for Ma and my little sister back in Vietnam who I hadn't even met. Ma gave birth to a baby girl, Tran Thi Thuy Ly, a couple of months after Ba and I left Vietnam. Ba and I were told the news after a couple of months of living in our first apartment. I remember when we received the letter from Ma, Ba and I were overjoyed. We imagined what she looked like. In Ma's letter, she talked about how she had been crying and worrying for us ever since we left Vietnam, while also worrying about the delivery. If Ba were still in Vietnam, he would've been the one to help Ma deliver this baby, just like how he helped deliver all of his children.

I was excited to meet my new half-sibling, however, I felt guilty not being able to be with the sister back home who didn't have a chance to meet her own father. She probably was not aware that she had another older brother in America who loved her very much and prayed every day to hold her.

On March 1, 1986, Di Yen gave birth to a baby boy. Ba named him Tran Vinh Thien Phong. Phong was a big baby, almost nine pounds at birth. The first time I laid eyes on him when Ba brought him home, I fell in love with his big eyes and chubby cheeks. Phong was such a happy and playful baby. He was so adorable that Anh Dung, Anh Bao, and I were fighting over how long we got to hold him. However, the fighting didn't last long when taking care of Phong became another tedious task of ours, especially when Phong cried more after a couple of months.

In the fall of 1986, Anh Dung entered his first year in college. He went to the same community college as Ba. Anh Bao became a freshman in high school and always hung out with his new friends. They would usually talk about girls and often excluded me as I was "only a kid." However, starting sixth grade was a transformation for me. I met Mr. Weissen, who was my homeroom teacher. After a few weeks in his class, he discovered that my math skills were more advanced than the other kids. There were times when Mrs. McKeever visited my class, and she always told him to give me tougher assignments.

One day, when I answered the problems so fast that he called me his "number one son." His constant reminder that I was his number one son made me feel more confident. Math homework didn't take a lot of my time so on days that I had extra time, I took care of Phong. Since Anh Dung and Anh Bao were in higher grades with harder homework, they were often excused from taking care of Phong or making the hair clips. In the end, I was left with a bigger load of chores I didn't want to do.

Phong was a cute baby to play with but looking after him was quite stressful. While doing my hair clip job, and watching Chinese dramas, I had to rock him back and forth in the hammock. At the very least, when he slept, I could stay focused on my movies, but whenever he woke up or wet his diaper, my peace was disrupted. I had never changed a diaper before. Back in Vietnam, I was too young when my siblings were infants. Ma took care of them all. It wasn't that hard as I remembered Ma used cloth as diapers for all of us. Luckily, Ba taught me how to change Phong's diapers, but I found it disgusting having to wipe him down every time he soiled the diaper. Through the unpleasantness, there was just something about this boy. As I wiped him clean, the big brown eyes above his peachy cheeks gazed into mine, and I felt that instant connection. He had a very innocent expression. Although I mumbled in my internal thoughts, complaining that I didn't sign up for all these tasks, the pure look on his face made it hard to be frustrated with him.

Taking care of Phong made me think about my younger brothers and sisters back home. I remember giving them horseback rides and playing hide and seek. Vu was always the first one to be found, being the youngest and still managing to balance himself on the concrete floor inside the house and the sandy ground surrounding it. The horseback rides would always put a smile back on his face. I carried Vu on my back and all my sisters were lining up behind me as we ran in circles, singing, and laughing while Ong Noi watched us. I missed them dearly, especially when the chance to see them again seemed impossible. It made me sad to think about it. The thought of them was constantly in my head. I even entered Vu's name instead of mine on the ATARI 2600 when I scored higher than Bang at his house on my break from making the hair clips. Whenever people asked if I had siblings, I'd always hesitate to answer, as it hurt me every time I had to reveal the fact that they weren't physically with me. The more I grew to love Phong, the more I yearned for my siblings.

Ba probably felt more of the pain. After all, he was the father to all these children. While they all waited for him, he was taking care of another. I wondered what was on his mind every time he held Phong. Although he never showed it on his face, I knew that he was in constant anguish. Understanding that much, I never asked him about my siblings or if he got letters from Ma. On top of everything, his schoolwork also took a toll on him. Ba told me he had a couple more classes left before he could get his associate's degree. His goal was to at least get a bachelor's degree in Engineering since he knew it would take more time and money if he pursued medical school instead. However, with more responsibilities, after Phong was born, Ba switched from working part-time to full-time and some additional overtime. This forced him to change his studies to part-time status. It was hard seeing him give up his dream, as he loved devoting his time to studying.

One night after getting home from work, I saw Di Yen give Ba a letter. He went into his room and then called me in after a short while. The silence filled the room as Ba tried to compile his thoughts. I wasn't sure what was going on but the expression on his face worried me. Ba's lips started to tremble and suddenly he was the most vulnerable I had ever seen him. His hands cupped his face as he tried his best not to sob in front of me. Not knowing what to do, I reached over and placed a hand over his shoulder. When he finished crying, he handed me a picture. It was a picture of a coffin. Without Ba's further explanation, I pieced together who it was. However, I denied that possibility. It couldn't have been him. It couldn't have been my beloved Ong Noi who I had been missing for the last five years. I looked at Ba, hoping that I was wrong, but his tears told me otherwise. I knelt to my knees and cried out loud. My vision became blurry as my tears swelled in my eyes, and my chest was in so much pain, feeling as if my heart was about to burst. It was hard to breathe. Within those five years, I wanted to be with my entire family. The thought of not being with Ong Noi during his last moments made me lose control. I was overwhelmed with guilt.

"He passed away a month ago. These were the pictures that Bac Thanh took and mailed to us," he said, attempting to conceal his emotions. I couldn't imagine what my father was going through. He decided to leave Vietnam without the rest of my family and never got to say goodbye. And on that day, he lost his last chance to say goodbye to his father.

"Remember what I have been telling you. We took a journey to come to America to find freedom. Promise me that you will study hard and become successful." Ba placed a hand on my cheek. His tears halted as he remembered our purpose in this new land. I assured him that I would follow his words.

Ong Noi's death left us heartbroken, especially Ba. I knew he tried to be strong and move on, but it wasn't easy, as Ba was Ong Noi's pride. I remember Ong Noi would always talk about Ba's achievements every time he got together with friends. Ong Noi was not one to brag, but it was indeed rare and difficult for someone from the countryside to get accepted into medical school. Being a doctor wasn't only Ba's dream, but also Ong Noi's. However, that dream left Ba when Ong Noi passed. Ba had new responsibilities, but on top of it all, he could not afford to grieve over the death of his father.

Life in that neighborhood was a lot tougher than in my old neighborhood, even though it was only half a mile away. Some of the Hispanic kids liked to gather in groups and scattered everywhere on the steps at the entrance of our building, especially whenever the weather was nice. They always gave Vietnamese residents a tough time entering and exiting the building. There was no way to get past them without asking them to move. These kids were aggressive and contentious compared to those we played basketball with at the park. They smoked weed, spoke foul language, and drank beer while blasting their music until midnight regardless of which day. Since we lived on the first floor, we had to endure the loud music, screaming, and laughter all night long. There were times they got so drunk that empty cans and vomit were scattered all over the stairway in front of the building. We couldn't complain to the superintendent as one of the boys was his son. As we remained quiet, they prey on the Vietnamese living in the building. There were times I looked out from the window to see some of them mocking an elderly Vietnamese. I was frustrated and wished that all the martial arts movies I had watched would prepare me to fight against them someday, but I knew for sure that there would be no way for me to come out unscathed if I encountered a group of so many.

  Whether we were Cambodian, Laos, Vietnamese, or Chinese, we were all grouped together. They would call us "Chinks" or "Ching Chong" as we walked by them. There was no point to turn back and respond to their mockery. It happened so often that we became desensitized to their insults.

  One day, while exiting the building and walking down the stairs with Bang, I saw three boys sitting on the steps. They weren't occupying the entire stairs. I thought we could pass by without asking them to move. Just as I thought it was my lucky day, I felt a sharp pain in my right wrist. Before I could process anything, I heard familiar laughs from behind. I ground my teeth and grabbed my wrist as I tried to ease the pain. Laughter arose as I turned around and saw those kids cheer as they were proud of what they did to me.

  "One of the kids just slingshot you," Bang angrily muttered.

  I looked down at the ground and saw a small piece of rock. It must've been what they used to shoot at me. I was so angry. I told myself I wouldn't put up with it anymore. I looked at Bang and it seemed like he was thinking the same thing. Without a word, we both glared at them.

  "What are you gonna do? I'll smack you in the face," one of them shouted.

The more I looked at them standing there laughing, the more I wanted to jump in and swing at their faces until my fists bled. I wanted them to feel the pain that I felt. Madness almost overcame me until I remembered Ba's advice to avoid getting into trouble with them. We also were outnumbered. Realizing the reality and the stakes, we rushed away before they could do anything else. However, the anger that we felt after we left the building made us pledge that we wouldn't let it go next time no matter how many of them there were. The pain on my wrist was still unbearable, I couldn't even clench my hand to make a fist. I held onto the pain and tried not to shed any tears as I didn't want to admit defeat.

That night, I told Anh Bao about the incident and made him promise not to tell Ba. I didn't want Ba or Di Yen to worry about me. Anh Bao said that Bang and I did the right thing by not fighting back and ignoring them. He understood how I felt but told me to pay no mind since getting involved with them wasn't doing us any good, especially since they were always in big groups.

For the next few months, every time I left the building, I stuck my head out of the window to scan if they were around. I was afraid to encounter any of them. Anh Dung and Anh Bao would usually accompany me every time we left the house.

Phong turned one year old and started walking. While it was nice at home playing and snuggling with him, I decided to take him to the park. I wanted to be around Bang and my friends. Di Yen permitted me to take Phong to the park and gave me money to buy milk on the way back. As I headed down the stairs to exit the building, one of the Hispanic boys was sitting there. I took a deep breath and hoped that he wouldn't do anything. I remembered that they only attacked whenever they were in groups. As I walked by, he stayed put.

I pushed Phong to the park and met up with Bang and my other friends. While playing softball with my friends, Phong was sitting in his stroller, watching us curiously as he enjoyed the outdoors as much as I did. When it was my turn to swing, the ball flew up in the air at least twenty feet high and headed in Phong's direction. All of us followed the ball with our eyes wide open and our heads bent as much as we could. It was so fast that none of us could run over to deflect it away from him. I felt a rush of panic as the ball headed straight down to his body. Amazingly, it landed right between Phong's hands. I was in awe that such a miracle took place, but moreover, I was relieved.

"Good catch, Phong!" Bang cheered.

After leaving the park, I pushed Phong to the grocery for milk. I hung the bag with milk on one of the stroller's handles and headed home. As I got closer to the building, I saw those boys again. The kid I saw earlier was now sitting along with his buddies. I sensed that trouble was coming and told myself that they wouldn't do anything to me since I was walking with a stroller.

"Excuse me, can I get through please?" I softly asked.

To my surprise, the boy I encountered earlier, who was around my age, got up and made way for me to walk through. With a big relief, I thought it was my lucky day.

"Thank you very much," I said as friendly as I could.

As I carried the stroller up the stairs, I felt an impact as though something struck the stroller. From the corner of my eyes, I saw droplets of milk falling onto my feet. The next thing I heard was the haunting laughter again. I turned around and saw the boy who made way for me was holding a stick which he used to strike at the milk. His friends all high-fived him. I stood frozen, processing what just took place. I knew the right thing to do was to simply go back home, but I had enough of being complacent.

"Why did you do that?" I shouted angrily.

"And? What are you gonna do about it?" He still laughed while looking over at his friends, searching for approval and validation. I remember this kid didn't have the guts to look at me. They were all truly pathetic.

"Stay here and wait for me. I will be back," I screamed.

I rushed back to the apartment with Phong. Luckily, Ba was inside his room studying. I apologized to Di Yen about the broken milk carton and told her I needed to go out for a while. I was so upset that I didn't care about being one man against a whole group. Without thinking of the consequences, I ran back downstairs and looked for that boy demanding justice.

"Come up here," I shouted.

"You come down here." He grinned.

"Come up here and fight!"

I screamed my head off as I felt the rage building up inside me. A recollection of all the times I was bullied by these kids flashed through my mind, and suddenly I couldn't take it anymore. I didn't know how I would fight against a bunch of them, but at that moment, I was so consumed with anger I didn't care about the consequences. As I stood my ground, the boy charged at me along with his friends backing him up.

The boy ran toward me, up the stairs, grabbed my shirt, and both of us fell down the staircase. We got into a wrestling match, and he managed to be on top of me. I felt my shirt was torn, but none of that bothered me as my emotions took over. I wanted to teach this kid a lesson. I continued to swing with all my might while on the bottom. I was relentless even if I missed. There was only one thing on my mind and that was to fight until the end. I wanted to show them I no longer was their prey.

Suddenly I heard a voice of a man speaking in their language. I didn't know what he was saying, but all of those kids who had been watching us stopped laughing and left the building. Even the boy I fought let go of me. I could see a slight look of embarrassment on his face as he silently followed that man up the stairs. That was all I wanted, even if it was only slightly. I wanted to make them feel ashamed for what they had done to me and all the Vietnamese people living in the building. Although my body ached, I felt like a winner because I got all the justice I needed. I found out later the man who broke up the fight was the superintendent, and the boy was his son.

As I walked up the stairs to my apartment, I hoped Ba was still in his room studying. I didn't want Ba to see me with the bruises scattered around my face, arms, and legs, along with a torn-up shirt. I was afraid he was going to be mad. I slightly opened the door and tried not to make any noise to alert anyone. However, Ba caught me at the door and was shocked to see me in that condition.

"What happened to you?" Ba worriedly asked.

"Those kids out there smacked Phong's milk and laughed at me," I said with tears in my eyes.

Ba hesitated to speak another word as he saw the look on my face. He took me to the bathroom, wiped the blood from my face, and gently placed a warm cloth over my wounds. I thought Ba would have been angry as he warned me to ignore them previously, however, he simply tended to me instead of being mad.

"Sometimes you have to ignore them," Ba said softly.

"I did, but they smacked the milk anyway, and now Phong doesn't have milk to drink!" I shouted. "They have been bullying me, Ba. It hurts."

Although Ba told me not to partake in a dispute with the kids outside my apartment building, deep down I was proud of myself for standing up to them. Instead of running away, I showed them that I could fight back too.

17 Karate

After the incident with the superintendent's son, I thought the bullying would cease, but they still called me names every time I passed through the group. However, they stopped occupying the entirety of the stairs, leaving a pathway for those to walk through. I guessed that change came from the superintendent. Although they were not as hostile, I still felt a sense of unpredictability. I wasn't sure if one day they would go back to their old ways and cause more trouble.

There were times when Anh Bao complained about the bullies and wished he was able to defend himself with the moves we watched in the martial art movies. He and I would watch fight scenes repeatedly, imitating the moves, and trying them on each other. One of Anh Dung's friends, Anh Son, saw us in the living room play-fighting with each other. He told us about his sensei, who was Vietnamese and taught free Vietnamese-style karate, Vovinam, at the Botanical Garden near the Bronx Zoo. He showed us a few moves, and I was caught off guard to see Anh Bao in excruciating pain from one of the punches from Anh Son. Scratching my head, I was piqued to see some more, as Anh Son showcased all the flashy moves he learned.

"Let's learn karate so we can protect ourselves against those jerks outside!" Anh Bao said excitedly.

"When can we start?" I eagerly wanted to learn.

Anh Son told us to go with him on Saturday at 7 AM since they started at 8 AM. I politely asked him if my friends would be able to join us. He gladly agreed to meet at the basketball court in the park before walking forty-five minutes to the Botanical Garden.

Anh Son allowed the idea of inviting friends to join us. Excitedly, I announced to Bang, Tam, Dan, and Hien about the free karate class I was about to partake in, and that the sensei would also welcome them. Saturday morning came, and Anh Bao and I were the first ones to wake up. We had to wake up early since the class started at 8 AM. It didn't take us long to get ready and dash out of the apartment to be the first ones at the basketball court. Surprisingly, within seconds, all the other kids were heading toward us. I could see everyone's enthusiasm as they exchanged moves to see who was stronger and more flexible. At 7 AM, Anh Son showed up, and we followed his lead. We walked along Fordham Road toward the Botanical Garden. Along the way, Anh Son suggested we all stop at White Castle.

"If anyone needs to use the restroom, take a break here," Anh Son said. "And if you are hungry, get some hamburgers. They're only twenty-five cents each."

There were more than ten of us, ranging from eleven to fifteen years old, taking turns using the restroom and buying hamburgers. I could see that the workers were wondering what we were doing out so early on a weekend. When I got my hamburgers, I was surprised by the small size that could be eaten in two bites. It didn't take us long until we continued walking again.

When we arrived at the Botanical Garden, some students were already there. Anh Son introduced us, and I recognized some of them were also Anh Dung's friends who I had met at our apartment. Anh Dung didn't want to join because he was never into martial arts. Just like Ba, he'd rather study. Closing his eyes and ears every time he went in and out of the apartment was his way to avoid trouble. To begin the class, one of the students ordered us to stand in lines of three. Then, a Vietnamese man in his early thirties headed our way.

"Hello. I am Sensei Hai, and welcome to Vietnamese karate - Vovinam." Sensei introduced himself loudly.

Bang and I winked at each other with excitement. As I stood there out in the open grass, surrounded by trees and flower beds, I felt the breeze blowing onto my face. I was mesmerized by the tranquility of the early morning. I felt as though I was in a movie scene where I was learning martial arts and zen up in the mountains with an old Sifu with long white hair. Suddenly, Bang whispered, "We are going to learn real karate now," and brought me back to reality. *I can't wait to fight back against these bullies. I can't wait to show them what I got.*

Sensei Hai started the class by having everyone repeat the class motto: "Karate is for defense, not offense." He also forbade us to tell people that we were practicing karate. He didn't want us to have too much pride and start showing off to other people. After all, his slogan said it all. Although we waited anxiously for action, the first fifteen minutes were all about training our minds to be calm.

Finally, Sensei had his senior students come up and demonstrate some basic moves that we would be learning. They looked so strong and skillful. In every move they generated, I could hear the snap of their uniforms. One senior student performed a flying kick onto another. I stood there watching, amazed that they were so well grounded and weren't afraid of taking hits. They made it look so easy and perfect. At one point, one senior student kicked another so hard, that he scraped the other's face. With blood dripping from his cut, I knew this was the real deal. All of us, the new students, were speechless to see these moves performed in front of our eyes. We wish we could do that someday as well.

After the demonstration, Sensei Hai had everyone line up in formation, to begin punching and kicking. It was so easy that some of us wished Sensei would teach us more advanced stuff. However, after hundreds of constant punching and kicking at different angles, it became quite difficult to maintain the same strength and speed. The routine became harder as our arms and legs wobbled. The sun rose higher, and we could feel the heat burning the back of our necks. I turned to look at others and saw they were struggling as well. I wanted to impress the sensei by trying my best and continuing to do what I was told. I gathered my inspiration by thinking of how I was bullied, and I needed to become stronger to fight back.

After the punching and kicking, Sensei Hai moved on to do shoulder ground rolling, cartwheels, and front and back flips. I was excited about cartwheels and rolling since these were what I did for fun at home. Yet, I couldn't picture myself performing a flip. The very first front flip I did, I fell right on my back and thought my lungs were about to pop out of my chest. The grass surface was hard. As I tried to get up, I heard a sound of a drop on the ground. I turned around, both Bang and Anh Bao were falling flat on their backs as well and were groaning in pain. None of us, the new students, were able to land on our feet. Sensei Hai had one of his senior students demonstrate it to us again. He did it with ease and that gave us hope that maybe it was possible.

We were split into small groups based on Sensei's assessment of how physically capable we were. He assigned his senior students to work with each group. Anh Bao, Bang, and I were in the same group, and we got a chance to train one-on-one with the senior student on what we had learned. After our three-hour session, Sensei Hai announced that he would teach us every Saturday and Sunday morning. We were incredibly happy because we could officially learn real martial arts from a real sensei. As we walked home, we felt sore and exhausted, but we kept our spirits strong.

Bang started punching and kicking while walking, but Anh Bao suddenly stopped him. "Stop! Sensei strictly said that we cannot let people know we are learning martial arts," Anh Bao said.

"I know, but I need revenge. I wanna give those bullies a piece of my mind," Bang argued.

I knew that following Sensei's orders was the right thing to do, but at that moment I couldn't help but agree with Bang. We had been bullied every day, whether verbally or physically. It was time to show these kids we could fight back because we were done putting up with it.

When Anh Bao and I got home, the first thing we did was practice the front flip. We wanted to get it right so we could show Sensei. Anh Bao tried to do a handstand, and I helped hold both of his legs. His goal was to balance his body while strengthening his arms, but when I let go of his legs, he fell and landed on his back, grunting in pain. I wasn't any better when it was my turn. We couldn't figure out how to land on our feet. We kept losing balance and fell on the hardwood floor. Our bodies were in pain and had bruises all over. Di Yen suggested we should go to the park to continue our practice before the tenants who lived below started complaining about our falling noises.

We walked to the park, and I asked Anh Bao if we should ask our friends to come train with us. I knew everyone would love to improve their skills so we could show Sensei our progress during the next class. Anh Bao agreed, and we split ways to go pick up our friends and then meet at the playground.

I ran to Bang's house and knocked on his door. He opened it while breathing heavily, covered in sweat.

"What happened to you?" I asked.

"I was practicing the punches and kicks that Sensei showed us this morning," he said while catching his breath. "I want to be ready tomorrow. I have to be at my best."

"Then let's go! We're all meeting up at the playground to practice," I said.

Bang and I rushed out of his building and there we encountered another group of bullies. They called us names and gave the typical expression of acting like they were the boss. I could see in Bang's face that he wanted to test out his karate and not hold back. I grabbed Bang and dragged us out of there before things got ugly. We had just started learning, so the odds of us succeeding were low. We did plan on demanding justice the minute we got better.

Anh Bao and his friends were already there when we got to the park. Since Anh Bao was the oldest, he took the lead and trained us. We went over everything that we learned. We pushed ourselves until our hands couldn't punch anymore, our legs got tired of kicking, and our backs became numb after so many falls. Luckily, we got to practice on a sandy playground rather than on hard asphalt.

After an hour of training, Anh Bao dismissed everyone. I asked if I could stay for a marble game with Bang since we hadn't played in a while. Anh Bao agreed. He told me not to stay out too late and then left. As we were playing, four Hispanic teenagers approached and demanded we give them our marbles. Bang grabbed the marbles, put them in his pocket, and told them straight up that the marbles belonged to him. One of the bullies tried to reach into Bang's pocket. Immediately, Bang pushed him away. To Bang's surprise, the boy lost balance and almost fell to the ground. I instantly had a bad feeling that something bad was about to happen to both of us. Thoughts ran through my head. Should we run to avoid problems, or should we stay and challenge them as we had always wanted? Every day was the same. Every day we got picked on and made fun of. All we wanted was to be able to play outside peacefully without being afraid of these bullies. So, I made my choice.

"Why don't we fight one on one?" I shouted.

Bang snapped his neck and turned to me in disbelief. He was always the one who got more heated than me. He was always the one who wanted to teach them a lesson. However, hearing this from me at that moment, he knew these kids had pushed me beyond my limit. Even they were shocked by my words. The one that Bang pushed seemed thrown off a bit but glanced at his group quickly for approval if he should take on my challenge. I stood there feeling my blood pressure rise and anger swelling up inside me. My rage was at an all-time high, and my head started swirling.

"Julio, why don't you kick this chink's ass?" said one of the boys to the one I challenged.

A familiar scene flashed through my head bringing me back to the fight with the superintendent's son. There I was again, another fight with another bully. I wondered if someone would break us up or if this teenager would beat me up until I couldn't walk and eventually beat up Bang as well. My heart pounded, my legs shook, and my lips became dry. With so much anger inside me, I wasn't thinking when I demanded we fight one on one. However, it was too late. I couldn't run away now, or they would catch up and hurt us even more. I had to live up to my words even if they were committed to breaking my bones.

I took a deep breath and got into the fighting stance that I just learned that morning. These teenagers laughed when they saw me get in position. I told myself not to get distracted but to focus and stand my ground.

"Kick that Bruce Lee wannabe in the ass real hard. Teach him a lesson," the same boy said.

Although my legs were shaking, I tried my best to keep them stable. I looked straight into Julio's eyes to cue I was ready. Without hesitation, he charged at me with a punch. I grabbed him, and we both fell to the ground. He kept on punching me, but I was able to get on top of him and wrap my arm around his neck. I put him in a chokehold until he screamed and cried.

He begged me to let go as he was out of breath. However, I tried to block him out because I wanted him to feel the pain, the injustice, and the fear that they had put us through. I wanted to hold on until he promised to leave me and my friends alone. Suddenly, thoughts of Ba being worried if he knew I got into a fight again popped into my mind. I got distracted and was caught off guard. I lost control and Julio was able to escape my arms.

While I was getting up and not paying attention, he swung a punch right to my face. His fist went up on my jaw and I saw stars. It hurt so bad that I thought I would faint. Luckily, he didn't continue charging at me, and I was able to gain consciousness.

His friends cheered him as they laughed and walked away. Although I got a punch from him, I believed my chokehold got him good too. Otherwise, they wouldn't have walked away and left us alone. Bang ran over to check if I was okay.

"You were really brave to confront him like that," Bang said.

"I was so scared, and my legs couldn't stop shaking," I said as I wiped the sweat off my forehead.

"That was awesome. You had him until he started begging like a little coward and cheated." Bang was angry that I got punched.

Bang felt bad that I got hit defending him. I knew he would jump in and fight them with me if it wasn't for the one-on-one challenge that I suggested. He kept asking me if my jaw was okay. Bang told me he would train hard so he could be as strong as me and stand up to these kids as I did. I could see he meant what he said in his eyes. We called it a night and went our separate ways. On the way home, I thought of Bang's words and felt great knowing I made an impact on him. He was looking up to me even though I was younger than him. The pain in my jaw was still unbearable, but I was happy that I stood up to the bullies and protected my friend. I wasn't sure if they would stop picking on us, but at least they knew we weren't such an easy target anymore.

When I got home, luckily Ba was still at work. Although Ba supported me in learning karate, he would be scared if he knew I got into a fight. I quickly went to my room. Anh Bao saw the bruise on my jaw and was able to guess what the cause was. I told him the whole story and he apologized for leaving me there alone. He took me to the bathroom to clean up and gave me a bag of ice to put on my jaw. Later at the dinner table, Di Yen and Ba saw the bruise, and surprisingly, they didn't yell or lecture me. Di Yen rubbed some salt on it, our traditional way to dissolve the bruise, and it worked like a charm. Ba hugged me and told me to continue studying hard and being a good boy.

That night it was difficult to sleep. My body was aching from the training and the fight. My empty stomach rumbled because I couldn't eat much for dinner. It hurt every time I chewed the food. I kept tossing and turning but wasn't sure if it was because of the pain, the hunger, or that I was eager to learn more from Sensei in the morning. I thought about the fight earlier and wished I was more skillful so that I could have blocked that punch. With that thought, I told myself that I should train hard to become better so I could protect my friends and family. By midnight, I was too tired and fell asleep but still managed to wake up at 6 AM to get ready for Sunday's class.

Once again, we met at the basketball court. However, only Anh Son, Anh Bao, Bang, Hien, and I showed up. The rest of the group was worn out from yesterday's training and gave up. Bang came up to me to check if my jaw still hurt.

"I'm going to give it all I got today, Linh. I'm going to train hard and get revenge for you," Bang said.

His eyes were different that day—full of determination. They were truly hungry for justice. We smiled and gave each other a high five. My jaw was still in pain as I moved my face, but I felt it was worth it because it brought out more courage in Bang. I was proud of him for not giving up like the others. We walked the same path and stopped for burgers at White Castle again. When we got to the Botanical Garden, Sensei Hai and his senior students were already waiting for us.

After repeating the class motto, Sensei pulled me aside for a small talk. I guess he spotted the bruise on my face. I honestly told him about the fight and sincerely apologized for disobeying his teaching. He quietly listened, and to my surprise, he didn't punish me. Instead, he taught me moves that I could use to defend myself in situations like the day before. I thanked him and sighed in relief as he understood.

That day, we learned our first kata, a sequence of movements for a karate form. The class was divided into three groups. Luckily, Bang and I were personally taught by Sensei. He made us perform the kata repeatedly until we memorized the entire sequence without his correction. Next, Sensei called one of his senior students up, and together with him, Sensei demonstrated how the kata was put into defensive and offensive usage. We were amazed to see the effectiveness of Sensei's skill. I wouldn't have been punched if I had even one part of Sensei's skill.

After a short break, the entire class rejoined for flipping exercises. Sensei knew we all had problems landing on our feet as he saw the prior day; therefore, he decided to give us some extra help. Sensei had one of his senior students lie on the ground. We would run towards him and place our hands on his knees instead of the ground and then do the flip. The purpose was for the senior student to push on our backs if he saw us coming down with our backs instead of the legs.

We were all excited about the new method that Sensei just showed us. We couldn't wait to do a full flip since no one could even do a half flip before. One by one, we took turns and followed Sensei's instructions. We were overjoyed as we were able to land on our feet for the first time. When it was my turn, with a little help from the senior student, I landed on my feet perfectly and it felt so good. After a few rounds of pushing us in the back, the senior student told us he wasn't going to brace our backs anymore. We had to be strong when using our hands. He wanted us to do it without any help.

We were a little hesitant, but we understood that we needed to learn how to do it on our own. To boost morale, we kept telling each other that we could do it and cheered on one another. After many attempts and grunting in pain, we got the hang of it. We all succeeded in landing on both of our feet without any help. Sensei gathered all of us in a circle for a final round of flipping. I was up first. I ran toward the ground, planted my hands, boosted my body into the air, and landed perfectly on both feet. The whole class cheered for me. We took turns and showed Sensei our best. We wanted to make him proud for taking his time and teaching us for free.

"Remember, to be great, you cannot stop! You did well!" Sensei said.

Sensei Hai's insight helped me a lot. He taught me discipline and determination. If I wanted to succeed in anything, I couldn't stop. It didn't matter how many times I failed to land. I practiced and practiced until I eventually succeeded. Along with teaching me how to physically defend myself, Sensei also taught me how to become mentally stronger.

18 The Separation

We continued to train with Sensei Hai every weekend, whether it was sunny or gloomy, either on the open grass area at the Botanical Garden or in a tiny hallway in Sensei Hai's building. We always trained with one purpose in mind: to be strong so we could protect ourselves. Although Sensei's motto wasn't to allow us to get involved in fights, after hearing our stories of getting bullied, he came to understand that we only wanted to defend ourselves.

Sensei Hai also had a goal, which was to pass down the art of Vovinam, the Vietnamese-style karate, to whoever wanted to train diligently. This explained why he was always dedicated and wholeheartedly teaching us with no fees accepted. As long as we wanted to learn, he would stay and train with us, regardless of the hours. However, Sensei had one strict rule—he only instructed Vietnamese students. Anyone else would be rejected on the spot. We didn't know what the reason was, but none of us dared to ask.

One Saturday as we were training, as usual, an adult was standing across the field from us, watching us attentively. He clapped as we performed our routine. We didn't pay much attention and thought he was just a passerby. However, on Sunday, he was quietly observing us again. He stood there and patiently waited until class was over then came over and talked to Sensei. His name was Juan, and he looked to be in his twenties. He was impressed with Sensei's karate and wished to learn under him. As expected, Sensei rejected him right away. Respecting Sensei's decision, he asked for permission to continue to watch.

For weeks, Juan would show up at the same time we did, and while we trained, he stood there watching. He didn't even mimic the moves since he knew he wasn't allowed to. Although Sensei turned him down, he wasn't bothered by it and showed respect to everyone. We all admired Juan for his forbearance, persistence, and good manners. In the end, even Sensei was touched. He broke the rule and accepted him as his student. We were happy for him and welcomed him to the class.

Unlike the other Hispanics in our neighborhoods, Juan was kind and polite and treated us like human beings. Meeting Juan made me realize not everyone was the same and that there could be good in anyone. I was happy to make a new friend—one who shared nothing in common with me. Juan knew that we had been bullied by a lot of Hispanic kids. He apologized to us on their behalf because he felt responsible somehow since he was also Hispanic. He told us those kids behaved that way due to a lack of guidance and support from their families. They acted out to get attention. The more I got to know Juan, the more I respected him for his wisdom. Both Juan and I hoped for those kids to learn and grow from their bad habits. Another thing that I admired about Juan was that he was a quick learner. Although he joined the class after us, he had caught up to our level. It seemed like he had been practicing on his own at home while watching us earlier. He picked up quickly whatever Sensei taught him.

As we became more proficient with the fundamentals, Sensei took it up another notch and taught us advanced forms and techniques. One of the specialties in Vovinam was the "number 8" flying jump kick. He would have one person doing a flying jump kick, while the other stood there to receive it. The receiver's job was to fall and roll once he felt the impact. After a few demonstrations from the advanced students, we understood what to do. Sensei split us up into groups. Juan was older and bigger, so he got to practice with bigger students. After fifteen minutes of practice, Sensei gathered us together to demonstrate our progress. We did well for a few cycles of "number 8," until Hien was the receiver again. For some reason, he wasn't as aware this time. Anh Son did the "number

8" as Hien was receiving it. Upon impact, Hien fell and twisted his shoulder in excruciating pain.

I felt bad for Hien as he continued to wince with pain. Anh Son and Anh Bao took him to the hospital. Sadly, he came back with a broken arm and had to be put in a cast for a few weeks. That was the last time Hien participated in karate. He quit right after because his mom wouldn't let him return. Although we were disappointed since we couldn't see Hien anymore, we still stopped by White Castle to get him his favorite burgers on our way back.

As the summer approached, I looked forward to my sixth-grade graduation. I couldn't believe sixth grade went by so fast. I remembered those first days at school: no English, no friends, and no confidence. Somehow, I survived. It was my last year at PS122. I thought I wouldn't miss it, but through the bad, there were some unforgettable moments. I was glad to meet a few good friends and especially Mrs. McKeever. She helped me tremendously along the way and I owed her so much.

On graduation day, I woke up early to get ready. Ba bought me new clothing at the thrift shop a few days earlier to get me ready to look my best. I combed my hair and sprayed some of Anh Dung's hairspray, which I never used before. When I walked into the living room, everyone looked at me and complimented my astute look. Di Yen generously offered my favorite - eggs on toast. While eating, Ba received a phone call from his boss. Unfortunately, someone got sick, and he had to cover that morning. The boss was in dire need of a replacement and Ba couldn't refuse as he was also new at this job. I was disappointed that he wouldn't be able to attend my graduation. Instead, he walked me to school. Although he couldn't be there, he kept congratulating me on my biggest accomplishment before dropping me off. I understood his situation, and we hugged each other as he left for work.

At the ceremony, I sat and watched the kids before me go onto the stage to receive their certificates. Each kid displayed a happy smile on their face, holding their diplomas, while their parents cheered them on. Looking at them, sadness took over as I wanted Ba to be with me so badly. I was hoping that Ba's boss would change his mind and that he would be in the crowd when it would be my turn. As I walked across the stage, I looked out into the audience. I didn't see Ba. My name wasn't cheered like the other students. The empty silence filled the auditorium until the next person was called. Upon receiving my certificate, I walked with my head down, continuing to go down the stairs of the stage, and back to my seat. While other kids were smiling as their parents snapped their cameras, I sat down in my seat continuously blinking to control my tears. Suddenly, I heard someone scream my name from the back. I immediately turned around to see that the voice came from Mrs. McKeever. She excitedly clapped her hands and cheered me on. I couldn't hold in my tears as I was thrilled to see someone - someone who believed in me.

When the ceremony was over, Mrs. McKeever met me in the back of the auditorium. She immediately hugged and congratulated me on my accomplishment. She then reached into her purse and took out something small.

"I have a little gift for your graduation." She grinned.

Having Mrs. McKeever at my graduation had already brought me joy, and when she handed me the gift, I became teary-eyed again. It was beautifully wrapped, and I didn't want to open it until she told me to. I slowly tugged the wrapping paper and saw a silver Cross pen. I instantly fell in love with it. She reached into her purse again and took out a folded piece of paper.

"Here is my address. I want you to use this pen and write to me about your progress in junior high school, or if you need my help with anything," she said as she put a hand on my shoulder.

I was so grateful to have her as my teacher. It was she who taught me how to speak English, made school fun, and reminded me to believe in myself. I made a promise to myself that I would treasure this pen and use it to write to her often.

School was over, but we continued to train in karate during the summer. I was happy to see improvements, and my passion for it had grown even deeper. I wished to train every day with sensei, instead of just the weekends. However, on weekdays, Anh Bao and I fervently practiced our katas in the living room. While making the hair clips and watching martial arts movies, we would yell out some of the techniques in the movies that were similar to what we learned. When the class resumed on the weekends, we would show some of the things that we had seen in the movies. The senior students laughed at our silly moves and told us to concentrate on what was taught instead.

One day before class, Sensei asked everyone to stay after class since he had something to announce. As the class went on, Sensei seemed distracted. He was quiet and there was a subtle sadness displayed on his face as he instructed us with less energy. At the end of class, Sensei gathered everyone in a circle. Slowly, he thanked us for being great students and for our dedication. He was also grateful to see that Vovinam would be taught in America and hopeful that all of us would expand the art someday. We felt strange after his speech and didn't know how to react until he went on with the news that saddened us all.

"I'm very sorry, I can't teach you, kids, anymore," he let out. "I'm moving to Canada to start a family."

We were silent trying to take in the news. We knew about Sensei's long-distance relationship, but since he rarely talked about it, we didn't think he would come to this decision. Although it was good news and we were truly happy for Sensei, we couldn't help but feel lost, like a part of our lives would be missing. I was really bothered by the news. I respected and looked up to Sensei since he was the one who made me realize my passion for martial arts. He taught me to be successful in anything - that I needed to push beyond my limit and always be confident in myself. I was hoping I could train with Sensei for a long time. It upset me that I had to say goodbye to another good teacher, a great mentor. We took turns hugging him and wishing him the best of luck in starting a new life in a new country.

Anh Bao and I went home that day feeling sad. We didn't feel like doing our routine practice in the afternoon, and even lost interest in our martial arts movies. Sensei's news was still shocking for us. Later that night, Ba came home from work and called me to his room. As I walked in, he handed me a picture. I held it up to my face, and for the first time after five years, I got to see Ma and all my siblings.

"How do you have this picture, Ba?" I asked in shock, holding back my tears.

"Bac Thanh just sent it to me," Ba answered as he looked out the window.

"They grew so much," I said, surrendering to the tears waiting to escape my eyes.

Ma looked sad while holding a baby girl, who I assumed to be my baby sister, Ly. Her other hand held onto Vu's hand, while the rest stood by her side.

"Will we ever see them again, Ba?" I hesitantly asked as I was afraid to hear the answer.

Ba didn't answer but let go of a deep sigh instead. He didn't know the answer. It was sad not knowing if our reunion would ever happen. At least I knew they were all in good health and doing well. I asked Ba if I could keep the picture; I wanted to look at it whenever I missed them.

After that night, Ba and Di Yen's relationship started to become troublesome. They had fought before, but it became more frequent. I didn't know what they were arguing about since it took place in their room. They always refrained from yelling, but I assumed it must have had something to do with Ma. We kids didn't know what to do, so we stayed quiet and hoped everything would be okay soon.

Toward the end of summer, Ba and Di Yen only communicated by bickering. There was always tension in the apartment. Anh Dung stayed over at his friend's place more often whether it was because of his new job that was near there, or because of the constant quarreling at the apartment. Anh Bao and I didn't have any place to go, so we witnessed the majority of it. We always looked forward to the weekend so we could get out of the house and go train karate. After Sensei Hai left for Canada, some of his senior students took over the class. They continued to train with us for free. However, their knowledge was limited, so unlike Sensei, we couldn't learn much from them. Eventually, the class became smaller and smaller since many kept quitting. One month after Sensei left, we said farewell to our class. It became the end of Vovinam.

One day, Anh Bao and I were playing with Phong in our room and suddenly heard screaming coming from Ba and Di Yen's room. That was the first time we heard them argue out loud. Phong was startled and started to cry. Anh Bao and I didn't know what to do. He picked Phong up and walked around the room, trying to stop him from crying. Phong continued to cry, and neither Ba nor Di Yen came out to soothe him. I wanted to run to their room and plead for the arguing to end. Before I could try, Anh Bao held me back and said there was nothing we could do. For all those years that we had lived together, I had never seen them argue this badly.

A week later, Ba told me we would be moving out. I didn't question Ba about his decision and the reasons, since the answer was obvious. I didn't know how Ba and Di Yen settled the matter, but only Ba and I were leaving. Phong stayed with her. I didn't feel right leaving Phong behind, but I didn't want to make the situation any harder for Ba. I was sad as I packed my clothing and nothing else. Anh Bao was just as confused as I was, but he was much older and realized this was something beyond our control. I would be missing the times we worked on the hairclips, watched martial arts movies, and stayed up late. Anh Dung and Anh Bao had grown to be more than just stepbrothers to me.

However, the saddest part was not being able to explain it to Phong. I wondered if he would ask for my goodnight kisses before bedtime. I wondered if he would look for me after waking up from his naps. I wondered if he would miss me as I would miss him. There were so many of these wonders in my head that I couldn't control my tears.

Ba and I moved into our new place in Astoria, Queens. It was a forty-five-minute train ride from our old place. The new neighborhood seemed nice and convenient. Our building was only one block away from the nearest train station. There were so many different groceries and stationery stores on the ground level along the block. There were six floors in our building, and our apartment was on the fifth floor. It was a one-bedroom apartment like the one we shared with Chu Chau and Anh Tri.

"Is it only the two of us again, Ba?" I asked.

"Yes, just you and me," Ba said.

This new place reminded me of the time we first arrived in the Bronx. A small apartment with just a father and son. Although I was about to feel the emptiness again in this apartment, I tried to adapt to the new living situation so Ba wouldn't have to worry about me. I never questioned Ba's decisions because I knew he had his reasons. After everything that we went through, I trusted him.

Although I missed Anh Bao, Bang, and all my friends in the Bronx, I was happy that I moved away from those bullies. The good thing about this neighborhood was that no troublemakers were sitting outside, blasting their music until midnight. I no longer had to put up with their bullying or get hit by them every time I went in and out of the building. I felt such a big relief, and so did Ba. He didn't have to worry about me fighting with them anymore.

Ba and Di Yen agreed to have Phong stay with her on weekdays, and we would have him on weekends. I was happy with the arrangement. I couldn't imagine not being able to see him at all. We would take the subway, pick him up on Saturday morning, have him spend the night at our place, and then drop him off on Sunday late afternoon. During that summer, Ba also attended classes at Pratt Institute for his engineering degree. His school and work took up a lot of his free time, putting a lot of stress on him. However, on the weekends, when Phong and I were in the apartment with him, I could see the joy in him as he cooked new dishes for us from what he had learned. He didn't want Phong to eat the same canned fish that we once ate.

Chu Tuan found out that Ba and I moved to Astoria, Queens, and so he came over to visit. There were times that he spent the night during the weekends when it was too late for him to take the train back to the Bronx, fearing that he might get robbed after getting off the train. After staying with us often, Ba asked if he wanted to move in with us since it would be closer to his work. A few weeks after he moved in, Anh Dung came over to visit us and asked to talk with Ba. Anh Dung got accepted to the New York Institute of Technology for his engineering degree. He also found a job at a restaurant near us. To save time on the commute between school and work, he asked Ba if he could move in with us. Ba gladly told him that he could do so anytime. One week later, Anh Dung moved in with me, and I was the first to be excited to live with him again.

The apartment suddenly became bustling with four of us living there. It reminded me of back when we shared the apartment with Chu Chau and Anh Tri. Ba and I slept in the bedroom, and Chu Tuan and Anh Dung slept in the living room. The only difference was that Anh Dung worked at a particularly good Japanese restaurant, and he became the cook for us. His teriyaki beef was his signature dish, which we always requested to make.

19 Astoria, Queens

On my first day going to Junior High School 204, I felt apprehensive about this new chapter of my life. *Would it be similar to PS122? Would I be able to do well? Would there be a kind teacher like Mrs. McKeever?* I was overwhelmed with these thoughts. When I arrived at the school, I saw students gathered in the schoolyard looking for their classes from the signs held by the teachers. I looked around and spotted my class: 7-B4 in the middle of the pack. While walking through hundreds of students to get to my class, I noticed that many of them were much bigger than me and some even taller than Ba. They had more facial hair and deeper voices. I was a bit intimidated by their sizes and looks. However, as I strolled through the crowd, I realized I was a seventh grader surrounded by eighth and ninth graders. *This must explain it,* I said to myself. I tried not to show fear as I walked past them to look for my class. There, I was relieved in seeing the majority of my classmates were my size.

After everyone lined up by the sign for their classes, we followed our teacher to our homeroom. Junior High School 204 was different from PS122. There was no assigned seat and we got to choose who to sit next to. Our homeroom teacher gave us the schedule of classes throughout the day, and I noticed that I would have to walk to each class instead of the teachers coming to us. I already liked this new system—walking independently to the next class instead of sitting in the same classroom all day long.

When I switched to the third class, music, I thought I was in the wrong classroom as I entered the room. It wasn't a typical table and desk format, but more like a mini auditorium with around fifty seats. In front of the class was a grand piano. I spotted an empty seat in the third row with no one on my left. I walked to the seat and saw two black students sitting behind me. They were my height, but much more built. Trying to make friends at the new school, I smiled and said hello while sitting down. As the teacher was taking attendance, I felt a kick on the back of my chair. I turned around and the two boys were looking at the teacher instead. *Maybe they hit my chair by accident*, I thought to myself. Then I felt something hit the back of my head. I reached for it with my hand to see what it was. I felt something wet, a nasty wet spitball filled with slimy saliva smearing between my fingers. Still disgusted by the saliva in my hand, I heard the giggling coming from behind. That unwanted, yet familiar feeling came to mind; I just got bullied. I thought I got away from it when I left the Bronx. I didn't expect it to happen again this soon, especially, on my first day of school.

The constant kicking and throwing of spitballs became unbearable. I told myself to ignore it and get through the class, however, it seemed like they wanted to test my patience. Their bothersome giggles that followed each time they messed with me brought me right back to the time I got hit by a rock from a slingshot. I couldn't take it anymore. I stood up and told them to stop. Although I told them off with a stern voice, they gave back a snarky reaction, only making me feel more agitated.

"What's going on?" the teacher asked.

"These guys are kicking my chair and throwing spitballs at me," I said.

"Why don't you move your seat." The teacher pointed to those empty seats on my left.

After telling me to move my seat, the teacher went back to teaching as if nothing happened. Not one word to those boys. I was shocked to see her reaction. Instead of questioning her, I obliged her request and moved my seat. As I got up to move, those boys pounded their fists into their palms as though they were ready to smash my face. Knowing nothing would make them change their behavior because even the teacher just let them be, I moved to the other end, which was at least twenty feet away from them. I wanted to be as far away as possible from them.

When the music class was over, I packed my bag and immediately got out of the room to avoid clashing with them. Out of nowhere, I felt a smack on the back of my head while walking to my next class. The sting from the strike made me stumble across the floor as I tried to maintain balance.

"Are you trying to get me in trouble, chink?" said one of the two black boys.

I was still shocked and confused as to why they wanted to hurt me so badly. The impact from the smack was much harder than the fights I had previously encountered. Either these guys were much bigger, or the sudden attack threw me off guard. As I tried to regain my awareness, I saw everyone staring at me and being screamed at. Then an older man, who I assumed was a teacher, ran toward us and demanded everyone leave the scene and head to their classes.

"You better watch out 'cause I'm coming for your ass," the other black boy said.

As I walked into my next class, feeling embarrassed from being hit, I kept my head down and grabbed the nearest seat to the door. I looked around and was relieved not to see those two boys. During the entire class, I was distracted and kept thinking about what would happen if we ran into each other again. I was worried and hoped it was just a one-time incident. I couldn't help but think it was somehow my fault for standing up to them. Had I controlled my anger and allowed them to throw spitballs at me, would the outcome be any different? The flashbacks of the fights in the Bronx came to haunt me again. I didn't want to get into another fight in this new environment.

During lunch, I was eating my food quietly at a corner table. I saw a boy carrying his lunch and heading toward my table. He sat next to me. I didn't know who he was, but I had seen him in a few of my classes.

"I'm sorry for what happened to you today," the boy said.

I was a bit uncomfortable seeing him sit down next to me since I wanted to be alone. However, hearing his words of comfort and seeing a friendly expression on his face, I felt at ease.

"It's okay," I said quietly. "Sometimes there's just nothing you can do about it."

He nodded in agreement. "My name is Eliazo. What's yours?"

"Linh. Where are you from?"

"The Philippines."

"I used to live there for almost six months until I came to America." I felt a good vibe from talking to Eliazo.

As we kept talking, Eliazo and I got along really well. I found out we had the same classes for the rest of the day. I took a chance and suggested if it was all right with him that we walk together to our classes. It would be safer with him around in the hallway since he had a bigger build and was taller than me. He quickly agreed as he understood my concern. The entire day, I didn't see those two boys again. I felt relief that they only shared music class with me.

At dismissal, Eliazo and I walked out of the school together, not knowing that we were heading in the same direction since we were into our conversation. I asked him where he lived, and to my surprise, he pointed to the building that I lived in. Shocked, I told him that my apartment was on the 5th floor. He smiled and said he lived in a townhouse across from my building. I was happy that we lived close to each other. I felt a good connection with Eliazo, so I asked to exchange phone numbers. We said goodbye as we got to our building and agreed to walk to school together the next day.

During dinner that night and since Ba was still out at work, I told Chu Tuan and Anh Dung about the unwanted incident on my first day at school. I didn't want Ba to know because he would be worried.

"What happened to all the karate you learned?" Anh Dung asked. "Didn't you try to use it?"

"Those kids were much bigger and stronger. Plus, I was only with Sensei Hai for less than six months. I probably would be dead if I gave it a try!" I explained.

"That's right! Stay away from trouble. It's not worth it to fight at that point." Anh Dung smiled.

For the entire week, I tried to stay out of those boys' sight. I found a different route going to and leaving music class to avoid seeing them. Although there were times I saw them talking with their group of friends in the middle of the hallway or flirting with girls. I was happy and went on my way as long as they left me alone. I was surprised that they didn't cause me trouble or tried to hurt me again.

The following week, on a Monday during lunch, I spotted a black student sitting at the corner of the table in the back of the cafeteria. He had been sitting at the same spot for the entire week. I also saw him in a couple of my classes. He didn't talk to anyone and hardly participated unless he was called upon. As Eliazo and I carried our lunch, looking for a table to sit at, I felt something pull me to walk towards that boy. He reminded me of myself during my first year at PS122. We got closer to his table. I suggested to Eliazo that we have lunch with him.

"Can we sit here with you?" I asked politely.

"Yeah, sure." I saw that he was taken aback.

"My name is Linh, and this is Eliazo. What is your name?"

"My name is Rufus."

Apparently, not only did Eliazo witness that I got hit by those two boys, but Rufus did too. Rufus told me that they lived in the same building as him. They were bad and liked to cause trouble with everyone. On the other hand, Rufus was a really good kid. He lived with his mom in a housing project for low-income families in Queensborough, which was in the opposite direction from my building. He always told us how much he appreciated his mom for working hard to provide for him since their circumstances were not well off. His mom had to leave early before he woke up for school and came home late at night. He had to take care of himself while his mother wasn't around. Hearing Rufus made me think of Ba and me. The more I hung out with Rufus, I admired his humility and patience. He always put on a genuine smile and avoided getting involved with any type of argument even when Eliazo and I disagreed on certain discussions.

Quickly, the three of us became best friends. On weekends, we would meet up at the park across JHS 204. I got introduced to a new sport: handball. I had seen other kids play this sport before in the Bronx, but I never tried it. The goal of the game was to hit the ball with a bare hand onto the wall and not let it bounce twice before hitting it again. I thought it was easy at first, but the first strike made me think twice. As I went all out to return a serve from Eliazo, my fingers went numb as I smacked the ball. It hurt so bad that I remembered the time when Sensei Hai conditioned our knuckles by making us do knuckle push-ups on hardwood or concrete. I couldn't feel my fingers for hours. However, the more I played, I felt like handball conditioned my hands to become an "iron palm," a term that we used in karate to build a hard-callous palm.

Besides hanging out at the park, we took turns inviting each other to our homes. Eliazo and Rufus knew that I lived with three men, so the apartment was often messy. Plus, I had nothing to entertain them but a small TV with no video games, nor any food to offer. Therefore, I rarely invited them over. Whether they understood my situation or didn't even notice it, they never asked about it. As for Rufus's place, I felt uneasy when I went there because I didn't want to encounter those two boys. Also, there were a lot of kids sitting outside of the building, giving us looks every time Eliazo and I walked by. This reminded me of those Hispanic kids at my old building in the Bronx. One time, one of the kids came up to Eliazo and me and demanded money as we were leaving Rufus's building. Both Eliazo and I ran as fast as we could to get out of there. After that incident, we told Rufus about it and didn't want to go back again. We mostly hung out at Eliazo's place since his mother and older sister loved us. They always prepared good snacks every time we came. Sometimes, we even stayed for a meal after long hours of playing video games.

All my friends (Bang, Eliazo, and Rufus), lived with their mothers. Seeing them being taken care of by their moms reminded me of Ma. I still frequently looked at the photo Bac Thanh sent to us and wished that Ma was there to give me the motherly love and care that I once had. At the time, Mrs. McKeever was the only female I was close to and was the closest mother figure to me. I would use the pen she gave me and write to her. I told her about my junior high school, about my new friends, Eliazo and Rufus, and about my everyday life. Somehow, it made me feel like I was talking to Ma. Mrs. McKeever always responded to my letters very quickly. She reminded me to believe in myself and never give up. She also talked about her everyday life, but mostly about her children and grandchildren. In every letter, she would always include coupons for McDonald's every few months or so; she knew that I loved McDonald's ice cream.

I thought the incident with the two black boys on my first day of school was over, but I was happy too soon. In the late fall of the school year, the bullies found me. I didn't know if they ran out of things to do and were bored, but those two kids started picking on me again. Throughout the entire day, it didn't matter how much I tried to avoid them by taking different paths in the hallway, I kept bumping into them. They would take turns blowing spitballs at me, kicking my backpack, laughing, and raising their fist to my face every time I walked past them. I was frustrated but tried to hold it in because I didn't want to make things more complicated. I knew I wouldn't be able to confront those two big guys.

One day, while walking in the hallway to the next class with Rufus and Eliazo, the two boys ran up and spit on my hair. That sent me to the end of my patience. I couldn't take it anymore. I turned around and screamed, "Stop it, man!" Then out of nowhere, there were so many of them running toward me yelling, "Let's beat the…"

I felt dizzy realizing I just put myself in an unbelievably dire situation. More than ten black kids were about to jump at me. My legs were trembling and my heart was racing. I knew right then that I would be beaten badly. I received a few kicks, a few punches, and at least one blow from each one. Luckily, Eliazo and Rufus jumped in and pulled me away. We ran to the next class as I was holding onto one of the backpack straps that got broken off during the beating. I looked like a mess. I was afraid to go to the principal's office to report them. Given the reaction from my music teacher last time, I doubted the principal would do anything to them. I was worried I would have ended up in even more trouble for reporting them.

I went home that night and didn't tell anyone about the incident at school, especially Ba, who was home that day. The last thing I wanted was to get him distracted from his school and work. I didn't want him to worry. The more I thought about it, there was nothing that Ba could have done if he found out. All the students saw the incident, and no one stepped in to help me, but luckily Eliazo and Rufus pulled me away safely. Right then, I knew I had to do something to protect myself.

After dinner, I told Ba that I needed to study and went to the room. I thought about what would happen to me at school the next day. These kids were worse than the ones in the Bronx and staying away from them was impossible. I couldn't sleep the entire night. I thought of ways to defend myself since no one could help me. Although I knew karate, I hadn't learned enough to fight them. These boys were much bigger and stronger. Suddenly, in the corner of my eyes, I saw a compass lying on my desk, and a thought occurred in my head.

I woke up in the morning and prepared for school. I took a long rope, placed the pointy part of the compass on my palm, and wrapped it with the rope onto my wrist. I put on a long sleeve shirt to cover the compass and felt ready for any bullying that day. While walking to school, I felt confident that I was ready if anyone picked on me. Instead, once I entered the school, my heart started pounding. The opposite effect took over. I felt nervous and hesitant to use this weapon. The fear that I might stab someone with it sent chills down my spine. I didn't want to hurt anyone but just wanted to stop them from bullying me. I walked around with my chest out and chin up as I switched classes, but part of me was praying I didn't have to use this compass on anyone. To my surprise, for the entire day, none of them did anything to me. It was like they knew I was prepared.

For the rest of the week, no one bothered me. I was perplexed and didn't understand the sporadic bullying from these guys, but I didn't mind that they stopped. However, that didn't last long. During the following week, just when I decided to leave the compass at home, those two boys approached Rufus and me. During recess, while we were playing handball on the wall behind the cafeteria, one of the boys ran over and snatched the ball from me.

"Come on man, don't do that," Rufus said. That was the first time I ever heard Rufus talk back to them.

"Whatcha gonna do about it?" one of the boys said.

"Give it back to him, man," Rufus demanded with a serious look on his face.

"Yo, guys, looks like this kid also wants to get beat."

Suddenly, the whole gang of them who had beaten me up ran toward us and surrounded Rufus. Instantaneously, one of them pushed Rufus to the ground. I ran over to help him get up, but Rufus got up and ran to his book bag. He took out a binder and removed the metal ring bar that held the paper. He ran back to the boy that pushed him and swung the metal part right into his head. Blood trickled down that kid's head, and others slowly backed away from Rufus. I had never seen Rufus lose his composure like that. The security guards ran over and held Rufus, taking away the metal bar. I told the guards that it wasn't Rufus' fault. I tried to explain the whole situation to them as a witness, but they didn't care. Rufus was escorted to the principal's office.

For the next hour, there were rumors in the school that these boys were waiting for Rufus outside of the school to get revenge. I was afraid for his safety and also for being in trouble with the school. He was still in the principal's office and hadn't returned to class. Eliazo and I were so worried, but later we found out that the police were informed. They escorted him home after meeting with the principal. Still, we didn't know if he was punished for fighting and injuring others at school. Eliazo and I wanted to visit him but were afraid to run into those boys at his building.

During the next two weeks, Rufus didn't go to school. His mom didn't want him to leave the apartment, afraid these boys would take revenge and hurt him. One day after school, I received a call from Rufus. He told me that his mom found another place to live, and he would be moving to another school as well to avoid confrontation with those bullies. I was so sad and broke into tears hearing the news from Rufus. No one had ever stood up for me like that before. Rufus was my hero that day. I would never forget his bravery as he defended me. He showed these boys that they shouldn't be pushing people to an impasse. When Rufus moved, we lost contact. I didn't know if his mom didn't want him to keep in touch with the people from his old school, but we never heard from him afterward. Eliazo and I talked about him every day and hoped to see him at the park. However, it seemed as though he never wanted to set foot back in Astoria ever again.

After that incident, the school increased security guards in each corridor. I still saw the bullies in my music class and the hallway. Whether they had been warned by the principal or Rufus had taught them a lesson, they stopped bothering me. Although I was happy that they left me alone, I felt like I paid a hefty price for it. The price that cost me losing my best friend.

After the next few weeks of seeing no sign of Rufus at the park, Eliazo and I stopped going there and concentrated on getting good grades in school. We studied together at his house. His mother was just like Ba, always encouraging her kids to study hard. I guess all immigrant parents had one goal for their kids—to get a good education so we could have a better future. Eliazo's mother, Mrs. Salinas, worked as a nurse while taking care of him and his sister, who started college. She reminded me of Co Lan and Bang's mom since they also loved to cook for their kids. It didn't matter how late she got home from work, she still managed to make food for them. Mrs. Salinas knew about my situation and just like Co Lan, she constantly offered me to stay for dinner before heading back to my apartment.

One day halfway through the school year, as I walked to my class, I saw Mr. Jackson, the Assistant Principal. He stopped me and told me to visit him in his office during my lunchtime. I was afraid I was in trouble. I couldn't think of anything besides the fights, but I hadn't been into any lately as I recalled. I was confused, trying to figure out what it could be. When I got to his office, I nervously sat down across from him. There he pulled out my report card and told me that I had exceptional grades.

"I am putting together a National Junior Honor Society, and I think you should be in it," Mr. Jackson said. "You should be proud of yourself."

"Thank you, sir! But what is the National Junior Honor Society?"

Although I didn't know what the National Junior Honor Society was, I was relieved knowing I wasn't in trouble. Since Mr. Jackson was also praising me, I assumed it must've been something good. After Mr. Jackson explained this to me, I felt a rush of adrenaline. I couldn't help but keep on smiling inside and out. I didn't know I could qualify for something this prestigious. I wasn't expecting any awards but just wanted to have good grades so Ba could be proud of me. I left his office and walked proudly to the lunchroom. I felt special, and all that hard work studying paid off. I couldn't wait to tell Ba.

That night, I anxiously waited for Ba to get home so I could share the good news. As Ba entered the apartment, I jumped with joy and told Ba about the conversation I had with Mr. Jackson. The ceremony was set for some time toward the end of the school year, and I made Ba promise to be there this time. Pleased and proud, Ba congratulated and commended me for my incredible discipline to achieve this award. Ba no longer had to bend down to my eye level to talk to me, as he no longer had to remind me to set my goals. Through the years of ingraining how education would be important for us, I didn't let him down and made him a proud father instead.

20 The Summer Job

In the spring of 1988, Ba was in his last semester of obtaining his engineering degree. Due to his class schedule being different every day, Ba had to quit working at the Pizza Parlor but was lucky enough to find another job as a security guard at a power plant facility, which allowed him flexible hours to adjust to his school schedule. On days that he had late classes, he worked in the daytime and vice versa. To balance work and school, Ba always had to make the most of his time. On nights when he came home after 10 PM and didn't want to spend time cooking, he went back to munching on dried noodles and drinking tea, so he could get on with his schoolwork.

Anh Dung had been taking more classes because he wanted to finish school quickly too. He seldom had time to cook for us anymore. Seeing Ba eating those unhealthy foods again made me worry that his stomach ulcer might flare up. However, I knew that this was his last year, and he would do whatever it took to reach his goal, including risking his life by taking the subway home late at night.

The train station near Ba's school, Pratt Institute, was in a secluded area and had frequent occasions of robbery attempts. Aside from robberies, people got beat up on the train all the time for random reasons. We didn't have a car, so besides walking, taking the train was the only other option. Occasionally, Ba was lucky to have friends drive him home, but most of the time, he had to take the train home. I would pray to Buddha to keep Ba safe on those nights that he had to take the subway home.

Although Ba's work gave him the ability to adjust to his time, he was required to work overnight shifts whenever there was a staff shortage. It was at least a forty-five-minute walk from our apartment to his workplace. Seeing him walking back and forth like that hurt me, especially when in the rain. Ba would get home all soaked in the morning, take a quick shower, and then head back out for school. I wished I could do something to share his burden.

One late Friday afternoon, Chu Tuan was on his day off, so we decided to surprise Ba at work. The walk to Ba's workplace seemed like forever. We had to cross many big intersections and many small bridges. I was breathing hard and my legs got tired. Chu Tuan told me we were only halfway there. I looked ahead and wondered how many more blocks we had to walk. Abruptly, an image of Ba walking on this road every day popped into my head. I felt guilty knowing what Ba had to do to support me. I picked up the pace and continued walking.

We arrived at the facility, which looked deserted. Trash was everywhere on both sides of the dirt road that was covered with weeds. We approached the gate and Ba was surprised to see us. He came out from his security booth and let us in. It was after working hours so only Ba was at the facility. I asked Ba to give us a tour around the place. This power plant provided electricity for the area located at the edge of the Hudson River. The whole place was built with many small buildings for the generators and power supplies. I could hear the loud engines running as we walked by.

We went back to the booth and had the dinner that we brought along. Chu Tuan stayed around for a while, then he went home. I wanted to stay with Ba to keep him company since Ba had to stay for an overnight shift. At every top of the hour, I walked with Ba around the facility, holding a flashlight, checking to make sure that everything was all right, then went back to the booth and checked off his routine walk. The booth had a big glass window viewing the entrance of the facility. There was no bed inside, just a table, a small lamp, and a chair.

"You can sleep on this side of the table tonight while I do my homework," Ba said.

"It's OK Ba. I am not sleepy yet," I said.

Ba gave me a small blanket that he brought to use when staying for the night shift and went back to studying. I watched him do his homework but kept checking the clock so he wouldn't miss his routine walk. I felt bad and loved him so much. At that moment, I wanted to do something to help so he didn't have to work so hard while going to school. A thought had crossed my mind; I wanted to get a job. I knew Ba wanted to get his engineering degree so he could make more money, and I wanted to help him get to his goal.

"I am going to save up some money to get us a car," Ba suddenly said.

"No, Ba, that's a lot of money. We can't afford that," I immediately countered him.

"Don't worry, I have been saving and we need one."

"But I don't want you to work too hard."

"It's okay. I planned things out."

Whatever Ba had planned in mind, I was hoping that he wouldn't be overwhelmed with all the responsibilities that he placed upon himself.

In May, I was informed of my participation in the ceremony for the National Junior Honor Society. I was happy that Ba and Chu Tuan were able to attend. As I was holding a candle, walking with my fellow awardees from the back of the auditorium, and passing by all the parents sitting on both sides cheering, I felt a profound sense of pride and accomplishment for all my hard work. I wanted to remember that moment as a reminder to myself—to work hard to achieve my dreams. When I got up to the stage to light my candle, I looked over at Ba and saw the proud look on his face. This was my gift to him for believing in me, for instilling in me to study hard and not give up. I would always be grateful for that.

A few weeks later, it didn't take long before it was Ba's turn to graduate. On June 3, 1989, Ba sat with hundreds of other students on the grass of Pratt Institute campus wearing his cap and gown celebrating a milestone. The day that he had been waiting for while working so hard had finally come. He proved that no situations or obstacles could stop one's dream once the mind was set. I stood in the back with Chu Tuan and some of his friends, watching him walk up to the podium to receive his Bachelor of Science in Electrical Engineering. I was so proud of him. It was picture perfect as I captured Ba reaching his hand forward to receive the degree he was determined to get ever since he set foot in America.

As the school year ended, I had another reason to be proud of myself. Eliazo and I were informed by Mr. Jackson that we would be placed in honors classes in eighth grade based on our report cards. We were happy and couldn't wait to share the good news with Ba and Mrs. Salinas. We knew how much this would mean to our parents to see their kids be successful in school. We were grateful for all the hardship that they went through for us to have a better future. Eliazo and I had been talking and we wanted to do something to repay our parents. As teenagers, we would want to do things teenagers would do.

"Let's get a job," Eliazo suggested.

That thought had been on my mind for quite some time. I wanted to make some money to help Ba with some of the expenses. Ba had applied for some engineering jobs but was still working as a security guard while waiting for those companies to respond. Ba wanted to save up to buy a car since it would be more convenient to visit Phong instead of taking the subway. We needed to cut down on spending and eating out. However, when Phong was with us on the weekends, Ba wouldn't say no when he asked for McDonald's.

Before starting to look for a summer job, I asked Ba if I could go visit Anh Bao and Bang since I hadn't seen them in a while. Ba hesitated for me to go by myself, but I convinced him that it would be okay since I had been on the train with him so many times to pick up and drop off Phong. I also asked Eliazo to go with me, but his mother didn't allow him to take the train that far, especially to the Bronx. I ended up going by myself. I got off at Fordham Road station and walked to Di Yen's place. After a delicious meal made by Di Yen, I sat to play with Phong in the living room and heard some strange news about Bang from Anh Bao.

Bang had changed quite a bit after I moved. He talked arrogantly, dressed differently, and even started smoking. He had gel in his hair and combed it straight back, looking like a gangster in those gangster movies. I was shocked after hearing it from Anh Bao. It had been a while since I'd seen Bang, and I couldn't imagine how my best friend could go astray.

Feeling worried, I ran to Bang's apartment. Di Lai was happy to see me and invited me in. After catching up, she started to cry the minute we sat down. Seeing tears on her face, I knew it had something to do with Bang. She hugged me and pleaded that I should talk to Bang. She told me he had changed a lot ever since he started hanging out with some new kids. She mentioned some of the names, but they were all new to me.

"Do you know any of the kids he's been hanging out with?" I asked.

"They're all Vietnamese, but they look like bad kids, and I don't want him to be around them," she cried. "He's never home. He just comes and goes whenever he pleases."

"When he gets home, please let me know. I will be staying at Di Yen's for a couple of hours."

Late that afternoon, I got a call from Bang, and we met up at the park. When I saw him, I noticed the change in his appearance. His hair was just how Anh Bao described and with a ponytail. He was wearing all black with the bottom of his jeans cuffed. I didn't know if he had been influenced by watching too many Hong Kong gangster movies, but he certainly looked like one that day. However, the kindness that he showed me when we first met was still the same. He didn't say it, but I could tell he was happy to see me. At the same time, he was a little awkward when he talked to me.

"You want to go to McDonald's?" he asked.

"Yeah, sure, but I don't have any money," I replied.

"Don't worry, I have money for anything now," he confidently responded.

Bang reached into his pocket and took out a pack of cigarettes. I was astonished to see him about to smoke in front of me. He had changed. Unaware, I felt sad I was losing someone close to me. Trying to hold my emotions back, I joked with him.

"Damn, you're learning how to smoke already?" I said.

"Wanna try?" he asked with a little embarrassment.

"Nah. My dad would kill me."

"All right, then you can watch me smoke."

He lit the cigarette like he had done it so many times. He seemed to enjoy huffing and puffing as we walked toward McDonald's. I couldn't stand the smoke blowing into my face as he puffed it out of his mouth. I had to turn away every time he exhaled the smoke. I wanted to ask him about the friends he was hanging out with, who taught him how to smoke, and why he was dressed like that. There were so many questions that I was curious about and wanted an answer to. However, I refrained and instead told him about my new friends in Queens.

When we got to McDonald's, Bang told me to order whatever I wanted. I felt strange and wondered where he got all this money. I worried, thinking of what I thought might be true. We sat down to eat our Big Macs. I told him about Rufus and how he stood up for me in front of a bunch of bullies.

"That's my kind of guy, man. You need to stand up for your brothers," Bang said angrily. "I'm sick and tired of being bullied. Nobody touches me now, man. I'll beat the heck out of them."

"How? With your flying kick from Sensei Hai?" I jokingly asked.

"Forget about karate, man. Only knives and guns will scare these kinds of idiots," he said, tightening his face and grinding his teeth. "From now on, let me know if they ever bully you. I'll bring my brothers and kick their asses for you."

After hearing what he said, I realized that Bang had joined a gang. The answer was right in front of me, but I tried to deny it. Remembering his mom's pleas, I wanted to talk to him but was afraid he might be offended that I tried to get into his business. I held back, thinking I would talk with him in the future under more appropriate circumstances. We finished eating and walked along the streets of Fordham Road back to the park. Although I tried to adjust to his new attitude, there was something that bothered me and made me feel uneasy. We parted ways and while walking back to Di Yen's apartment, I kept thinking of the knives and guns that Bang mentioned. I hoped he wouldn't get himself into trouble.

A week into the summer had passed, and it was time to find a job. Eliazo and I went to a supermarket, which was a few blocks away from my building, and we asked to see the manager. Eliazo did all the talking since he said his friend worked there. After a short interview, we were hired and would start working the next Saturday. The manager agreed to pay us $3.35 an hour. We were happy thinking finally we could do something for the family, feeling useful as a "grown-up." I didn't want to tell Ba that I found a job, afraid he would insist I focus solely on school, but I trusted my capabilities to give back to him.

The next Saturday, I told Ba that I was going to Eliazo's house to play games. Ba knew Eliazo was a good kid, so he didn't mind that I spent time with him. I went to his house, and we walked to the supermarket at 3 PM as we were told. Our first task was to rearrange boxes in the basement. It was dark and damp with boxes of food scattered everywhere as we walked downstairs. I heard rats running around and chewing on the boxes. Next, we carried some of the frozen items from the freezer, which was the size of my bedroom, in the basement up to the main level of the supermarket and stack them on the cold shelf. After those cycles of being in and out of the freezer, my whole body was numb. I turned to Eliazo and told him to take a short break in which he didn't argue.

When we finished the work in the basement, the manager sent me to the back of the dumpster to clean the garbage. I had to jump on top of the dumpster and kick the garbage to distribute it evenly to the other side. The dumpster was at least six feet high and ten feet wide. I had to grab onto the top edge of it to pull myself up. When I stood on the top panel of it, I looked down to see those nasty garbage bags filled with rotten food and brown water dispersed from one bag to another. The smell was rancid, and I wanted to vomit as I jumped onto those bags to distribute them evenly in the bin.

By 7 PM, the manager gave us a mop and told us to take turns going up and down the aisles. There were twenty-four aisles in that supermarket. Eliazo and I needed to finish half of it, while two other men mopped the other half. We had been continuously working since we came and weren't given any breaks. By that time, we both were thirsty and tired. I asked the assistant manager if we could have one can of orange soda, which we had reorganized many of them in the basement. She sternly said no and told us to drink the water from the faucet in the basement. There was no way I would drink that nasty water. I'd rather be thirsty. However, Jose, Eliazo's friend, came to the rescue. He secretly grabbed two cans and gave them to us. I gulped mine as fast as I could in order not to get caught. I needed that juice before mopping that floor for another hour.

That night, walking home, I thought I was walking on clouds because I couldn't feel anything in my body. It was the most tiresome job I had ever done in my life. After five hours of constantly moving heavy stuff and dealing with nasty things, I was beaten and wanted to quit. At that moment, I thought of Ba and his plan of getting a car, so I gathered my strength and told myself I couldn't quit. I wanted to do something to help Ba and to show my gratitude to let him know he wasn't in this alone.

On Sunday, I used the same excuse, hanging out with Eliazo, to get out of the house. We showed up to work at 3 PM. We were sent to the basement for more cleanup. Around 5 PM, the manager gathered all the workers in front of the store. He had seven of us line up six feet apart. I wondered what this formation was for. There, I saw a truck pull in with a lot of boxes.

"Here comes the real work. It will be a good workout for you guys," Jose said.

Two of the big guys jumped on the truck and everyone in line got ready. It was like they all knew the routine. I was the last one in line next to the loading cart, and Eliazo was the second from the truck. As soon as the guy from the truck threw a box to the first one in line, the work began. Boxes were passed down by throwing them to the next person. After I caught a box, I had to stack it on the cart. At first, it was kind of fun, like we were playing catch. However, when the boxes got heavier and I became more fatigued, it became a tiring job. The guy before me threw it at me and I didn't realize how heavy it was. For not preparing in advance, I was hit in the chest, and that sharp pain took me to the ground. I fell holding my chest as I couldn't breathe. The manager ran over, helped me up, and pulled me aside to rest. The corner of the box broke, and I could see liquid detergent bottles falling out. After a short rest, the manager came to check if I was okay, then asked me to get back to work.

Around 8 PM, the manager came to look for both of us while we were in the basement stacking boxes with Jose. He handed Eliazo and me $30 each.

"All right boys, thank you for working," the boss said. After a pause with uncertainty, he continued, "but I don't think this job is meant for you two."

"It's OK. This work is tough for you boys. He doesn't want you to get hurt." Jose tried to comfort us.

After just two days of work, we got fired. We were disappointed since we planned to work the whole summer to save more money. For me, it was to help Ba with buying a car and for Eliazo it was to help with his sister's tuition. It was sad walking home that night since our goals were cut short. Yet, that $30 made us proud knowing we earned it with our own hands. I felt great even though my chest still hurt.

On Monday after school, while Ba, Chu Tuan, and Anh Dung were still at work, I took my money and went food shopping. Since $30 wouldn't help much with buying a car, I decided to help out with the food for the family. I bought cereal, chicken, vegetables, bread, and eggs. I didn't forget to grab two big boxes of ice cream since we all had a sweet tooth. After paying for all of that, I still had a little left. I brought the food home and put it in the refrigerator. When everyone got home, ready for dinner, Ba was surprised to see all the food when he opened the fridge. I told him that I bought it with the money that I made over the weekend.

"What?" he screamed. "How did you get a job?"

"Eliazo's friend works there, and he introduced us to the manager who gave us the job," I explained. "I'm sorry, Ba. I lied to you that I hung out with Eliazo. I wanted to help you with buying a car so you don't have to work so hard."

Ba held me for a long time and then patted me on the back. I knew he was proud of me. Although he didn't say it, the look on his face told me he felt bad that I had to work.

"You don't have to work. Enjoy your summer," he said in a cracking voice.

"We got fired, Ba. They said we were not strong enough," I said sadly.

"That's good. But at least you got the experience." Ba laughed with relief.

"I also have good news to share." Ba paused for a moment and with a big smile on his face, he said, "I got an offer. A real job!"

We were so happy for Ba. We congratulated him and wished him luck with his new job. It was an exciting summer for us. Ba graduated from college, I made it to honor class for 8th grade, I experienced my first job, and Ba got his first engineering job in America. I couldn't believe how much our lives had changed ever since we stepped foot on that small fishing boat. Ba set out to search for freedom and a better life. Here we were, in America, building our new lives and our dreams. Everything was starting to fall in place. I couldn't wait to see what awaited us.

21 The Phone Call

Ba got a job at the Department of Environment Agency in Flushing, Queens. I was happy that Ba was no longer working the night shift or taking the late train home. Every morning seeing Ba put on a shirt and tie to get ready for work made me proud of him and motivated me to do better in school. After knowing about our two days of working experience, Mrs. Salina and Ba didn't want Eliazo and me to find another job. Ba wanted me to enjoy the summer and study hard to prepare for the honors program in 8th grade. Mrs. Salina also wanted the same thing for Eliazo. For the rest of the summer, I went to his house every day to study with him in the morning and play video games afterward. Thanks to our hard work during the summer, the entire year of 8th grade went by smoothly and brought us some accomplishments that made our parents proud. Both of us enrolled in honors classes and made it to the honor society again.

In the fall of 1989, I attended Aviation High School. This school had more than 95% male students and it concentrated on both academic and technical learning. The thing that interested me most was that they taught students to fix aircrafts. I didn't know anything about airplanes, but after hearing there were actual small airplanes and helicopters at the school's hangar, I was intrigued and wanted to give it a try. On the other hand, Eliazo wanted no part in a school with mainly boys and getting his hands dirty fixing airplanes. He ended up going to Long Island City High School, which was only a fifteen-minute walking distance from our place. Aviation High School was a bit further. It took me thirty minutes by train to get there.

Two weeks before starting school, I was hanging out at the park, playing basketball with some friends who went to Aviation HS and I was warned about Freshman Fridays, where seniors picked on freshmen and gave them wedgies. Usually, it took place outside after school for them to avoid getting in trouble. I wasn't happy to hear about this. I wondered why there was always something to fear every time I entered a new school. I should have joined Eliazo at Long Island City HS to save all the headaches. Nevertheless, it was too late to change schools now. I had to come up with a plan to protect myself. For the next two weeks, I worked out to build more muscle. I went back to self-train all the karate forms that I learned from Sensei Hai. I realized I needed to be stronger to boost my confidence to prepare for future unwanted situations.

The first day at Aviation High School was intimidating. The boys around me were much bigger. I had flashbacks of the first day at JHS 204. Walking to my class, I sat down quietly and minded my own business. I didn't want to encounter any more commotion with anyone in the class. Luckily, the first day went by without any incidents. In fact, throughout the week, nothing happened and I even made new friends. I began to like this school a lot. The students seemed friendly, and the teachers were helpful. I also enjoyed fixing those airplanes. When I took the plane to America, I only saw it from afar. I remembered wondering how it could carry that many people, flying in the air for such long hours. I was amazed to find out the answers to my curiosity at this school. Even though these planes were much smaller, I was so glad to understand their mechanisms.

The first Freshman Friday came by, and I hoped it was just rumored to scare the freshmen since no one picked on me so far. Still, I was petrified the entire day every time I walked in the hallways. I kept reassuring myself that I was stronger and that I could fight back since I had prepared for it. At the end of class, to avoid going home alone, I tagged along with my new friends, Carlos, a freshman like me, and his older brother Alex, a sophomore. They lived three blocks away from my building. While taking the train home, as we were standing waiting for our stop, two older black teens, who I assumed were seniors since they were carrying a backpack, approached us and were fixated on me.

"Give me your money!" one of the guys said.

"I don't have any," I confidently responded, but my mind was conjuring fear.

The inevitable struck. Instead of giving me wedgies, they demanded money. They both moved closer to my face and looked down into my eyes since they were much bigger than me. I had to brace myself not to fall backward. I was shaking as I clenched both of my fists. I knew I wasn't ready for this, but I didn't want to back down. It had been too long, ever since fourth grade since I got bullied. I didn't want to put up with this anymore as my patience had worn out. I was ready to take them on even if it was a losing battle.

Alex suddenly spoke up. "Leave him alone, man."

Alex was a sophomore, but he was tall and built just like those two guys. Three of them were staring at each other in silence. I was worried for Alex but somehow felt secure since there were three of us and only two of them. After a few seconds, the two seniors looked at each other and walked away. I turned to Alex and thanked him for standing up for me. Alex didn't say anything, just nodded his head and patted my shoulder as he had my back. I was envious of Carlos for being lucky to have a brother who could protect him. After that incident, the three of us took the train together every day. I introduced Carlos and Alex to Eliazo and we became good friends. It was nice to have Alex watch our back every time we hung out at the park.

One night, I was studying in the living room. Ba called me into the bedroom, had me sit down on the bed, and handed me a letter from Ma. It was in Vietnamese and at least three pages long. It would take me a long time to finish reading it, so I asked Ba to fill me in instead.

"Ma and the entire family escaped Vietnam a month ago," Ba said.

"What? How? Did they take the boat like us too?" I was shocked.

"Yes, and they are now in one of the refugee camps in Hong Kong."

In disbelief, I was dazed by the image of Ma and all my siblings in a little boat going through the same ordeal that we did. I had experienced the horror of the nights at sea, especially when the vicious storms came as they wanted to engulf our small boat in the sea. I couldn't imagine how afraid my siblings were and how Ma had to wrap five children in her arms to keep them safe in that ferocious South China Sea. I couldn't stop asking Ba questions to ease my mind. Ba told me that the escape was organized for months by someone in the village. A lot of people from my village followed Ba and my footsteps. Ma decided to join them, hoping for a chance to reunite with us. While listening to Ba, I wondered what gave Ma the strength to endure all that hardship. However, I was grateful to know that Ma and my siblings were safe and now staying at the Whitehead Refugee camp in Hong Kong, a new camp that was established after Ba and I left. It appeared that the Hong Kong officials weren't as strict as when Ba and I were there. They allowed the Vietnamese refugees to go out of the campsite and work. Ma and her friends worked as house cleaners to earn money while living there.

Ba told me he would apply for the paperwork to bring them here. I was overjoyed to hear that. Finally, I could see Ma and my siblings again. Our family could finally be reunited. I looked over to Ba and saw the excitement on his face, but also the underlying signs of worry. I wasn't sure what was in his mind, and I was uncertain as to how Ma would react to the news of Di Yen and Phong. Although Ba and Di Yen had been separated for quite a while, they still had to keep in touch due to Phong. *Would Ma be able to accept that? Would Ma be able to accept Phong?* I was supposed to be over the moon, as this was the moment that I had been dreaming of, being with my family, being in Ma's arms, something that I yearned for every day. Instead, I was unsettled thinking of the future. I tried to convince myself that everything would be all right, but there was a part of me that felt anguished for unknown reasons.

The next day after school, I was surprised to see Ba home before me. He told me to put my backpack down and follow him. As we got out of the building, he pointed to a silver Ford Tempo parked across the street.

"There it is, our first car, Linh," he said with a big smile on his face.

"Wow, that is so cool, Ba." I was just as delighted.

I knew he had been talking about buying a car for some time but didn't expect it would happen this fast. Ba told me he went car shopping with Chu Tuan and found this. The car had more than 60,000 miles and cost $1,500. Since Ma and all the siblings would be here soon, Ba thought it would be more convenient for a family of eight to ride in a car, rather than taking the train.

"Let's go for a ride!" Ba excitedly said.

I couldn't wait to get in the car. Although it was used, I somehow still smelled the scent of a new car. The inside looked so clean that I made sure to sit with both my feet on the mat. As Ba drove us along the streets of Astoria, I rolled down the window to feel the breeze blowing on my face. I remember taking the taxi with Ba and Co Kim from the airport to the hotel in Manhattan when we first arrived in NYC. That was the first time a country boy like me got to experience a car ride. I dreamt of the day we could have one for ourselves. There we were, sitting in our car, bought with our hard-earned money. Ba and I had come a long way as I reminisced about our journey to America to search for freedom.

The following week, while I was having dinner with Ba and Anh Dung, the phone rang. It was Anh Bao looking for me. He rarely called us unless Di Yen wanted him to relay a message to Anh Dung. I felt strange as this call was for me. I picked up the phone but couldn't tell if there was a bad connection, or if his voice was shaky. I couldn't make out any words from him. I kept saying *hello, hello,* until I finally understood him through his somber voice.

"I have some bad news," he said.

My legs shook and my mind was clouded with anxiety. *What was it? Did something happen to him or Phong?* If that were the case, he would speak to Ba instead of me. I became more anxious as he took a long pause.

"Bang is dead. Bang is dead." He broke down.

I was stunned and fell to my knees bawling. *How could this be? What happened to him? Not Bang, not my friend.* So many questions were running through my head as I tried to deny the reality. Everyone was shocked to see my reaction. Anh Dung came over to help me get up and hear the news from Anh Bao. Ba and Anh Dung were astounded as they were speechless.

"Are you still there?" Anh Bao asked.

I heard him from the other line, but my whole body shut down. I couldn't move or talk as I was in disbelief. My first friend. My best friend, who made me feel welcomed, who saved me from being alone in the apartment, and who was gracious enough to give me that first marble, passed away. I tried to gather my strength and grab the phone from Anh Dung.

"How did he die?" I asked, trying to hold in my emotions.

"He was shot along with two other gang members in a parking lot. It was on the news," Anh Bao replied.

My heart shattered. What I had worried about had happened. I stood there frozen as I was angry at myself for being timid the last time we met. I should have talked to him. I should have made him stop hanging out with those kids. I should have made him leave the gang. I should have done what a friend would have done. Then he would still be here. I wouldn't lose my best friend and his mom wouldn't lose her son. I couldn't imagine the pain Di Lai was going through now. Her children were everything to her.

The next day, I told Ba I wanted to go visit Di Lai. I took the train to the Bronx, got together with Anh Bao, and headed over to Di Lai's apartment. When she opened the door for us, her puffy red eyes and pale face struck sadness within me. She couldn't stop crying the minute she saw us. We followed her into the living room and there it was, Bang's altar, built with his picture leaning against the wall and a small cup holding incense in front of it. Anh Bao and I couldn't hold in our tears looking at his picture. We stood still at his altar but couldn't believe that he was gone.

"He really loved you two," Di Lai sobbed. "He talked about you all the time, Linh. Ever since Linh moved to Queens, he started hanging out with the wrong crowd. He said he felt more powerful while he carried knives, and nobody dared to touch him." She continued sobbing.

I sat there, feeling guilty that I couldn't say anything to Di Lai. I felt ashamed for not fulfilling her pleas. I would never have thought when we said goodbye that day after eating at McDonald's was also our last goodbye to each other. Bang would always be remembered as my very first best friend who I cherished.

On the way back to Di Yen's apartment, Anh Bao asked me about things in high school. I told him I went back to self-training karate and doing pushups and pull-ups to build my strength and confidence. That was how I was able to stand up to those guys on the train. Anh Bao was happy that I knew how to protect myself. I asked him about college. He hesitated for a while and told me he wanted to take a break from school. He wanted to work to make money. I was shocked by his decision. I didn't know the reason why he was in dire need of money and making this choice. It was sad to see a good student drop out of school.

Bang's death and Anh Bao dropping out of school put me in a bad mood. I didn't even feel like playing with Phong. We sat on the couch watching whatever was on the TV while waiting for Di Yen to make dinner. Phong seemed to understand my feeling. He sat quietly on my lap and enjoyed the show. Suddenly, he turned around and hugged me. It felt great since that was what I needed. As I held him in my arms, thoughts of Ma popped into my head. I was scared to think of what would happen when Ma arrived. I hoped Phong wouldn't get hurt being stuck in this complicated situation.

A week later, while I was doing my homework, the phone rang. I ran over to pick it up. The operator said there was a collect call on the other line and asked if I wanted to accept it. I found it strange to receive a collect call and wondered who it could be. Usually, collect calls were from someone who didn't have money to make the call, and the receiver would be responsible for the fees if accepted. Ba always told me not to accept a collect call since it was expensive. However, something was telling me to find out who the caller was.

"Who is the collect call from?" I asked.

"It is an international collect call," the operator said.

"I don't know anyone inter—"

"Linh? Is that you?" A familiar voice of a woman. "Linh? This is Ma."

It had been roughly seven years since I heard Ma's voice. Within a few seconds, which felt like an eternity, I was still trying to grasp the reality that my mother was on the other line. I suppressed my emotions, sealed my lips, and responded.

"Yes, it's me, Ma," I said.

"Linh, this is Ma. I'm living in Hong Kong right now. I miss you so much," she cried.

I could feel her tears as the operator continued to ask if I wanted to accept the call or not. I accepted the call. As Ma continued to ask me questions, her cracking voice from containing her cries traveled to my ears and hit me straight to the heart. I couldn't hold it anymore and broke down with her. We both hung on to the phone. Not one word was said, only the sound of us crying. She sounded so close to me yet so far. After a few seconds, I regained my composure. I wanted to talk to Ma. I wanted to know about her and my siblings' situation.

"How are you, Ma? How are my sisters and brother?" I asked.

"They're all well and miss you too. Is Ba home?" she asked.

"No, Ma, Ba is still at work. I will let him know that you called when he gets home."

I continued our conversation by telling Ma how I lived there with Ba, how we went to school there, and how much we missed her and all the siblings. Ma told me about life at the camp with the kids, how everyone acclimated to the new circumstance, and how they were all excited to see Ba and me again. When we were about to hang up, Ma reminded me to tell Ba to write to her more often.

Later, when Ba got home, I told him about the phone call from Ma. I told him I still recognized Ma's voice even after seven years. I was a little upset that I couldn't talk to any of my siblings. They must have grown a lot since I last saw them. I was talking non-stop about how they lived at the refugee camp. I was excited to fill Ba in and almost forgot to ask Ba how Ma knew our phone number. Ba told me that they had been writing to each other and Ba gave it to her.

"I just got news from the immigration office, and if everything goes well, they'll most likely be here in the next two months," Ba said.

Based on Ba, the reason Ma and the kids could be here early was that Ba sponsored them directly and not through any organizations as we had back then. Hence, they could go straight from Hong Kong to America. As long as Ba could prove that he was able to support his family when they got here, they would be exempt from going to the Philippines. That night, I couldn't sleep thinking of the day our family would be reunited. How I wished two months would go by fast so we could pick up where we left off seven years ago. Although excited with all those ecstatic thoughts, I felt something unpleasant was slowly taking place.

22 The Reunion

Things were going smoothly at Aviation HS. I made a lot of new friends, got good grades in my academics, and was focused on getting my FAA (Federal Aviation Administration) license as a certified mechanic. Aviation High School allowed students to take the license examination upon completion of the classes. I was planning on studying for it.

The bullying also subsided. No more Freshmen Fridays. Besides the incident on the train where Alex stood up for me, nothing happened after that. High school seemed different. I didn't know whether I had gotten bigger and fitter, or these students became more mature and wanted to focus on school rather than picking on others. For the first time, I could relax and enjoy my time at school.

In October 1989 Ba told Chu Tuan and Anh Dung about my family coming the next month. They somehow knew that Ma was in Hong Kong and would be there soon. Chu Tuan understood the situation and mentioned moving out. On the other hand, I was concerned about Anh Dung's feelings. I didn't know what he was thinking but I could see a little resentment. Even though he agreed to look for another place to stay, I felt that he was holding back questions for Ba. I was sure his mom's feelings and Phong weighed a ton on his mind.

After a few weeks, Anh Dung moved in with his friends to a place a few blocks away from his school. I was glad that it turned out to be more convenient for his commute. As for Chu Tuan, he moved in with his girlfriend, who he was seeing during the time he lived with us. His wife in Vietnam remarried a few years after he left. He found out and decided to move on. Sometimes, I felt like Ba's and Chu Tuan's fates were playing a joke on them. I hoped they both could find their peace in the end. Chu Tuan didn't move far since his girlfriend lived within a few subway stops. They came by to visit us on the weekends. I was glad that Ba's best friend was still around to keep him company.

After Chu Tuan and Anh Dung moved out, the apartment became quiet, and once again, I found myself living with Ba in a lonely one-bedroom apartment like when we were in the Bronx. It reminded me of Chu Chau and Anh Tri as I wondered how they had been. We lost contact after they moved and didn't know where to find them. I wouldn't want that to happen with Chu Tuan and Anh Dung. We'd been living together for almost three years and those fond memories of eating in the living room, strolling around the neighborhood, and staying up late watching wrestling, will always be cherished. I knew them moving out was bound to happen, but I couldn't help feeling somber.

Despite all the sudden changes in everyone's living situation, Ba and I didn't miss spending the weekend with Phong. We drove to the Bronx on Friday afternoons to pick him up and bring him to Queens. Phong was getting cuter as he got older. His chubby cheeks were irresistible to pinch. Ba told me to stop doing it otherwise his cheeks would sag. I couldn't help it and did it anyway. Phong was almost four years old and very observant. He kept asking me about Chu Tuan and Anh Dung since he didn't see them around. I told him that they moved out and he looked confused. I didn't know if he understood, but I was sure he would be more confused if I told him the whole situation. Looking into his adorable eyes, I wondered how Ma would react to him. For the last four years, he was the brother who helped me cope with the separation from my other siblings. The more I thought of it, the more I prayed for the best.

As the days got closer to Ma's arrival, there was a lot of mail between Ba and Ma as well as from the immigration office. Ba was busy running back and forth making sure there were no missing documents that might cause a delay. He excitedly updated me on the process every time he got back from the immigration office. We were anxiously looking forward to the day to come. I hadn't seen my siblings for more than seven years, but only saw the pictures that Ma sent from Hong Kong. I couldn't believe how much they had grown since the last time I saw them. Although they were getting taller, they hadn't changed one bit. Their faces still looked the same as how I remembered when I left. I couldn't wait to meet my baby sister, Ly. She was just adorable like Phong. They could play with each other since they were only four years apart. Suddenly, the thoughts of Phong saddened me as I wondered how Ma would react when she saw him. I thought of Mrs. McKeever and wrote her a letter. I told her about the good news of Ma and my siblings coming to the U.S. I asked for her advice on how to talk to Ma about this matter. I had shared with her about Phong and our situation in previous letters. She always responded with encouragement that I should think positively and that everything would be okay. However, I was afraid that I would need more than just words of encouragement this time.

November approached and Ba told me we needed to buy more mattresses and bunk beds, as well as some household items to prepare for Ma and my siblings' arrival. Thanks to our favorite shop, the thrift store, we got everything we needed after a couple of trips there. As we brought the stuff home, I couldn't imagine how a family of eight would fit in a one-bedroom apartment. Ba suggested that I should sleep in the living room. I didn't mind, since I slept there with Anh Dung before while staying up late watching TV. I just wondered how everyone else would fit in the bedroom. However, Ba had it all planned out by putting the bunk beds on both sides of the wall for the kids, and the parents' bed in one corner of the room.

Finally, the day we all had been waiting for came. Ba and I were excited, yet nervous, heading our way to John F. Kennedy Airport in his Ford Tempo. I kept talking incessantly as he drove along the Brooklyn-Queens Expressway. Within the forty-minute ride, I told Ba I admired how Ma took care of my siblings in the last seven years without us and how they survived the boat journey on that treacherous sea.

After we got to the airport, Ba and I stood in the arrival waiting area. The door where the passengers exited was about a hundred feet away from us. I stood there, anxiously waiting to see those familiar faces. Ba was pacing back and forth as he anxiously waited for this moment. I couldn't imagine what was going through his mind; those years of him missing his wife and children must be hard. As the door opened and people walked out one by one, my heart pounded and my eyes started to tear. There they were. Ma held Ly's hand while the others walked alongside her, pulling their luggage. I recognized every single one of them. Ma looked around trying to find us. At the moment that our eyes met, Ma called out my name as she hurriedly walked toward us. Once she was within arm's reach, I ran over and held her tight. I didn't want to let go because this was what I had been longing for. Being held by her reminded me of the times I rubbed my eyes onto her soft silky hair to get rid of the chili pepper stain. I couldn't believe this day was here for me to once again be held by my loving mother. I felt my Ma's tears as they constantly dripped onto my shoulder. Once both of us stopped sobbing, I looked to Chi Trang, the older sister who I cherished, who was now a few inches shorter than me. She pinched my two cheeks and told me I had grown. Once again, my tears built up and rolled down my face as I turned to hug her. I looked over to my younger siblings, Trinh, Anh, and Vu, who were crying their hearts out, holding Ba, a father who was absent from their lives for seven years. As much as Ma was holding me, Ba wrapped each one of my siblings into his arms and the happy tears continued to trickle down their faces. My poor baby sister Ly was so confused as she wondered why everyone was crying. She grabbed both of her hands to Ma's, hiding behind her and curiously looking at me, a brother who she had never met. I knelt, opened my arms to her, and within a few seconds of hesitation, she ran over and gave me a big hug. Ba walked over, held Ma tightly, and thanked her for taking care of his parents and the kids while he was gone. Ma broke down as she couldn't say a word. His arms wrapped around her tightly as they both continued to sob. I turned around and saw the shyness on my siblings' faces, possibly because they hadn't seen me for a long time. I rushed over and hugged them all. Just like that, we couldn't stop hugging and crying in the middle of the airport. People cheered for us. Some even congratulated us. They probably figured it was a reunion of one big happy family.

As we walked out of the airport, I looked at my siblings' faces and saw myself seven years ago, walking out of the airport with Co Kim. We had the same reaction, curiously looking at everything around us. When we got to the car, I was worried about how all of us would fit in a car that was made for only five people. To my surprise, we made it. Ba had Ma sit in the front with Ly on her lap. All five of us were able to squeeze ourselves in the back with Vu sitting on my lap. The ride home was so uncomfortable that we couldn't even move, yet I felt the coziness of having them right next to me. Those sleepless nights missing them were behind me now.

The next morning, I was awakened by my siblings' screaming. They were excited by the white particles that were falling from the sky and had covered the roads outside. Looking at them being curious about the snow brought me back to my first time seeing it and how I wished for them to be there so we could compare our footprints. I gathered them up and put a couple of layers on each of them since Ba didn't get a chance to get them their winter clothes. I knew they weren't properly dressed but I didn't want them to miss out on the fun since I was sure they wanted to experience it too. We ran out of the building, and the first thing we did was catch the snow. Vu and Ly even stuck their tongues out trying to taste it. Seeing the smiles on their faces made me so happy. After comparing our footprints, we rolled up snowballs and chased each other along the block. We ran after each other just like how we played horse riding back home in our front yard. The instantaneous bond between us made me feel like we were never apart. However, after fifteen minutes, they all started to shiver and their fingers became numb. I knew it was time to get back inside before the frostbite overtook their fingers. Inside the house, we warmed ourselves with cups of hot chocolate. To keep them entertained, I turned on my martial arts movie collections. Little did I know, Vu also had a love for martial arts. He was glued to the TV every day just like I was.

Ba wanted all the kids to start school right away, and he had everything planned out. Anh, Vu, and Ly entered an elementary school that was two blocks away from our apartment; Anh was a sixth grader, Vu was in fourth grade, and Ly was in second grade.

Trinh went to JHS 204 as a seventh grader. Since it was my old school, I helped Ba take her there and showed her around before she started. As for Chi Trang, she was enrolled as a senior at Long Island City High School where Eliazo went. She didn't want to go to my school because she had no interest in fixing airplanes. It was tough for my siblings in the first few weeks at their schools. Understanding what they were going through, I tried to help as much as I could. Every day after school, I would sit and help them one by one with their homework. I also asked Eliazo to look out for Chi Trang at school and assist her if needed.

While all the kids were in school and Ba was at work. Ma was the only one at home. I could empathize with Ma as she had to adjust to the new culture, language, and even friends and neighbors. Her life in Vietnam was simple, taking care of her family, helping her friends, or chatting with the neighbors. Ba knew that Ma coping with the new lifestyle would be difficult in the beginning since he felt the same when he first came. To make her feel better, Ba and I took her to Chinatown, hoping the bustle of the market with Asian goods and people would make her feel like back home. Ma bought a lot of food as she planned out what to cook for the family. I reminded her not to forget the special spices for her signature fish dish.

During those weeks helping Ma and my siblings settle down, Ba and I didn't pick up Phong. We wanted to let Ma know about him first before bringing him home. Although I missed him, I knew it wasn't something that Ba could just blurt out to Ma. He needed to do it in a way so she wouldn't get hurt but could understand his situation and accept Phong. Ba was looking for the right moment, so I needed to be patient and wait for him. I just hoped it wouldn't take too long.

The moment had come. That day, Ba asked Chu Tuan to take all the kids out for ice cream and he had a talk with Ma at home. By the time we got back, the atmosphere in the house was tense and Ma was upset. I didn't know how Ba broke the news to Ma, but given the situation, it didn't matter how he said it. Ma wouldn't be okay after one conversation with Ba. In the following days, things became tenser between Ba and Ma. Although they tried to act normal in front of us, we could feel there was something wrong. The love and affection that Ma showed Ba when she first came here were gone.

There was sadness and disappointment every time their eyes met. Ba kept quiet as he didn't want to agitate her. All my siblings were confused as to why the mood in the house changed so quickly. I wanted to comfort Ma but was afraid of what she thought of me. *Was she mad at me, thinking I betrayed her too?* I felt like I was walking on eggshells every day.

One afternoon, after I got home from school, Ma asked me to go into the room to talk with her.

"Was she nice to you?" Ma asked.

I had been expecting this from Ma. I worried there might be things she didn't want to hear. Yet I was glad she decided to talk to me. So as not to make matters worse, I carefully chose my words.

"Yes, Ma, she was nice. She took care of me while Ba went to school and worked," I said, hoping it wouldn't upset Ma.

"Did she ever yell at you or hit you?"

"Well, she yelled when I was wrong, but she never hit me."

"How about that little boy, Phong?" She spoke louder and faster.

My heart pounded profusely as I didn't know how to answer that. I didn't want to say the wrong thing that ended up giving her a bad impression about Phong. Thoughts ran through my head, but nothing seemed right. I just gave her my honest answer.

"Phong is a cute little boy. You will like him. So please give him a chance, Ma." She didn't respond but looked at me disappointedly.

At that moment, I knew I made matters worse. Ma broke down with both hands holding her face and kept saying, "Why, why, why?" I didn't know what to do but let her vent her heart out. I stood there, patiently waiting for her to let go of all the anger and frustration. I didn't know how long it was, but it seemed like time had stopped for Ma to grieve her pain. Ma reached for my hands and asked the same question while sobbing. It hurt me to see Ma in agony. I held her tight and broke my silence through my tears.

"Ba loves you and his children. Therefore, we moved out. They had been separated for the last three years. Ba ended the relationship before knowing you would come here. But Phong was innocent. So please open your kindest heart and accept him."

Ma's crying slowly subsided. She finally raised her head as I continued to confirm to her that Ba loved his family. I told her how tough it was for Ba when we first arrived in NYC. How hard Ba had to work to make money so he could send it home for her, and how much he suffered when his stomach ulcer attacked. Ma sat quietly listening to me. I didn't know if she felt my words, but she seemed calmer. I sat with her for a little while, then she told me to go on with my homework as she wanted to be alone to think.

  Walking out of the bedroom, I saw all my siblings standing in front of the door with uneasiness projecting on their faces. I knew they heard our conversation. Chi Trang pulled me to hear my explanation. We took a walk outside of the building since we didn't want to confuse our younger siblings more than they already were. I told her the whole story and felt so relieved because I no longer had to hide it from anyone. I told her I loved Phong just as much as I loved all my siblings, and kindly asked her to accept him too. This news was probably too unexpected to her, and it would be selfish of me to ask for her understanding of Ba. I hoped she could sympathize with Ba's difficulties as he managed to take care of me while striving to get an education and work so that he could provide for all of us.

  Chi Trang didn't say much but told me that she needed time to process and went back to the apartment to check on Ma and the kids. I decided to hang around in front of the building to wait for Ba. I wanted to give him a heads-up in case Ma broke down again. As I saw Ba getting out of his car, I ran up to him and briefly filled him in on what happened at home. Ba patted my shoulder, nodded his head, and told me it was time to talk with everyone.

  Ba and I entered the apartment. Ma was in the living room crying again with all my siblings surrounding her. I thought my interpretation earlier helped ease her pain somehow, but I guess her emotions still lingered and she wanted more answers. Ba took a deep breath, cleared his voice, and asked everyone to sit down as he had something to say. I looked around the room and saw my siblings' innocent faces questioning why Ma kept on crying. It made me wonder if they could process what Ba was about to tell them. I got nervous, thinking what if it wouldn't end well? What if Ma blamed his infidelity? I didn't want any of his children to hear about it, especially since they were too young and had just reunited with their father.

After a long pause, Ba started to tell them how he came to the decision of leaving his family behind and that it ended up becoming the toughest choice he made in his life. Not knowing where the journey would take him or even being able to make it, he didn't want to risk everyone's life, so he only brought me along. Coming to the United States, he only had one goal in mind, and that was to make money so he could provide for his family back home. He knew only through education he'd achieve that goal. However, he struggled with school, work, and taking care of me. At times he wanted to give up. Then Di Yen came along. They met in a tough time and helped each other to overcome it. She shared his burden and helped take care of me. With the thought that our family would never be together again, we became family with Di Yen and her sons. Then two years later Phong was born. However, the relationship ended a year later, and we moved out. Ba took a break and turned to Ma to see her reaction. Looking at Ba facing his dilemma while Ma and all my siblings were crying, I felt a sharp pain in my heart as I didn't know what to do to make them ease their pain.

Ba took another long pause and then begged Ma for her forgiveness. He assured her that the relationship was long over before she arrived. Nevertheless, Phong was still his child, and he had the responsibility to take care of him. He asked her to open her heart and give him a chance to fulfill his duty as a father. He then turned to my siblings and begged them for their forgiveness as well. He told them that he loved every single one of them just as much as he loved Phong. He asked them to welcome him as their brother because they were all his children.

Ba sat there silently, waiting for Ma's reaction. She regained her composure, stopped crying, and softly acquiesced to have Phong come over to see us. Ba and I were surprised to hear that and elated that she made that decision. Her approval not only made Ba happy but the agony that I had been carrying in my mind was finally quietened. However, I felt a little apprehensive that Ma came to that decision so quickly. I didn't want Phong to be caught in a situation where he would never be able to see Ba again.

The following weekend, Ba drove to the Bronx to pick up Phong. I stayed behind in the apartment to help Ma cook. To keep Ma in a good mood, I bragged to her about how I cook for Ba when he was out late with school and work. I told her about when we prayed to Buddha for rain on the boat, how Ba climbed the fence at a refugee camp in Hong Kong to find work, and how much I missed her after seeing Co Tram take care of her son when he got hit playing *Oc Tan*. She hugged me after listening to me. I could see a transformation in Ma's outlook and attitude. She was happy and enthusiastic. She praised me for being a good boy throughout the journey with Ba.

Then, we heard a knock on the door. Ma and I went over to open it. There he was, Phong, standing next to Ba with those chubby cheeks and a big smile. He was so happy to see me since we hadn't seen each other for a couple of weeks. I was about to hold his hand to take him in, but Ma stepped up and without hesitating, she bent down to his level and held his hand. I saw the same affection on her face that she would have with her children. I was thrilled that Ma offered her warm welcome to Phong.

Phong spent every weekend with us after that. Ma and all my siblings treated him like one of us. Ma fed, bathed, and took care of him as her own child. There were times I felt bad that she had to take care of many of us. I told her to let me bathe Phong, but she voluntarily took over the task. Ba was happy to see Ma willing to accept him with open arms. As for Phong, he seemed to enjoy being with us as well, especially Ly, who was four years older than him. Since they were close in age, they played with each other the most. Yet, when the night came, he would ask to sleep with me in the living room.

On March 1, 1990, Phong turned four years old. Di Yen invited our family over to her place to celebrate his birthday. Ba and I were delighted that Ma agreed to it. After two months of seeing how Ma treated Phong, we gradually worried less and appreciated Ma more. As we got to Di Yen's apartment, the adults happily greeted each other. It made me believe that everything was resolved. I was happy to see them on good terms, otherwise, it would be difficult for Phong, being stuck in the middle. I introduced Anh Dung and Anh Bao to my siblings, and they all got along well. I felt a big relief that the constant distress on my mind had lifted off my shoulders. We gathered there to celebrate Phong's birthday, but to me, it was a celebration of a new beginning. We ate and laughed as though we were meant to be together.

During the drive home, there was utter silence in the car. I felt strange but thought maybe everyone was just tired since all my siblings had fallen asleep. Ba and Ma didn't say a word to each other and the forty-minute drive back to our apartment was awkward. I tried to remember if anything went wrong at Di Yen's place, but there was nothing I could think of. Everyone seemed to have a good time there. Even the adults chimed in to sing happy birthday to Phong. I couldn't figure anything out but told myself I was thinking too much. However, a big storm awaited us.

As soon as we entered the apartment, Ma shouted, telling everyone to sit down in the living room.

"As of today, I don't want to hear Phong's name." Ma breathed heavily.

I was aghast to hear that from Ma. *Where did it come from? What initiated this?* I turned to Ba, and he was just as shocked.

"I want to have my own family." She continued with an outburst of cries.

My poor siblings—they all looked confused, wondering if something had happened while they were sleeping in the car. Ba told everyone to go clean up and get ready for bed. As I was about to get up, Ma gave her final stern demand.

"From now on, I don't want either of you to set foot in that lady's place."

Ma's words hit me like a ton of bricks. *How could I accept that?*

Asking me not to go to Di Yen's place was the same as asking me not to see Phong. Just like all my siblings, Phong would always be my family. I could never comply with her request. Within minutes, Ba and Ma were at it. She continued to accuse him of his selfishness, for having an another relationship while she was taking care of his children back home. My mind was racing with confusion as they continued to scream. Only a couple of hours ago, I was over the moon thinking what I feared most was gone. I thought Ma opened her heart and let bygones be bygones, but my conjecture of her forgiveness was transient. As Ma continued to make her point, Ba looked down onto the floor willingly allowing her to release her anger. I knew right there that we just lost Phong. That birthday party was a farewell party instead. I walked to the room to be with my siblings.

23 The Pair of Gloves

After the day that Ma forbade Ba and me to go to Di Yen's place to see Phong, there were constant arguments at the apartment. Whenever Phong's name was brought up by accident or whatever reminded Ma of him, she would start a fight with Ba and it would go on for hours. Those arguments became unbearable. There were times that I wished I could stay in school all day, so I didn't have to witness the quarrels. I could feel the same for my siblings being distracted from their studies and wondered if my parents would ever resolve this. We were constantly on our toes watching out for Ma's mood.

Things got worse when Ma became doubtful of all Ba's actions. On days that he didn't finish the food that she packed for him before he left for work, she would assume that Ba went to Di Yens and ate there. When he got stuck in traffic and got home later than usual, she would think that he stopped by to visit Di Yen and Phong. As long as he was with her, everything seemed fine, but the minute he left the house, her suspicion took over and a big fight awaited him. It didn't matter how much Ba tried to prove to her that there was nothing between him and Di Yen anymore, Ma still questioned his honesty. At times, I wondered why she couldn't believe him. Ma was too distressed to listen with her heart and instead, she let her anger fly every time she felt uncertain. She needed time to ease her pain and help her heal.

For the next two months, my siblings and I focused on preparing for our finals. Luckily, the bickering subsided and we concentrated on studying. I didn't know whether time did its magic for Ma, or if Ba tried to come home on time and finish his packed food, but Ma seemed happier. The house was filled with more laughter again. Ba didn't ask me to visit Phong, and I was afraid to ask him as well. We both didn't want to create more chaos, not at least until we could come up with a better solution.

Summer was break time for us kids, but it was working time for Ma. She was constantly in the kitchen cooking and cleaning. There were six kids to feed and three meals a day. Ba took Ma food shopping every week. With an entry engineering level income and a family of eight to support, Ba struggled. Although Ba never said it, Ma understood and only bought the food that was needed. Seeing the difficulties of our family, Chi Trang and I wanted to get jobs so we could help. I asked Eliazo for summer work again, hoping that his friend could hook us up at the supermarket since I had grown bigger. However, he said his mother wanted him to concentrate on summer school, and his friend also resigned from the supermarket.

Some Vietnamese ladies recently moved into our building. I often saw them coming back late in the afternoon from work. Chi Trang and I spoke to them often when we were out getting our mail. One day, while waiting for Eliazo, I saw these ladies walking in. As usual, we greeted each other and as the conversation went on, they mentioned that they worked in a clothing factory nearby. I took a chance and asked them if the factory would hire me for a summer job. Cheerfully, they told me to go with them tomorrow to meet the boss.

I came home and told Chi Trang about it. She was happy and hoped that the boss would offer us a job. The next morning, we met up with those ladies in front of our building and left with them. The factory was less than a fifteen-minute walk from our apartment. It was hot and steamy when we entered the place. There were no air conditioners, but many big fans blowing across the open space. Although all the fans were running, they only circulated the stifling air from outside, since all the windows were open. The ladies introduced us to the boss, Chu Minh. He was also Vietnamese. After a quick interview with him, we were hired and asked to start the same day. Chu Minh walked us around the factory and showed us what kind of work they were doing. It was a chain factory from sewing clothes to ironing and bagging. Since we didn't have any experience, Chu Minh told us to work in the bagging section. He showed us how to take the ironed shirt and cover it with a plastic bag to prepare for shipping. It looked easy enough, so we just jumped right in. For every ten bags we did, we got paid five cents. We didn't even bother to calculate how much we would make. We were happy that we got to work. After eight hours of breathing in hot circulated air, we each made twenty-five dollars from the bagging. Chu Minh said we would get paid every other Saturday. That night during dinner, Chi Trang and I told Ba and Ma about the job at the factory. They were concerned about the air circulation, but we reassured them that we could handle it.

For the rest of our two summer months, Chi Trang and I were at the factory working every day. However, Chu Minh had us work sporadic hours. There were times I would stay a full eight hours while Chi Trang got partial hours and vice versa. The reason was if the sewing and the ironing weren't done quickly, the bagging wouldn't be needed. In the end, my earnings would depend on how fast the people worked upstream. Although some days I just sat there making little money because there was not much to do, I was content that my little hard-earned money could help get some more food on our table.

Summer seemed to end quickly this year since I was busy working. With us going back to school, I asked Chu Minh to allow us to work on weekends only. I wanted to go home after school to finish my homework, as there would be more assignments in my sophomore year. One day at work, looking at the people next to me ironing the clothes, I was curious and wanted to try. It paid more than bagging, and I could make up for those lost hours due to school. Chu Minh agreed and had one of his workers show me the process. It had two steps: first, put the shirt under a large press of steam, followed by using a typical iron and flattening any missing areas. I watched him and thought it was simple enough. The steamer was big, at least six feet long, and when it opened, I had to reach high to pull the lid down. The longer I stood there doing it, the hotter it became. Luckily, it was fall and the weather was getting cooler. I couldn't imagine these workers having to do this throughout the summer.

One night after dinner, Ba asked me to go with him to Brooklyn, which was around thirty minutes away from Astoria, Queens. Ba said we were going to a clothing factory. I was confused as to why we had to go there at this hour. Seeing my reaction, Ba continued that one of his friends introduced him to a side job, which was similar to making hair clips that we did before. He would prefer Chi Trang and I do this job while Ma and the kids were at home than for us to work at the factory under tough conditions. We could earn extra income for the family by working from home. As much as I was happy that we could make more money, I felt dread thinking of doing that job again. Besides, I was worried that it would take up my time and not allow me to concentrate in school. I didn't like the idea one bit but didn't want to tell Ba otherwise. I just played along and followed Ba's lead.

Ba and I brought home four large trash bags of fabric. Ma didn't seem surprised when she opened the door. It looked like Ba already discussed it with her. Ba gathered everyone in the living room and once again, tasked us with our part—the same routine of cutting and assembling the metal clips to the fabric. After a few weeks, the factory gave us different stuff to work on. We started making all kinds of things from ties to hair clips to shirts. I also quit Chu Minh's factory and stayed home to help. Gradually, Ba not only brought work home, but he also ended up bringing home a professional sewing machine. The manager at the factory liked our work, and he sold Ba one of his machines for a fair price so we could produce more. He knew our situation and was willing to deduct the price of the machine from the money that we made. Ba and Ma took turns sewing, while six of us continued cutting the threads, folding the ties, and assembling the shirts. Just like at Di Yen's place before, we all sat in front of the TV, working, and watching Chinese drama series.

School was getting harder with more homework and assignments since I was taking honor classes. I became frustrated every time Ba brought home more of those fabric bags. Although Ba told me to finish studying first, I didn't feel right seeing my siblings working while I was studying. Besides, the living room had become the working area, which was also my studying and sleeping space. It was uncomfortable enough that I slept on a military-type bed with canvas held by metal rods on four corners. Now, with all those ties, shirts, and hair clips lying around, I felt cluttered. As a result, my grades suffered. I worked hard just to maintain a B average during the first quarter. However, thanks to those late nights and weekends of laboring, we got back to our bonding times. No more disturbances in the house and we kids were thrilled to see that. The extra income certainly made our lives more enjoyable. Ma bought more treats for us at the supermarket, and for the first time, we got to shop at a department store for our new clothes.

It had been nine months since I last saw Phong at his birthday party. I missed his chubby cheeks and wondered how he was doing. In consideration of Ma's feelings, I hadn't visited Phong nor called him. I honestly hoped that Ma would calm down and take back her words after seeing how much we respected and cared for her emotions. Ba and Ma had been on good terms for the last few months. Ma hadn't dwelt on Di Yen or Phong lately. At this rate, I hoped that Ba could change Ma's mind about Phong soon.

One Sunday afternoon, we were in the living room working. I heard the doorbell and went to open the door. It took me by surprise to see Di Yen and Anh Bao at the door. Politely, I asked them to come in but didn't feel good about their sudden visit. Ba was shocked to see them both. Ma and Di Yen didn't have good expressions on their faces either. To give the adults privacy, Chi Trang took the kids out for ice cream. Anh Bao also asked to talk with me outside. We went to the park nearby, and Anh Bao was upset about our disappearance for the last several months. He wondered what happened and why we were neglecting Phong. I apologized and explained our family situation to him. He wasn't happy about it, but he understood our difficulties and hoped we could find a solution soon because Phong had been missing us. I was glad that we spoke about it so that at least we could clear up some of the tensions between the two families.

We walked back and saw Chi Trang with my siblings in the main lobby. Thinking that the adults should be done talking since it had been a while, we all went up to the apartment. As we opened the door, we regretted coming back too soon. Ma and Di Yen were screaming at each other. They were taking turns accusing one another and it seemed like neither one would give in. Anh Bao and Ba intervened and tried to calm them both. Before things got worse, Anh Bao grabbed Di Yen's coat and told her to leave. Without saying anything, they left the apartment. Ma broke down again and it didn't matter how much Ba tried to explain, not one word was going through her ears. I stood there contemplating how I could convince Ma and make her pain go away, but the more I tried to come up with a plan, the only answer was that it was all up to her.

The days that followed were long and miserable at the apartment. Ma couldn't stop crying and self-pitying. It was so stressful every day at home. None of us could concentrate on our homework, let alone, work on the hair clips. Ba kept silent, trying not to agitate her. However, it triggered her more. Fight after fight ensued, regardless of how Ba reacted to her mood. In the end, Ma gave Ba an ultimatum, her and the kids, or Di Yen and Phong.

Ba was even quieter the next week. I didn't know what he was thinking but the agony was showing on his face. I couldn't imagine the pain he was going through. How could he possibly choose when they were all his kids? Whatever choice he made, he would end up carrying that guilt his whole life. Ma wasn't backing down. She was even sterner than last time. At this point, nothing could ease her mind except a decision from Ba.

The next Saturday, Ba and I were on our way home from dropping off completed work at the factory. Ba made his way toward the Bronx and told me we were going to see Phong. I was shocked, but seeing the serious look on his face, I just nodded my head with no questions asked. Although I kept my silence, curious thoughts were driving me crazy. *Why are we going to see Phong? What was the purpose? What was Ba's decision?* It was like a puzzle to me, and I couldn't get any answer from Ba either. The more I thought about it, the more I feared the choice Ba might have made. Suddenly, wishful thinking popped into my head. Perhaps, Ma changed her mind realizing she was irrational the other day. Thinking so, I felt assured everything would be okay and couldn't wait to pinch Phong's chubby cheeks again.

When we arrived at Di Yen's place, she was surprised to see us when she opened the door. As we came in, Ba told me to play with Phong in the living room and asked to have a talk with Di Yen in her room. Phong was so happy to see me and kept asking about his other siblings, Chi Trang, Trinh, Anh, Vu, and Ly. I was impressed that he was able to remember all their names. I didn't know how to answer him but told him they were busy with school.

He took out a folder under the table and showed it to me. They were pictures of him taken with us during his birthday. I couldn't hold my tears as he pointed to the picture and named all his siblings. After nine months of not seeing us, he still recognized every single one of us. As I flipped through all the pictures, I saw a duplicate one of me holding him. Not knowing the reason why, I decided to take it along, with another one of him wearing a birthday hat.

Suddenly, I heard Di Yen screaming from inside the room. I didn't know what was going on, but it gave Phong a scare. I held him tight and tried to comfort him. Ba came out of the room and asked him if he wanted to go get ice cream. Without any thoughts, Phong nodded his head, got up, and followed Ba. Di Yen didn't say anything but just stood there with a sad face. Ba got him dressed and put on his favorite pair of gloves as we headed to the McDonald's at Fordham Road.

The three of us had a late afternoon meal. Ba sat quietly with a wistful look on his face watching both of us eat. I felt like he was fighting with his conscience. I didn't know what Ba and Di Yen argued about, but Ba's expression told me it was about Phong. I was scared to ask Ba, afraid he would give me an answer I didn't want to hear.

"Linh, you have to love Phong no matter what," Ba said in a cracking voice.

Ba's comment felt strange to me. I doubted my wishful thinking that Ma forgave him, but at the same time, I refused to believe it. I felt a sudden pain in my heart as I looked at little Phong eating his ice cream.

"Of course, Ba. He's my brother. I love him as much as I love the others," I said, trying to hold back my emotions.

Although I gave Ba my answer, I felt like it wasn't what he tried to tell me. It sounded more like he was asking me to take care of Phong instead of just loving him. At that moment, I couldn't understand what he meant, until later.

After our meal at McDonald's, Ba drove Phong back to Di Yen's apartment. I hugged and kissed him goodbye, then Ba walked him up to drop him off. I waited in the car for about ten minutes. I saw Ba come down with both hands wiping his face. He didn't say a word as he got in the car and drove away.

"I had a great time eating with you and Phong today, Ba." I tried to break the silence.

Ba just nodded his head but remained quiet.

"I hope Ma wasn't serious the other day. We are still seeing Phong, right, Ba, because he is my brother no matter what." I continued, hoping for an answer from Ba.

"Yes, he is your brother and I'm glad you think that way. As for your mother, I don't want to hurt her anymore. Most importantly, I don't want all of you growing up seeing us fight like that." Ba broke his silence as tears were falling.

Finally, I understood why Ba and Di Yen were fighting earlier, and why she had that anguished look on her face. I also understood why Ba was saying those words to me at McDonald's, and why he was wiping his face after dropping Phong off. I broke down in tears realizing I could never see Phong again. Ba had made his decision. A decision to be an irresponsible father to one child, so he could raise the other six. A decision that would torment him for the rest of his life. I felt pain in my heart as I thought of Phong. However, Ba probably felt it tenfold. I glanced over to Ba. He remained silent with tears in his eyes.

As we got back to our building and Ba parked the car, I turned to Phong's seat and saw his favorite pair of gloves. I wondered if he purposely left them there so that I would never forget him. I picked them up and put them in my pocket. When we got to the house, I hid the gloves in the corner under a pile of clothes in my closet in the hallway. I made sure no one could see it. I was afraid Ma would find out and make me throw them away. That was the only memento of Phong for me as a keepsake. After securing the gloves safely, I sat down in the living room and continued making hair clips with everyone.

24 New Home

A month had passed since I said goodbye to Phong. Although things seemed to be okay at home, we needed to be extremely careful when it came to Phong. We were forbidden to mention his name or anything that was related to him. It seemed like every trace of him was erased as if he had never existed. I didn't know whether my siblings were afraid to upset Ma or if they were overwhelmed with the arguments about Phong, but they never asked about his whereabouts. I understood their feelings and didn't want to force anything on them. I told no one about our last trip to see Phong and showed no one Phong's birthday pictures that I took from him. I knew keeping peace in the family was the main focus. However, it saddened me that once again, I was separated from another sibling of mine and didn't know when we could be reunited.

    Since the living room became my bedroom, I often took out Phong's gloves and his birthday pictures to look at when I couldn't sleep and thought of him. There were times I wanted to call to see how he was doing but was afraid Di Yen wouldn't let me talk to him due to what happened at her house the last time. She probably wanted to cut ties with us as well. Part of me didn't want to impose on Di Yen, and the other part didn't know how to explain to Phong about our disappearance in his life. I began to write in a diary. It was always hard to start a new entry without tearing up first. Some nights, I stayed up until one in the morning so I could express my emotions in a small notebook, even though I had to wake up early for school the next day.

On September 19, 1991, our family was excited to welcome a new member. Ma had given birth to a baby boy, Tran Vinh Edgar. Whether Ma wanted Ba to forever forget Phong by replacing him with another child or not, Edgar did bring joy and happiness to our family, especially Ba and Ma. We were happy to see they were able to heal their relationship. Taking care of Edgar was like deja vu for me; he had so many similarities to Phong. The first time I saw him at the hospital, I thought I was looking at Phong when he was a baby. I wondered if Ba saw the resemblance too. As Edgar grew up, he looked more like Phong. They even had the same chubby cheeks. Every time I snuggled with him or changed his diapers, it brought me back to those days when Phong helped me cope with my separation from my siblings. It was ironic that it was Edgar's turn to help me now.

One day, I overheard Ma's conversation with her friends in the living room. Ma made friends with some Vietnamese women who lived nearby. She was talking about Edgar looking more like Phong by the day. I wasn't surprised that Ma noticed that too. At that moment, I felt optimistic about her recognition of the resemblance. I was hoping that their resemblance would ease her pain and help open her heart to Phong. Nonetheless, the reality wasn't what we hoped for. Frustration, disappointment, and resentment filled Ma, making her become a different person whenever she felt vulnerable. I guessed it was her way to protect herself from getting hurt. That night was the beginning of an endless quarrel in my family.

"You went to visit someone and that's why you're home late?" Ma sternly asked as Ba entered the door.

"I got stuck in traffic," Ba said, taken aback.

Within a couple of minutes, the bickering accelerated into screaming and slamming doors. We didn't know why there was a sudden fight. They had been happy with each other. Edgar was crying and wanted Ma to hold him. However, Ma was too busy accusing Ba of visiting Di Yen. She brought up his other relationship and couldn't stop blaming him for causing her pain. It didn't matter how much Ba tried to explain, nothing seemed to soothe her anger.

The argument kept going until Ba couldn't suppress himself anymore and left the apartment. Her frustration hadn't subsided, and so Ma turned to me and continued to unload.

"Have you been visiting Phong?" Ma asked with a stern voice.

"No, I haven't," I raised my voice.

For the first time, I felt anger at Ma. I had been obeying her demands for the last two years. Living my life respecting her difficult request, putting the peace and happiness of the family first, and even pushing Phong aside. Yet, she still couldn't let go of her resentment. Right then, I wanted to tell her to stop lingering with her emotions, but those letters from Mrs. McKeever flashed through my mind, telling me to be patient with Ma because her wound was just too deep. I held back and continued letting Ma accuse me of not stopping Ba from meeting Di Yen. As much as I wanted to scream back to ask her, "How could I, an eight-year-old kid?" I kept quiet so she could release her indignation.

Those arguments became a monthly episode at our house. Ma got ticked off easily with everything that might cause suspicion to her. Whenever she was done with Ba, or when Ba was at work, I was next in line. She would either accuse me of going to visit Phong or blame me for not stopping Ba and Di Yen's relationship. Her rant would go on for at least one or two days, but things went back to normal the minute her mood improved. It irritated me so much. I couldn't concentrate on my school or anything else during her meltdowns. Eventually, I either had to block her out or go to the main lobby of the building and sit by the windowsill when her mood got worse so I could focus and finish my homework. I was in my junior year of high school. I couldn't afford to fail since I knew how important education was for me. I told myself I needed to stay on track and finish high school. With that in mind, I managed to study under whatever conditions were thrown at me.

Fortunately, I was able to finish my junior year on Honor Roll. Halfway into my senior year, especially with college around the corner, I worried if I could survive continuing to study like this. Some of my friends at school were talking about dorming in college. The idea was so amusing to me, and I wanted to try it. At least I wouldn't be distracted by Ma. I was very tempted to ask Ba if I could do that. However, after I looked into the tuition, room, and board of some universities that I had in mind, I had to let go of the idea because Ba couldn't send me there on his salary. I didn't want to add another burden for Ba.

In spring 1993, Chi Trang brought her boyfriend, Anh Robert, home and asked to talk with Ba and Ma. Anh Robert was also Vietnamese. He went to the same school and graduated at the same time as Ba as a civil engineer. Coincidentally, both of them worked for the Department of Environmental Protection, but in different areas. Chi Trang and Anh Robert had been dating for almost three years, and now Anh Robert wanted to ask Ba and Ma for their permission to marry. We were shocked that they wanted to get married so soon, especially Ba. He felt that Chi Trang was still young and needed to finish college first. Ba and Ma still didn't know how to respond to his request. They both gave another surprise saying that they wanted to have a small wedding in the summer. Although Ba was hesitant to give his blessing, in the end, Chi Trang's happiness was more important to Ba than anything else. Ba and Ma accepted their marriage.

The next day, I asked Chi Trang for a walk. I wanted to make sure Anh Robert was the one for her. As we strolled along the neighborhood, Chi Trang told me how kind and responsible Anh Robert was. Most importantly, he made her happy. She believed he would be a good husband. Listening to her, I knew she had found her true love. I sincerely congratulated them both and wished them a lifetime of happiness. As for her plans after the wedding, she would be moving in at Anh Robert's place, which was only fifteen minutes away from us by train. Suddenly, I felt a sense of loneliness. She was always there to comfort all of us when Ba and Ma fought. She was always there to console me after Ma yelled at me. She would be missed dearly by all her siblings when she moved out.

As the high school year was almost over, I needed to decide on college enrollment. Stony Brook University in Long Island was on my list. One Sunday, I asked Ba to drive me there so we could check out the campus. It was a little more than an hour's drive. Most of my friends planned to dorm there. As for me, I wanted to see if the school would be worth the commute. Being in a car alone with Ba, there was a moment I really wanted to ask about Phong. It had been almost three years since we last saw him. I wondered if Ba had been in contact with Phong. Instead, Ba surprised me with the idea of buying a house. The apartment that we had been living in was too small for all of us. With Edgar being another addition, the bedroom was so cramped having eight people squeezed in there. Having only one bathroom in the house was always a challenge for us in the morning.

"How are you getting the money to buy a home?" I asked worriedly.

"I can get a loan since my job is stable now," Ba excitedly responded.

Buying a house had been his long-term dream. He wanted to give the family a more comfortable living situation. The well-being of the family was always his priority. Just like how he worked hard to buy a car before Ma and my siblings came to the U.S. Although buying a house would be more difficult than a car, I couldn't even imagine how he would manage that, but I trusted Ba. He would find a way like he always had. I stopped asking him more questions and cheered on the exciting news with him.

When we arrived at Stony Brook University, it was a break away from New York City. There was no noise and congestion that we dealt with every day. The campus was a big open area with scattered buildings. The scenery was breathtaking with trees on both sides of the walkway and fountains at the end. I imagined myself sitting on the grass field in the middle of the campus and studying for my classes. I saw students riding their bikes along the pathways to get to the next building. Immersed in the serenity, I slowly walked to the building in front of me to get more information about the university. I enjoyed the atmosphere so much that I wanted to tell Ba I wanted to attend school there. However, the thought of Ba buying a house held me back from my desire. There was no way that Ba could pay for my tuition and the mortgage at the same time. Having to take care of a family of nine, and with the house on the way, I didn't want to overload him with my self-preference. I felt despair from not being able to attend there, but I knew I needed to be responsible and realistic so that Ba would have less stress from me.

During the drive back home, Ba asked if I liked the school. He kept reminding me how college would be paramount for my future. I needed to make a good decision regarding where to go and what to study and let him take care of the financial part. I didn't want my school choice to interfere with his plan of buying a house. I told him I still had a couple more schools to check out before making my final decision. He then asked if I had chosen my major. I told him possibly engineering since math and science had always been my strongest subject areas. He paused for a bit and suggested if I should consider pharmaceuticals. I guessed he wanted me to do something related to the medical field since he couldn't. The suggestion was entertaining, and I told him that I would keep that in the back of my mind when I filled out my college applications.

One day early in June, as I just got home from school, Ba asked me to go for a ride with him and Ma. I didn't know what was going on, but Ma was smiling happily, which meant something good. Seeing the curious look on my face, Ba told me we were going to see a house in College Point, Queens. He had been looking and found one that was suitable for our family. Ba surprised me again, just like when he bought the car. He acted on it so quickly that it amazed me every time. Ba drove us to College Point, which was thirty minutes away from our apartment. It was different from Astoria. There were no train stations nearby, only bus routes. The nearest subway station was at least a thirty-minute walk from the closest bus station. The homes in College Point were much nicer and quieter compared to Astoria. There were other buildings, but mostly single homes. As Ba circled the neighborhood, he mentioned that his work was only ten minutes from there. I could see the convenience for Ba to buy a house in this area.

Ba pulled up to a house with white siding and red shutters. It was a single home separated by a small pathway of approximately four feet wide from the adjacent homes on both sides. In front of it were bushes next to the three steps of stairs going into the entrance of the house. Ba turned to both of us and excitedly asked, "What do you guys think?"

"It's nice. The neighborhood is quiet and peaceful," Ma said.

"Is this gonna be our home?" I joyfully asked.

"I want to see what Ma thinks before proceeding further." Ba looked over to Ma, waiting for her confirmation.

"I think it looks really nice." Ma was impressed by what she saw.

As Ba and Ma walked around the outside to check on the house, I stood at the front wondering if this was a dream come true.

Who would have imagined that ten years ago Ba and I were roaming around those dumpsters on the streets in the Bronx finding used furniture and now we were about to buy a house? After all the hardship that we experienced coming here, we finally got to live our American dream. Through hard work and determination, Ba was able to achieve his goal. I felt grateful that our family wouldn't have to cram into a tiny place anymore. I no longer had to sleep on the small tight military bed in the living room with no privacy. Finally, we could have our own space to study. Ba and Ma returned to the front. I could tell they both were pleased with the house. Ba said he would call the real estate agent for us to see the inside before putting in an offer.

That night, while feeling excited and happy that my family would be moving to a new house soon, I suddenly thought about Phong. We had cut him out of our lives for the last three years. With my family situation and trying to survive myself, I let time pass and neglected him. I wondered how he had been doing. *Was he still in the Bronx?* Did he still remember us? I felt a great sense of guilt toward him. I wanted to be a responsible brother to Phong but didn't want to cause Ma pain. At that moment, I made a promise to myself that I would go look for him and ask for his forgiveness after I graduated from college. At least by then, I could make my own decision and would be able to take care of Phong as an adult. I loved and respected Ma, but I hoped she could empathize with my decision when that time came.

In June 1993, I graduated from Aviation High School. Four years of diligent learning had paid off. I finished top in my class with an honor roll and passed advanced placement (AP) math and science classes to prepare for college. I was extremely excited. I wrote to Mrs. McKeever to tell her about my achievements and asked if she could come to my graduation. Due to her busy schedule, she couldn't make it. However, she congratulated me and wished me all the best in college. On my graduation day, Ba pulled me aside while I was getting dressed for my big day.

"I've been waiting for this day," he said with proud eyes.

"Me too, Ba." I clenched my lips holding back tears.

"Good job, Con. You did it. Another journey will start for you. Keep doing what you've been doing and continue to make me proud of you."

I turned to give Ba a hug. By now, I was a little taller than Ba. Yet I still felt like that little boy holding his hand walking along the beach back home during that afternoon in 1982.

Ba, Ma, Anh Robert, and Chi Trang came to attend the ceremony at my school. As I walked across the stage, I could hear Chi Trang and my friends screaming my name and cheering for me when the principal gave me my diploma. I reminisced about my first day in second grade, not knowing much English, being teased as "the swallow stick boy" in third grade, and getting bullied all the way up to high school. Nevertheless, I triumphed over them all and proudly entered the next chapter of my life. I looked over to my family and friends who were clapping their hands and whistling at the top of their lungs for me. I saw that same look on Ba's face like at my junior high school graduation, smiling brightly at how proud he was of me.

Shortly after my graduation, Anh Robert and Chi Trang got married. They had a small wedding with only a few friends and my family. Anh Robert's family was still in Vietnam. As I watched Chi Trang in her wedding gown, walking down the aisle with her husband, I couldn't hold my tears, feeling happy for both of them. Albeit she was married, in my heart she was still that sweet big sister who carried the water from the well with me home for our family to use.

Chi Trang moved in with Anh Robert after the wedding. One Sunday, Ba drove Ma and all of us to go visit them. They lived in a basement one-bedroom apartment. The stairs to their apartment were dark since it was underground. The apartment was small and with my family over, there was not much space to move around. While Ma, Chi Trang, and all of us were cooking in the kitchen, Ba and Anh Robert went outside for a talk. I didn't know what kind of conversation they were having, but after coming back, Ba announced that Anh Robert and Chi Trang would be living with us. We were all confused as to where this newlywed would be sleeping since our apartment wasn't any bigger than theirs. Ba further surprised us with news that he just bought a house. The one that he took Ma and I went to see the other day. Anh Robert and Chi Trang could join us in that house. Ma was the first one to jump with joy. Chi Trang seemed a bit surprised that Anh Robert hadn't discussed it with her. However, it didn't take long after Ma planned everyone's living arrangement that Chi Trang was just as excited.

By the beginning of August, Ba told us that we would be moving into our new home in a week. None of us kids saw the inside of the house except for Ba and Ma. Nevertheless, we were excited and couldn't stop smiling from ear to ear. On moving day, Ma made Ba drive her there first so she could have her traditional prayer, asking for everyone's good health and blessing us in the new house, before having the rest of the family come inside. The house had two bedrooms on the first floor, which were a little smaller than the bedroom at the apartment. Ba, Ma, and Edgar would occupy one room, and the other would be for Anh Robert and Chi Trang. A full bathroom was in the middle of the two rooms. There was a living room in front as we walked in and a kitchen in the back. On the side of the living room was a circular staircase going up to the room in the attic. Trinh, Anh, and Ly would be staying up there. It was the same size as the bedrooms downstairs. In the kitchen area, there was a staircase going down the basement. Ba told me that Vu and I would occupy that area. As I walked farther into the basement, I saw an open space bigger than the bedroom above. It could fit two twin beds, one on each side. There was also another full bathroom in the corner of the room. I stood there looking around the room and couldn't believe that I would finally be sleeping on a real bed and not be disturbed, unlike when I slept in the living room. That night, my whole family comfortably enjoyed their sleep in their own semi-private space.

25 The College Years

After the day Ba took Ma and me to go see the house in College Point, I had an interest in Queens College and decided to apply there. Knowing Ba would buy a house for the family soon, I wanted to pay for college myself. I planned to apply for a student loan but also didn't want to graduate with big debt. Therefore, Stony Brook University was crossed off my list; the tuition was too expensive for me. I also needed a car to drive there since there was no other type of transportation to the university. With Queens College, I could take a train or bus since it was close to College Point, and the tuition was much more affordable.

A few days after settling into the new house, Ba stood in the backyard smoking. I came out and told Ba I had decided to major in pharmaceuticals just as he suggested. Ba was content to hear the news. However, when I told him I would be attending Queens College, he was surprised that I didn't choose Stony Brook, given how much I liked the school the last time we were there. I told him that the commute to Queens College was more convenient for me since it was only twenty minutes, whereas Stony Brook would take an hour. In addition, I planned to stay at Queens College for only two years to save money, then would transfer to St. John's University since it had a good pharmaceutical program. Ba seemed to understand the reason behind my decision. He patted me on the shoulder with his head looking down. He took a long pause before talking to me again.

"You are the first child attending college. I want you to be a role model for your siblings," Ba said softly.

"I know Ba," I reassured him.

"As for the tuition, I will take care of it."

"It's okay, Ba. I can take care of myself in college. You take care of my siblings."

There was another moment of silence from both of us. Ba stopped taking another puff of his cigarette, and I saw his eyes turn red while swallowing his saliva.

"If you need money for transportation and food, let me know."

"I may reach out to you for that." I smiled.

That afternoon, I reached out to Suchanh, a friend who went to Aviation High School with me. I remembered he mentioned that he worked at the New York Public Library on 5th Avenue, Manhattan, and they were hiring students. Suchanh gave me the number of the supervisor and told me about the flexibility of this job. Immediately, I dialed the number and spoke to the supervisor, Mr. Kruger. He asked me to come in for an interview the very next day.

During the interview with Mr. Kruger, I told him that Suchanh and I were classmates in our high school years. When he asked about my college intentions, I told him that I would be enrolled in Queens College. Since he recognized that the commute from Queens College to the New York Public Library would be long, he was concerned if that would restrict my working hours. I told him that I could be flexible during the weekdays, but he requested that I work an entire day on the weekends. After the interview, he hired me and said that I could start the following week. I was excited to leave his office, and during the commute back home, I felt relief that I didn't have to ask Ba for transportation or food money for college. Although I only got paid $4.25 per hour, I was satisfied with it.

At the beginning of the fall 1993 semester, I started my first day at Queens College. I was taking five classes in the first semester: calculus, chemistry, physics, English, and anthropology. Juggling between school and working hours was arduous. There were days when I had to leave school right after my first class, which ended at 10 AM, and head straight to the library for work. After four hours of work, I went back to school and finished up the night classes. The commute was long with the bus and train routes. I tried to manage my time by doing homework and catching up with any assigned reading materials during the commute. On days that I didn't have to work, I felt less overwhelmed and took advantage of the school library to catch up with my sleep.

Although I tried my best to accommodate between work and school, my grades suffered. I was getting all C's in every class after the first test. This could not continue since retaking these classes wasn't an option for me. I was mulling between cutting down on working hours or completely stopping work to concentrate on school. However, I couldn't afford to do either. I took out a small loan for my tuition because I didn't want to owe too much after I graduated. I needed to work to pay for whatever the loan didn't cover, as well as my everyday expenses. Halfway through the semester, I continued to struggle and didn't get the same grades I used to get in high school; I wasn't on an honor roll scale. Instead, I was desperate to keep my head above water. If Ba was to find out, he would be extremely disappointed in me. Nevertheless, I was disappointed in myself. I gave Ba my word to set a good example for my siblings, but I couldn't keep it up only a few months into college.

One day, after getting my test back with another C, I walked to the courtyard at the back of the school. Feeling hopeless as I didn't know what to do to pull my grades up, I wondered how Ba managed to do so much back then; taking care of me, working, and going to school at the same time. As I sat there contemplating my situation, I figured there was no point in complaining, but I had to fix the problem. Ba had shown me that he didn't sit there feeling pity for himself; he kept moving forward until he achieved his goal. I pulled out my wallet from my back pants pocket and looked at Phong's picture. As I continued to look into his eyes, I reminded myself that whatever it took, I needed to finish college and find him.

After that day, I made sure not to waste a minute of my time. I woke up early to go to school so I could have more time to study. I did my homework during lunch. I took every opportunity I had to study, even at work. It was a good thing that my job was very flexible. I worked as a library page in the vault. There were two pages placed on each floor of tens of thousands of books. We needed to put the books back on the shelves when they got returned every hour. When I was done with my tasks and had nothing else to do, I took out my homework and studied. Luckily for us, Mr. Kruger was thoughtful. He knew all the pages at the library were college students, so as long as we got our work done, he was fine with us studying.

With all the effort and persistence that I put in, at the end of my first year at Queens College, I was happy to end up with B's. Although it wasn't the grade I set out for, I was motivated to see my improvement. However, it was also a time when I solidified my decision of becoming an engineer instead of a pharmacist. I realized that I wanted to do something that would require hands-on experience, rather than sitting in the lab. When I told Ba of my decision, I could see the disappointment on his face. Nevertheless, Ba was supportive of the choice that I made.

I decided to forego St. John's University and applied to the City College of New York (CCNY) for a chemical engineering degree. When I got to the CCNY registrar's office, I was told that none of my science and math classes were transferrable since they were geared towards a science major and not for engineering. The information hit me like a ton of bricks. My entire year was wasted. *How could I let this happen? Should I continue with pharmaceutical school and avoid losing a year?* It was a back-and-forth assessment as I was ambivalent as to what to do. In the end, I had to choose what I would be best at and that was being an engineer. Due to my indecisiveness in a major, I lost an entire year taking the classes at Queens College.

In the fall of 1994, I began my first semester at CCNY, which was in Harlem, upper Manhattan. Mr. Kruger gave me the same work hours as the previous year. However, I felt overwhelmed by the constant commute between school and work. In the morning, I had to leave as early as six to be on time for my morning class. During the day, I would go to work from school and then back to school after work. By the time I got to go home, it would be around 10 PM. The train commutes increasingly became my studying time.

The environment of CCNY was no different from the Bronx. Each time I got off the train station, there would be groups of teenagers standing there, either smoking weed or picking on the passersby and stealing their money. I was their victim quite a few times. I was angry that I had to give them my hard-earned money, yet there was nothing I could do other than take a longer route along different streets after getting off the train to avoid them. On those nights walking home on the longer route, I thought about Stony Brook or St. John's University. I wouldn't have to put up with those petty crimes if I had gone there. However, I knew Ba had a whole family of nine to take care of. I couldn't be selfish thinking only for myself.

One of my favorite classes at CCNY was FORTRAN, a computer class for engineers that started at 6 PM. On the first day, the professor walked in with his long white hair and his beard extending down to the middle of his chest. He looked around the class and slowly said, "My name is Professor Left, not right." The entire class started to burst into incessant laughter. Professor Left always made the class more interesting than it actually was. He often came up with funny jokes to make the whole class laugh. However, it wasn't only Professor Left that made the class memorable for me. In this class, I found my two best friends. Sitting next to me were Chee Chong and Tang. Chee Chong was from Malaysia. He came here with an older sister, and both had student visas. Tang, on the other hand, was an immigrant, just like me. He came here with his mother and younger brother from Thailand a long time ago.

The three of us became friends after our first day of FORTRAN computer class. Although we only took some general classes together since Chong and Tang were studying mechanical engineering, we hung out together at lunch on days when I wasn't working or between classes to study together. One time during lunch, the three of us sat at our regular spot, on the balcony of the science building, eating our packed food. Tang looked at mine and Chong's food and was curious.

"What are you having today?" Tang asked

"Leftover sautéed chicken that my mom cooked," I answered.

"Leftover chicken lo-mein," Chong said.

"Here, try some of mine," Tang offered.

"Wow, what is this? It's so good." Chong and I both said.

"It's chicken basil," Tang smiled.

That was the first time in my life tasting Thai food. The taste was similar to Vietnamese food but somehow different and unique in its own way. It was very delicious and I loved it. The most interesting thing was how Tang cooked it. Tang had an exceptional talent for cooking. All his dishes were amazing. From then on, we agreed to share food at lunch. However, Chong and I ended up eating Tang's food and only the rice that we brought was shared.

Chee Chong lived fifteen minutes from me with his older sister. They rented the first-floor level with a two-bedroom apartment. Tang and I came to his place sometimes to study together. His sister was wonderful as she always offered us dinner. Chong's situation was better off than mine, but he still needed money for his expenses. I introduced him to Mr. Kruger and got him hired. The following week, Chong was placed on the same floor as me. At that time, we both got paid $6 per hour. As I got to know Chong, I felt like I had a brother who I could share things with. I told him about my family's situation, and how Ba and I came here by boat and later reunited with the rest of the family. I also told him about Phong. He sympathized with me and told me to be patient with Ma. My family matters had improved ever since we moved to the new house. Ma seemed happier, resulting in fewer arguments in the house. However, as we were joyfully living in this new home, I felt irresponsible and guilty toward Phong, not knowing if he was doing okay or maybe struggling somewhere. I told Chong about my plan to go look for Phong after college. He supported the idea and wished me the best.

One day, while walking to one of my classes, I saw a flyer posted on the door in front of the science building, *American Karate Federation*, followed by *Free Karate*. It had been more than six years since I took lessons with Sensei Hai. All the good memories of us doing karate in the Bronx flashed back through my mind. I missed those times training with Anh Bao, Bang, Hien, Tam, and Dan. For the last couple of years, I either trained by myself or with my younger brother, Vu, since he had a love for the art as well. I taught him all the things I had learned from Sensei Hai. However, I always wanted to take more lessons, but all the karate schools were so expensive, and I couldn't afford them. After seeing the "Free Karate" sign, it was like my wish had been granted. I wrote down all the information and ran to our lunch spot to meet up with Tang and Chong. I told them the exciting news, thinking they would be thrilled and join me. In the end, it wasn't their cup of tea. They told me they would cheer for me instead.

On the first day, as I entered the karate class, it was vastly different from Sensei Hai's class. It wasn't only Vietnamese students like Sensei Hai pushed to have. Instead, the class was truly diverse. In addition, all the students were in their white uniforms with white, green, brown, and black belts scattered across the room. I was the only Vietnamese student with a T-shirt and shorts. I had never been to a real karate school besides Sensei Hai's class. He was very casual and no dress code was required. I didn't know the real class could be this formal. I stood there, feeling so awkward that I was about to leave. Then I saw a man with a mustache walking in, wearing a black belt around his black karate uniform. He looked tough, and in an intimidating voice, he told everyone, "Line up!" Quickly, the whole class was quiet and followed his order. I knew right then that he must be the sensei. One of the black belt students started to line up all the newcomers. We were told to stand still with one hand crossed over to grab the other fist.

"Remember, don't wipe your sweat, or the whole class will be penalized!" he said in a stern voice.

After giving out that order, the sensei didn't waste any time, not even introducing himself. He jumped right in with all the exercises. There was no talking besides everyone taking turns counting the repetitions of push-ups and sit-ups. Sensei was also doing them along with us. A brief break happened between each exercise, yet we had to stand still with one hand grabbing the other fist. I stood there with the sweat dripping down my face, feeling so uncomfortable. I tried to fight it off, but the next thing I knew, we were down on the floor, doing more push-ups because I just wiped it off. We ended up doing 500 jumping jacks, 200 sit-ups, 200 pushups, and other calisthenics due to all the penalties. There was no karate taught that day besides some punching and kicking toward the end of class. I wondered if I was attending a karate class or preparing for the military. This Sensei was a lot stricter than Sensei Hai. I felt that his training method was too extreme for me. There was no philosophy or true martial arts involved in this class; it was just pure body training.

After class, while in the locker room, I saw the black belt who lined me up at the beginning of class. Wondering about the sensei's ridiculous rule, I tried to start a conversation with him.

"Sorry for causing the class to get punished. But why can't we wipe our sweat?" I humbly asked.

"We follow Sensei's order. We don't ask questions," he answered sternly.

"He is tough. What is the "tough" guy's name?" I tried to be funny to ease the mood.

"Who are you calling 'guy'?" he bellowed. "The teacher's name is Sensei Dombrowski."

I was startled by his loud voice. I didn't mean to offend him or disrespect Sensei, but I tried to be friendly to soothe his seriousness. I apologized for how I misspoken and left the locker room. On the way home, my whole body was sore. I was having doubts as to whether or not I should continue training in this class. Sensei and his students were too intense, and I had never trained this way before. I missed Sensei Hai, Anh Bao, Bang, Dan, and Hien. I missed training with them at the Botanical Garden while having fun at the same time. Unlike that class, I wasn't allowed to even wipe my sweat. Although I was debating whether to come back or not, I found myself showing up for the second class. Just like the first day, Sensei screamed and penalized all of us whenever one of us wiped his sweat. During one session, we had to do pushups several times because someone forgot the absurd rule. Once again, I was one of them.

On the way to the locker room, I felt bad for making the class suffer due to my mistake. I didn't know how to ignore the sweat. Maybe I just wasn't good enough to keep up with Sensei's standards. After changing my clothes, I turned around and saw Sensei. He also changed to his regular clothes, and without the black uniform, he didn't look as tough. I mustered up my courage and walked up to him.

"I am sorry, Sensei. I just couldn't help but wipe my sweat," I said while controlling my panicking.

"Did it bother you?" he asked with a softer voice.

"Yes, Sensei, the sweat was right in my nose and it was extremely itchy."

"But if you leave it alone, it will go away. You should be the one in control and not let it control you. The sweat is a distraction. Learn to put distraction behind you and focus on your goal."

Sensei's words enlightened me. I finally understood his reason for enforcing the preposterous rule on us. Sensei wasn't only teaching us free karate, but he was also giving us the most valuable life lesson. His wisdom helped me change my perspective in everything that I did. Waking up early in the morning wasn't that tiresome anymore, but just gave me more time to get my tasks done. Going back and forth on the train for work and school wasn't as much of a burden since it helped to train my endurance when facing obstacles. A long walk home to avoid those bullies just helped me prepare for my endurance (strength) during the next karate class. I took control and ignored hurdles that came to mind. These thoughts no longer became a distraction to me. I became more focused on the bigger picture, and that was to get things done. Thanks to Sensei's insight, my grade reports started to look more like the ones in high school.

As I understood Sensei Dombrowski's philosophy of training, I valued karate class even more. Sensei had brought me to another level of thinking and realization of a true martial artist. Every time I came to class, I implemented Sensei's instructions and philosophies in my training. I ignored my sweat by letting it drip down from my forehead and onto the floor. At the end of each class, I checked on my progress by looking at the amount of sweat I generated on the floor. This kind of discipline was what I needed during my first year at CCNY. I lived my life carrying his valuable lesson.

One day towards the end of the second semester, Tang and I were having lunch at our regular spot. Tang told me the shocking news that made my heart sink. He had to quit school to tend to his mother's care. His mother was sick, and he needed to find a job to pay for her medical bills. I felt bad knowing that there was nothing that I could do to help because it was beyond my abilities. I wanted to ask if he wanted to join Chong and me by working at the library. However, I knew with our minimum wage salaries, it wouldn't be enough for him to take care of those medical bills.

"What do you plan to do?" I sadly asked.

"A taxi driver and also making bagels at the bagel shop in midtown," Tang said.

After that day, Tang terminated his education and started a new path in his life. Chong and I visited him often at his apartment. We didn't want to lose our friendships just because Tang was no longer in school. His mother's condition gradually got better. However, seeing how hard Tang worked to support his family made me respect him more. I realized we all had our battles to overcome. Tang sacrificed his college education to take care of his mother. I felt a similar difficult situation of not seeing Phong to maintain my family's well-being.

In the summer of 1995, Ba and I went to his workplace to pick up some of his work documents. During the ride, Ba made another announcement. Ba enjoyed surprising me with his big news every time we rode together.

"I am going back to college," Ba suddenly announced.

"What do you mean, Ba?" I was startled.

"I want to get a master's degree in environmental engineering."

"Really, Ba? When and how do you have time for that?"

"I am going to apply at your school, CCNY, and will be taking night classes."

I was astounded by his news. Going back to school after a few years of absence, and especially at his age, wasn't easy. Ba set no limits when it came to learning. It made me respect him even more. As I was excited for Ba that he could go farther on the path of his education, I was concerned that he would be overloaded with a full-time job and being a graduate student at the same time. Thinking back, he went through a tougher situation back then when we first arrived in America. At least now he didn't have to take care of me, and his English was much more fluent. I was sure Ba would be fine, especially when he had already set his mind on it.

As our conversation went on, Ba asked me about my progress in school. I happily informed him that I finished my second year with A's and B's. Ba seemed pleased with my report. Since the mood was cheerful, I courageously decided to ask Ba a question that I had been holding inside for so long.

"Have you seen Phong?" I nervously asked.

Ba was shocked to hear that question. He turned to look at me as to why I brought Phong up all of a sudden. We both looked at each other, and I could see the sadness in his eyes.

"No, I haven't," Ba responded after a long pause.

"Would we ever see him again, Ba?"

Ba let out a big sigh without responding to me. The agony was showing on his face as he tried to hold onto the tears that were brimming in his eyes. I wasn't pleased about not getting an answer from Ba, but the expression on his face made me feel pity for him. I realize he was the most miserable in this matter. Ba probably had to live like a sinner to Phong for the rest of his life. I thought after having Edgar, Ma would ease her anger and forgive Ba. However, that wasn't the case. From time to time, whenever Ma was irked at something, she would bring up Ba's other relationship and lambasted him. I saw the irritation from Ba each time Ma brought it up. Sadly, whenever Ba was not around, I would be the scapegoat for Ma to release her anger.

After summer was over, Ba and I started the fall semester together at CCNY. That year was special for me. I got to go to school with Ba and I got my first car. Since all my siblings were bigger now, we needed a van so it could fit all of us. Ba bought a used Dodge Caravan and gave me his old Buick Century that had more than 140,000 miles on it. As for the old Ford Tempo that he first bought, he donated it to charity a few months after we moved into the new house. Driving my "new" car to school saved me at least thirty minutes compared to taking the train. The previous year, toward the end of the semester, Chong also bought a used car. He often came by to pick me up and drop me off. It would be my turn to be his driver now that I had a car. The car ride saved us a lot of time and hassle going to school and work. However, parking at CCNY was extremely hectic if I ever wanted to park near the school. There was street parking in the back of the science building, but it depended on street cleaning days—parking wasn't allowed for a couple of hours for sweeping. The best time to get to school and find a decent parking spot was between 6 AM and 8 AM. Any time after that, it was tough to find a spot. I had to park a couple of blocks away from the school. Yet, we still preferred our car ride to taking the subway.

Parking on the street behind the science building came with one dreadful thing: since it was a long street, part of it was next to a secluded park, where drug dealers and users hung out. Students and teachers got robbed and beaten up every semester regardless of day or night. The safest part of the street was between the science building and the engineering building. The farther out in the park, the more dangerous it was. Therefore, I tried my best to arrive at school early so I could park in the safe zone. There was a time when I got there late due to traffic, and I had to take a risk and park farther out next to the park. Once I got out of the car, I had to run fast and look out for anything suspicious. On days that I had late classes, I had to run to my car and move it closer to the engineering building to avoid the risk that I might face walking to my car at night. One time, Chong jokingly teased me about why I was afraid since I was training in karate. To be honest, I told him karate wouldn't help if these guys had guns.

Fortunately, Ba didn't have problems with parking since his classes started at 6 PM. By that time, a lot of the students had gone home, so the safe zone became more available. This was why I could move my car there. After re-parking my car, I would sit in front of the engineering building and wait for Ba. I hopped in his van and we had dinner before our classes. Ba stopped by home after work to pick up the food that Ma packed for both of us.

"How is school and working full time, Ba?" I asked.

"I am doing fine," he said.

"I do admire your dedication, Ba."

"You are the oldest son. I want to see you graduate college to set a good example for your siblings."

Ba always felt bad that Chi Trang didn't finish her education. She got pregnant after the wedding and decided to drop out of school and stay home as a housewife. She wanted to dedicate her time to taking care of her husband and her baby on the way. Therefore, Ba had lofty expectations for me. He wanted me to be a role model for the rest of my siblings. Understanding his concern, I gave him my word. No matter what, I would finish college and make him proud. After dinner, we said goodbye and headed to class.

26 Last Year of CCNY

During the next two years, nothing changed much as Ba and I continued with our education at CCNY. Chong and I still worked at the New York Public Library, and both of us got a fifty cents per hour pay raise. On most weekends, we visited Tang at his apartment or sometimes at the bagel shop. Tang enjoyed being in the kitchen. Although he was standing in a tiny, sweltering kitchen making hundreds of bagels, he was still funny as always while talking to us. We told him that he should consider a restaurant business for his career. Just as we thought, years later, he opened a Thai restaurant in Astoria and has been very successful to this day.

As for our family, we welcomed another baby boy. Chi Trang had given birth to her son, Bryant Phan. Since Bryant and Edgar were close in age, they were like buddies, always fighting over toys or taking turns drawing on the wall with crayons. The house became more bustling with all the laughter that those two brought to us. However, Ma still had her moments once in a while when Ba and I got home late from school or didn't finish our food. Her suspicion took over, and once again, Ba and I were the ones to be blamed for making her life miserable. The accusation would last for a few days until her anger subsided.

In the fall of 1997, I began my fourth year at CCNY. After looking at the curriculum, I realized I still needed forty-two more credits to complete my degree. It required more classes because I went for a Bachelor of Engineering, and not a bachelor of science. I knew I had to rush it if I wanted to graduate in a year, which meant I needed to take seven classes each semester, in both fall and spring. That thought scared me. I wasn't sure if I could handle it while having to work on top of the heavy school load. However, I had already wasted one year at Queens College taking pre-pharmaceuticals classes. I didn't want to waste any more time.

The next day, I went to the dean, who was also one of my chemical engineering professors. I told him about my situation and asked if he could permit me to take seven classes this semester. He looked at my schedule and was concerned since five out of seven classes were chemical engineering disciplines.

"Professor Taros, please let me take these classes," I begged him.

"But that's a lot for you to handle," he said.

"I can do it, you can check my grades," I said, as I continued to convince him. "I need them to graduate on time."

He pulled up my grades from his computer and after a long pause, he turned to me and gave me his consent.

"If you feel overwhelmed in the first few weeks, you will have to drop some classes."

"Thank you, Professor Taros, thank you very much. I won't disappoint you."

I ran straight to the registration office and registered for the seven classes. After that, I stopped by the school library, found an empty table, and took out my organizer. I planned out a schedule for all my classes and work. I wanted to make sure I still had time for homework. Failing these classes wasn't an option since I had set my goal. Most importantly, I needed to keep my word to Professor Taros.

That night, I told Ba about my schedule for the fall semester. He was flabbergasted with it. I explained to him the reason for those extra credits was because of my degree. He was worried that I would overload myself and suggested that I take some of these classes in the summer, instead of compressing them all in two semesters. I had never gone to summer school because I didn't want to waste money. I preferred taking advantage of being in full-time status and took up to eighteen credits to save money. I assured Ba I could handle it because I didn't want to delay my graduation. Ba took my words and went on to surprise me with his news.

"I got a job offer!" Ba smiled.

"That's great. What company, Ba?" I asked excitedly.

"At the Patent and Trademark Office in Northern Virginia."

"What? Virginia? How are you gonna do that?" I was shocked.

"I will stay at a friend's place in Virginia on weekdays for work and drive back to New York City on the weekends," Ba explained.

"You have a friend in Virginia?"

"Yes, he's my college friend, who also introduced me to the job."

"But how about your school?"

"I talked to my professors. They excused me from coming to class and all I have to do is just complete my assignments."

I was astounded by Ba's news. I didn't know how he would manage to do this. He was already busy with work and school. It would add more to his plate with the four hours of driving each way every week back and forth between New York City and Virginia. The reason he couldn't forgo this opportunity was that the pay was higher and there was room for growth through frequent promotions within the agency. He planned to put up with the hassles of driving back and forth for another year until he finished his master's degree. After that, he would have the entire family move to Virginia. I was amazed by his determination not to let obstacles get in the way. I wondered if he and Sensei Dombrowski were friends as they shared the same kind of thinking.

The following week, going to school felt a bit different not seeing Ba in the early evening. I missed having dinner with him in the van before our night classes. Coincidentally, we ended up having the same professor for our engineering classes that semester, except mine, was at a bachelor's level. At the end of each class, the professor always kindly reminded me to tell Ba to hand in his homework and project on time. Indeed, Ba didn't need any reminders. He was always on top of his game. Every time he was home on the weekends, he was either working on his project on the computer or studying. There was never a time that I saw him sitting around doing nothing.

It was a tough semester for both Ba and me. Just like Ba wasn't home on weekdays, I rarely came home also. There was even more homework and senior projects that I felt swamped with at times. I ended up staying late at the school library trying to finish or going to Chee Chong's place to study with him. Although we didn't have the same engineering major, there were still some classes that were required for both majors. Knowing how important this semester was for me, I put in my best effort. After a tough fall semester, with work in place, I managed to pass all seven classes with A's and B's. As for Ba, I didn't know how he did it with driving to Virginia on Sunday night and back to New York City on Friday afternoon, even at times driving during snowfall. Even so, he was able to complete his assigned projects and took leave from work to drive back for his exams. In the end, Ba and I survived the semester.

At the end of the fall semester, I went back to professor Taros and asked for his approval to take my last twenty-one credits. This time, without any questions asked, he signed the paper and told me I was the man. I thanked him for giving me a chance to carry out my plan. Walking out of his office, I couldn't help but feel excited as graduation was near. The journey of a little boy who didn't know much English in a new land had finally reached his destination. I felt a sense of pride for how far I had gone. The promise that I made to Ba, I was about to fulfill, and so was the promise that I made to myself. It had been more than seven years since I saw Phong. He must have grown a lot now. There were times I wanted to go see him, but I held back that thought. I kept thinking when I could be on my own and capable of taking care of myself, then I would reach out to him. Otherwise, it wouldn't do any good knowing there was nothing I could do for him. During break time at work, I would go outside to Bryant Park behind the library and sit on a bench to write in my diary. The only thing that I could do was to tell him how much I missed him through the words written in the diary.

In spring 1998, I asked Mr. Kruger to allow me to switch to Fridays and the weekends as I didn't want to risk doing poorly in any of my classes. As my working hours were cut down, and with twenty-one credits each semester, I had to borrow more from the loan to pay for my tuition and expenses. Ba offered to pay for both semesters, but I refused. He already had a family to take care of, in addition to his tuition. I couldn't take his money knowing what he had to go through every week to make more money.

One day, my cousin, Oanh, who lived in Boston, came to visit. It was during midterms, so Ba took a week off from work and stayed in NYC to study for his exams. It was Sunday and I was at the library working late. As I entered my basement through the back door, I saw Vu watching TV, but he looked at me differently as I talked to him. That strange reaction from him gave me a bad vibe. I changed my clothes and walked up the stairs. I saw Ma sitting by the dining table with her fiery eyes burning into mine. She let go of her anger before I could open my mouth to greet her.

"So that is how you wanted to write about me?" Ma screamed.

As soon as I heard the word "write," I knew what had happened. My heart pounded profusely, and I was sweating through the skin on my palms. It confused me as to how she managed to find my diary and understand what I wrote since everything was written in English.

"What are you talking about, Ma?" I said.

"Don't play stupid with me," she screamed louder. "Oanh read it and she told me everything."

I turned to Oanh in disbelief at how she could do this. She not only invaded my privacy, but she also festered a wound that my family had been trying to heal for years. She destroyed my last hope that Ma would understand and accept Phong. I was angry and wanted to shout at Oanh, but it was useless now that Ma was on her side.

"I didn't write anything bad about you in that book. I haven't gone to see Phong in many years because I respect your feelings," I cried, feeling it was unfair.

"If this family is broken, it is because of you! You wanted me and your dad to be separated. It is you that is the problem!" she screamed back.

I stood there befuddled. I couldn't believe the words that came out of my mother's mouth. Keeping the peace in the family was always my priority. I did all I could to take care of myself and not be a burden to the family. *How come I was the problem? Didn't Ma read my diary?* I never mentioned anything about breaking up the family. Ma continued to rant that I betrayed her, that I wanted

Ba and Di Yen back together, and that I only thought of Phong and not my siblings. For years, I endured so many accusations from her every time she felt anger. I told myself it would be all right for her to release her anger on me if that helped heal her pain. However, that night, I no longer let her stab me with her allegations. I refused to be punished for something that wasn't warranted. I left the room without wanting to explain myself. I went back to the basement, but the screaming and yelling continued.

I sat in the basement as I tried to study for the midterm the next day for one of my engineering classes. My mind couldn't focus on anything as Ma was constantly shouting upstairs. I kept telling myself I needed to block these noises and concentrate on the test. I needed to follow through with sensei's teaching, keeping distractions away. Mostly, I needed to graduate. I packed my backpack, went to my Buick, and drove to a nearby streetlamp. I parked my car and started to study. As I looked at the words, my mind raced with questions and anger. Nothing I read absorbed in my head. No matter how hard I tried to tame it and go back to studying, the words that Ma shouted at me tormented me.

The next day, while walking out of the classroom, I knew I tanked my midterm. During the test, all that was in my head were Ma's words about how I was the cause of her misery. Instead of focusing on the exam, I let myself get caught up in Ma's anger and ended up jeopardizing my graduation plan. As I kept walking while my head was still spinning due to lack of sleep from last night, I felt like the world was crumbling in front of my eyes. After all the endeavors of working and studying diligently day and night, the finish line seemed so far away again. I got to the cafeteria and felt empty inside, losing my appetite. I bought a cup of coffee and sat in the corner of the room. Chong came over and saw the expression on my face. He knew something was wrong and offered his ears. I told him what had happened and how I messed up on my midterm. Understanding my emotions, he suggested we go to his house after work so I could release them. That night at his house, I unbound all the dejected feelings that I had been holding inside. I kept on drinking as if there was no tomorrow. I wanted to be drunk to not face my reality.

Strangely, the more I drank, the soberer I was. After Chong fell asleep, I frozenly sat in the living room feeling lost and lonely.

I didn't know how much longer I could endure this behavior from Ma. What could I do to make her happy and have her love me back? I missed that motherly love that I once had. I missed the caresses and comfort that she once gave me. I remembered how I longed to be held in her arms every night in my sleep when we were apart. I used to wake up crying and prayed that I could see her again. Then my prayers were answered, and I thought those forlorn nights were far gone now that we reunited. Ironically, there I was, still longing to be held in her arms although we were together. I understood what Ma went through and felt her pain. Still, I did no wrong in this whole matter. I was only a kid who couldn't change anyone's fate. I wished Ma could use the love of a mother to handle this situation rather than let her need for vengeance take over.

Sadly, Ma was too angry to see it through and pushed me to the edge. I lost the love of my mother; I lost the goal that I worked so hard for, and I lost the will to live. A thought crossed my mind. I looked on the floor and saw an empty bottle laying there. One broken piece of it could help me end all the pains that I've tried so hard to endure. I leaned over and reached for that empty bottle. At that moment, the whole journey of coming to America flashed through my head. Those days stuck at sea, risking my life with the ferocious waves, months in Hong Kong and the Philippines facing loneliness, waiting for the day to get to the land of freedom and opportunities. After years of facing hardship, surviving, and being determined to get to my goal, I thought about the people who had helped me along the way, making me feel proud and confident about myself - the people who believed in me. I couldn't end my life like this. I couldn't repay my benefactors this way. More than anything, I couldn't do this to myself. I overcame so many hurdles and made it this far. I needed to get back up and keep moving forward with what I had set out to do. My mind started to ease as the anger also subsided; I put down the bottle as the thought of taking my life drifted away.

The next morning, I asked Chong to drop me off at the bus station so I could go home. I didn't want to go to school with my head still pounding from drinking. Instead of taking the bus, I walked along the dilapidated part of College Point. There were run-down factories and junk yards on both sides of the street. The walk from there to home would take me at least thirty minutes. Even so,

I needed that air to clear my mind and figure out a way to talk to my professor about the midterm. Halfway through the walk, I heard someone honking. I turned to see Ba driving Ma across the road. He made a U-turn and told me to get in. Inside the car, Ba asked where I was last night and told me that I should be home no matter how late. Ba seemed to understand my feelings. He didn't talk much or question how I was not at school. Ma didn't say anything to me as she still looked angry. I didn't want any company from her either given the situation. I looked out the window and kept quiet during the whole ride home.

I entered the basement, feeling tired due to the sleeplessness. I laid down on the bed, hoping the pounding in my head would stop. Then I heard a knock. I opened the door and saw Oanh. Enraged to see her, I wanted to slam the door and go back to sleep as I had nothing to say to her. Nonetheless, I didn't want to be one without manners, and she seemed to have something to say.

"I am so sorry for all of this," Oanh said.

"How could you? That's my diary. You don't go around reading people's stuff," I sternly told her.

"I saw it on your desk and your mom wanted me to read it while I was down here with her," she tried to explain.

I knew it wasn't her intention to invade my privacy, yet she should have known better when it came to another's business. One wrong word could destroy the peace of a family. Oanh said she didn't mean to cause me trouble but couldn't deny Ma's request. I accepted her apology and went back to bed. In truth, I wasn't as mad at her as much as I was with Ma. How could she accuse me of something like that? Regardless, I was still her son. Emotionally, she had been causing me great damage. This time, even my future was affected.

Back to school the next day, and just as expected, I flunked my test. At the end of the class, I came up and admitted to the professor that I had gone through personal problems and got distracted during the midterm. I asked him if there were side projects or anything I could do to boost my grade. He told me to do well in the final design project and the final exam, then he might consider that. I felt a big weight lift off my chest as I thanked him for his understanding. I was so happy knowing that I could get back on track. I promised myself not to let anything deflect me to fail another class. I needed to stay focused to finish this last semester.

For the next two months, I spent most of my time at school, work, and Chong's place. I went home late at night and left early in the morning. I tried not to be at home as much as I could. I didn't want to get into another dispute with Ma. One evening, after finishing all my homework around 10 PM, I left the engineering building and walked to my car. I came back late from work earlier so I parked a few blocks away from the building, which was out of the safe zone. As I got to the corner of the building, out of nowhere, a black man with a hood over his head appeared in front of me.

"Give me your money!" he said in a deep voice.

Luckily, I was always on the lookout knowing how unsafe this road was when walking at night. Immediately, I took a few steps back, trying to maintain at least ten feet away from the man.

"Sorry, I don't have any money, sir," I said.

"I said give me your money now!" He raised his deep voice and approached closer.

I took a few more steps back, getting ready to turn around and run. Then I noticed the movement of his arms and saw a handle slipping through his sweater's sleeve. *It's over. He has a gun*, I thought to myself. At that moment, all sorts of thoughts flipped through my mind just like when I was drowning back home in Vietnam. I looked over his shoulders and saw more than five black men charging in my direction. Suddenly, a voice inside my head told me not to give up. There were things I still hadn't accomplished yet. I couldn't die like this. I couldn't let these men rob my life from me. The handle that protruded out of his sleeve became more visible. It wasn't a gun, but a hammer. I was relieved it wasn't what I thought it was, but I was still in danger. I turned around and instead of running back on the sidewalk, I took a chance and ran across the street with all the incoming cars. I thought they wouldn't follow me, but they all ran after me and, surprisingly, none of us got hit. With every ounce of fight I had left in my body, I ran as fast as I could and finally got to the school security post. They followed me almost to the school but stopped as they saw me talking to the guards. I told the guards that I was chased for money by these thugs. The security officer contacted the police and then drove me to my car.

At my karate class the next day, I told Sensei Dombrowski and everyone in the class about the incident so that they could be cautious while walking alone at night. Sensei emphasized what I did was right and was glad that I didn't get hurt. Although he wanted us to train hard, for our minds and our health, he didn't want us to become egotistical and end up putting ourselves in a wrong fight. Sensei reminded us that a practitioner of Okinawan Karate never strikes first. It was for defense only. Finally, I realized Sensei Dombrowski and Sensei Hai weren't so different after all. They both wanted to train their students to have a strong mind, not an egotistical one.

After this incident, the school improved its safety system. More security guards drove around the campus after dark, which made all the staff and students more at ease. On days that I parked my car farther away, I could always count on the security officer to drive me there. As the semester was winding down, I made sure I wasn't behind with any assignments, especially the final design project for the engineering class after I failed the midterm. I studied days and nights to prepare for my final examinations. During the final week, Ba also took a few days off from work and drove back to NYC to prepare for his exams. I gave Chong's phone number to Ba so he could call me if needed since I would be staying at Chong's place to avoid any incidents with Ma, as her mood was unpredictable.

At the end of the semester, I walked to each classroom to check for my grades that were posted on the door. Nervously, I walked to the class where I failed the midterm. As I approached the door, I could feel the shakiness in my knees. My heart was pounding profusely while I clamped both hands together to my chest praying to the Buddha. I scrolled to my ID number and looked over to its right. I was in disbelief. A big B was next to my name. "I did it!" I screamed in my head. Running out of that building, I couldn't hold back my tears of excitement. This was the class that I feared most. I continued to go from one class to another to check my grades. As I expected, I ended up with mostly A's and some B's. After I found out about my grades, I went to the courtyard and looked up at the sky. I embraced the moment that I finally accomplished my goal. I could picture myself walking proudly with my cap and gown during graduation. Mission accomplished!

In June 1998, the day that Ba and I had been waiting for finally arrived: graduation. Ba drove the entire family in his van to CCNY. I drove alone since I promised to go celebrate with my friends afterward. On the way to school, I couldn't stop smiling, knowing that the long wait was over. In front of me was a new beginning, and I couldn't wait to see what my future held. At the ceremony, while I was lining up to get to my seat, I looked over and saw Ba in his cap and gown, standing there waiting as well. It brought me back to those nights sixteen years ago when Ba was holding my hand, walking under the snow to attend his night class. Those nights, sitting in the back of the room doing my homework, waiting for him, helped mold who I had become today. Fast forward, there we were, graduating from college together. I thanked Ba for his guidance and encouragement throughout all these years. However, Ba no longer had to hold my hand to show me the path, as I now could spread my wings and create my own future.

27 The Meet-up

A few days after my graduation, I went back to karate class. Sensei and everyone in class congratulated me on my achievement. We trained as usual until almost the end of the class. Then Sensei had everyone sit down and called me up on the deck. After training under Sensei for a while, we all knew his way of testing us. Unexpectedly, he would randomly call on his students and ask them to perform on the fly. Therefore, we were always prepared and ready every time we came to class. That day, when my name was called, I knew I was being tested. Sensei had me stand in front of him and a panel of black belts. He wanted me to perform all my katas, or forms, and ten pushups between each kata. Excitedly, I took on his challenge since this was what I had been waiting for.

On the deck, I gave it my all. I did everything that I had learned from Sensei when I first joined the class. There was no break in between because Sensei wanted to see focus and tenacity with each move. Yet thanks to the "military training" from him, I was able to get to the last kata. It was an intense demonstration with full power for almost fifteen minutes. By the time I finished, I looked down at my feet and saw a puddle of sweat. I knew I didn't waste Sensei's effort.

After my demonstration, Sensei made me spar with other black belts for the second part of the test. I was then asked to leave the room while Sensei congregated with the panelists. As I stood outside to catch my breath, with sweat dripping off my forehead, I felt the satisfaction of what I had done, regardless of the result. About ten minutes passed, and one of the black belts called me in. As I entered, there were four panelists, including Sensei sitting at the front. He motioned me to sit in zazen, sitting knees bent with buttocks resting on top of the heels of the feet and hands on top of the quadriceps.

"You have shown your strength, skill, and discipline that was required to be a Shodan, first-degree black belt. Congratulations!" Sensei smiled.

"Domo Arigato Gozaimasu!" I said thank you in Japanese as we always did in class.

Sensei stood and had me walk toward him. He handed me my certificate and a beautiful black belt.

"Put it around your waist. You deserve it." He patted my shoulder.

Getting a black belt was also part of my goal besides the chemical engineering degree. I couldn't have been happier now that I had completed both. Those nights of staying up late to study and finding the strength to endure the tough training from Sensei the next day had made me realize my grit. I put on the belt and felt proud of myself for knowing what I had done to earn it.

One week later, Ba and I were out running errands, and habitually, Ba surprised me with news again. He informed me that our family would be moving to Virginia in two weeks. I knew it had been his plan ever since he got a job in Virginia. However, I didn't expect it to be so soon. Ba explained since he was done with school and his job in Virginia was more stable, it was best to have the family settle there so he wouldn't have to deal with the long commute every weekend. Also, the reason Ba rushed with the move was so Edgar, Ly, Vu, Anh, and Trinh could start their new school year there.

"What are you gonna do with the house here?" I asked.

"Your sister and Robert will take over the house," Ba said.

I understood his reason for moving, but I still couldn't wrap my head around it, as many thoughts ran through my mind. Ba read my mind as he saw a pensive look on my face. He told me now that I had become an adult, he would let me make my own decisions. Whether I wanted to stay, move with the family, or apply for a job in Virginia, he would respect that. I told Ba to give me time to think about it.

Ba had talked to me several times about Virginia. It seemed to him that the cost of living and the housing market there was more affordable than in New York City. Moreover, the job that he currently had was paying much better and had more growth opportunities. The family would enjoy a peaceful life there since it was less traffic and a quiet neighborhood. Most importantly, Ba wanted to reassure Ma, since she still picked fights with him bringing up Phong and Di Yen whenever she was in a bad mood. Ma couldn't let it go. It seemed the only way for Ba to get out of that rut was to move away from New York City. I hoped with the distance, Ma could finally put her mind at ease.

As for me, New York City was where I spent most of my time growing up, even longer than in Vietnam. It felt like I would leave behind my whole life if I moved. Above all, I still hadn't fulfilled my promise—I needed to stay to find Phong. Leaving New York meant I could lose a chance of reconnecting with him forever. Ba may have had no choice. However, I had my choice, and that was to stay behind to be a brother to Phong and to look after him. I told Ba since I had applied for jobs around New York City, I wanted to stay to see how it worked out.

In July 1998, my whole family moved to Virginia, except Chi Trang's family and me. I helped Ba drive a big U-Haul filled with all their stuff, while Ba drove Ma and my siblings in his van. Ba planned to buy a house there, but he wanted the family to get to know the place first before deciding on the location of the house. Hence, Ba rented a two-bedroom apartment in Alexandria, Virginia, which was near his workplace, to settle temporarily. Although it was an apartment complex, the neighborhood was much quieter and nicer compared to College Point. It was sad to see my family move, but I felt Ba made a good decision. I could see my family growing their roots there.

Back in New York City, there were only Anh Robert, Chi Trang, their son, Bryant, and me. The house used to be noisy and cramped, but now it was quiet and empty. I felt lonely and missed Vu since we were always either doing karate or playing video games together in the basement. Anh Robert seemed to understand my feelings, and he told me to move up into my parents' room. I was thankful for his gesture, but their family of three had been squeezed into one tiny bedroom for so long. Moreover, I felt bad that they didn't have a chance to enjoy their newlywed time together. They moved in with us right after their wedding and didn't get to enjoy being alone. I told them I got used to the basement after living there for a long time, and Bryant could now move over to my parents' bedroom.

A month after I graduated, I was still unemployed. Unfortunately, during that year, there was limited opportunity for chemical engineers. Also, I restricted myself from applying out of state, since I wasn't willing to leave New York. I went through the newspapers every day looking for jobs. I sent out a bunch of resumes, but I still hadn't heard any response. Luckily, Mr. Kruger still loved to have me at the library. He said I could work there as long as I wanted. Even so, being a page at the library during my entire college years was more than enough. I was eager to get a real job, which was why I went to school. I needed the money. I needed to repay my student loan and the rent. I didn't want to live rent-free with Chi Trang and Anh Robert now that Ba had moved out. I told them that I would pay my share, but Anh Robert was nice enough to tell me not to worry about it until I got my engineering job.

One day, as usual, I was job hunting in the newspapers and saw an interesting ad from Cutco Vector, a cutlery company. It was hiring college students and the job was guaranteed to make good money. I was desperate and would do whatever was available. I wrote down their information and decided to attend their seminar. The next day after leaving the library, I drove to the seminar in Woodside Queens. As I entered the room, I saw more than twenty people about my age sitting around. I found an empty seat and quietly sat down. A few minutes later, three people, a gentleman and two ladies in their mid-twenties entered the room. They introduced themselves and started their presentation of the business. They placed an elegant shiny briefcase, the size of my backpack, on the table. When one of the ladies opened the briefcase, I was astonished to see so many varieties of knives. The only knife that Chi Trang and Ma would use at home was a butcher knife that would chop any tough meat or bones. However, as the presentation went on, I got to see and learn about more than ten distinct types of knives with well-designed construction of the handles and different shapes of the blades. By the end of the seminar, they convincingly told us that these knives should be in everyone's kitchen. They taught us how to be a successful salesman by letting the knives do the talking. All we had to do was go from door to door and show potential customers these knives. They reassured us that there would be a mentor to assist us along the way so we could make money as they guaranteed in the ad. I was skeptical, but since I had no other options, I decided to give it a try. The downside was that I might lose the two-hundred-dollar deposit that they asked for, but they promised I would get it back once I started selling.

  I brought the knife set home and showed it to Anh Robert and Chi Trang. They were impressed by the quality of the knives after I did the demo. Nonetheless, they didn't make any purchases as they had enough knives in the kitchen. I didn't want to push them since they didn't take my money for rent. Plus, these knives were more expensive than the ones they usually got at the Asian market. Still, determined to make a sale, I moved on to my neighbors. I knocked on Mr. and Mrs. Mel's door, who lived next to my house. They welcomed me in and let me present to them. To my surprise, they bought two knives from me and invited me to stay for dinner. That night, I got my first sale and a free meal. Feeling enthusiastic, I thought this job was easy and could help me survive during the actual job-hunting process. Little did I know that I couldn't make another sale for the next two weeks. I walked to nearly every house in my neighborhood and even drove to some houses farther away. Most of them knew me and allowed me in to show them the knives, but at the end of the presentation, I got free cookies or drinks, but not a sale, as they all said they had enough knives. No matter how determined and diligent I had to be, as I told myself every morning before leaving the house, I always came back disappointed and unmotivated at night.

  One afternoon, while driving home feeling hopeless after another day with no sales, I remembered what those representatives told me at the seminar. They made their first sale on the same day and within months, they became the "top salesman of the year." Meanwhile, I only sold two knives in two weeks. I wondered if I had no skill in selling. Maybe persuasive communication was what I was lacking. As I entered the house, I heard the phone ring. It was from Pall Corporation, a filtration company out on Long

Island where I had sent my resume. They wanted me to come in for an interview the next day. I was so happy that finally those years of studying in school weren't wasted. I called up one of my friends from college who worked at Pall Corporation and asked her to give me advice on things I needed to know about the company. I spent the whole night practicing so I could present my best.

The next day, I drove for forty minutes to head toward Long Island for the interview. During the drive, I talked out loud and rehearsed potential questions that could be asked. When I walked into the building, a secretary greeted me and asked me to follow her. She took me to a room down the hall and inside were two gentlemen sitting there waiting for me. They introduced themselves, shook my hand, and started with their questions. The very first thing they asked was how much I knew about Pall Corporation. Good thing I did my homework, as I gave them an answer that they seemed pleased with. Following generic questions about why I wanted this position and my strengths and weaknesses, I thought my answers were well delivered. To wrap up, they asked me why they should hire me. I honestly told them that I needed the job and that if I was given a chance, I would not be afraid of challenges and not let obstacles hold me back. After an hour of the interview, I thanked them for the opportunity and politely asked when I could expect a decision from them. They told me it probably would take a couple of weeks for them to decide. I got home and called Ba to let him know how I did at the interview. He was happy after hearing some of the answers that I shared with him during the interview.

While waiting for a decision from Pall Corporation, I continued working at the library and selling Cutco knives. One day, I called Tang and Chong, to ask them a favor. I wanted to show the knives to Tang's boss to see if he wanted them for his bagel shop. As for Chong, I was hoping he could introduce me to his sister's boyfriend, whose family owned a restaurant, to see if they might be interested as well. Mostly, I wanted to catch up with them since we hadn't seen each other after graduation.

We met up at the bagel shop in Manhattan, where Tang worked. He had become the bagel chef master and managed the whole store. Tang took Chong and me to the back and showed us how to make bagels. While watching him diligently knead the dough and make the bagels, one by one, I wondered if he ever regretted his decision of quitting school.

"Are you happy?" I asked Tang.

"When you have a family to take care of, your happiness is not a priority," Tang quietly said.

"You are a good man."

"I am sure you would do the same if you were in my shoes."

Hearing his comments, I admired how he sacrificed for his family. He was truly a good man, who always stepped up when needed. I was glad that we were good friends.

Although I couldn't make any sales either to Tang's boss or Chong's sister's boyfriend, I was glad I got to spend time with my friends. Chong, like me, struggled to find a job. Tang was better off than us since he had a job that could bring home money. Although it wasn't his dream job, he still put in a full effort to do his best. He told me he would go back to school one day to finish where he left off to fulfill his dream. I admired his patience and optimism. He made me realize never to throw in the towel under any circumstances.

After I got home, I picked up the phone and called Human Resources at Pall Corporation. I asked to speak to Mr. Larry Johnson who was one of the interviewers.

"Hi, Mr. Johnson, this is Linh. I'm calling to check on my status since it has been more than two weeks," I politely said.

"Hi, Linh. I'm in the middle of something. Let me get back to you," he said.

He hung up the phone after his short response. I thought it was time to go buy more newspapers and send out more resumes. As I was about to head out, the phone rang. Mr. Johnson called me back to offer me a job with an annual salary of $33K and a start date of two weeks from then. I couldn't have been happier and quickly accepted his offer. After thanking him for giving me the opportunity, I hung up the phone and called Ba to tell him the good news. Ba congratulated me and I heard the happiness in his voice. That was the first time Ba wasn't around to pat my back telling me I did well.

That weekend, one of my friends from college asked me to attend an event that was held by the Vietnamese Students Association at Baruch's College, which was located on the lower east side of Manhattan. We hadn't seen each other since graduation and since some of us just got job offers as well, we decided to get together to celebrate. At the party, while I was waiting in line to get my drink, I was shocked to see a familiar face heading my way. It was Anh Bao. I was so excited to see him, but at the same time, I was afraid he wouldn't want to have anything to do with me. The last time I saw him was at the park near my apartment, asking him to give us time to settle our family matters first. Since then, we had disappeared without a trace. Seeing him then, I was ashamed to face him. He stood in front of me with the same friendly smile as when I first met him, and I let go of all my thoughts.

I happily greeted him. "Hi Anh Bao, how are you?"

"I'm doing great. How about yourself?" he asked.

"I'm good. I'm so happy to see you here."

"Me too. Go see Phong if you have time. He would be happy to see you too."

The words that came out of his mouth left me stunned. He had every right to curse me for being irresponsible for all those years, yet he gave me another chance to reconnect with Phong. His benevolence put me to shame. I was speechless by his compassion. He walked up to the booth where they served drinks, borrowed a pen, and wrote something down. He came back and handed me a piece of paper.

"Here is my number. Phong would love to hear from you."

"Thank you, Anh Bao. I will call him."

I gave Anh Bao my number as well. We ended up hanging out together just like old times the whole night. It seemed like things had taken their course. While struggling to survive, I had put my promise to Phong on hold. However, fate did its magic and brought Anh Bao to me. That night while driving home, I was overjoyed. I felt like everything fell into place for me. I graduated from college, got my black belt, got my engineering job, and finally was given a chance to reunite with Phong. I couldn't have asked for more now that all my wishes had been granted. I kept thinking about Phong and wondered what he looked like. Those big eyes and chubby cheeks of his appeared in my head and brought a smile to my heart. Anh Bao told me that Phong asked about me and Ba often. I was happy knowing he was still thinking of me.

The next morning, I woke up feeling happy, thinking I would call Phong later in the afternoon since I had to drive to Long Island to do some paperwork for Human Resources at Pall Corporation. I thought about calling Ba to let him know about my encounter with Anh Bao and his invitation to see Phong. However, with Ba moving to Virginia, I didn't know if it was a good idea to bring up Phong. I doubted he could do anything about it and probably would put him in more misery. As for Chi Trang and my siblings, I was also hesitant to tell them. I didn't know how they felt about Phong after all these years since none of them ever mentioned Phong to me. I decided to hold onto that thought and wait for an appropriate time. I called Chong and Tang to tell them the news instead, as they also knew about Phong. It was Tang's day off so both of them took me out that afternoon to celebrate my finding a job and my brother. I got home around 9 PM and the phone started ringing. I picked it up and it was Anh Bao on the other line.

"Hi Linh, it's Anh Bao."

I planned to call him after hanging out with Tang and Chong, but once again, he was one step ahead like how I met him at the party.

"Hi Anh Bao, how are you?" I held my breath, anxiously waiting for what he would say next.

"I'm good. Phong is here and he wants to talk to you."

My heart sank as Anh Bao said his name. After a short pause, I felt a sharp pain when I heard a voice at the end of the line. The voice sounded different, yet familiar, saying hello to me. I stood still, holding onto my tears as I wanted to respond to him, but I couldn't manage what to say. It had been eight years since we said goodbye in Ba's car that night. That little boy was now almost a teenager. The guilt that I couldn't be there for him all those years made me at a loss for words. I tried to compose myself and responded to him.

"Hi Phong, how have you been?" I asked, still trying to contain my tears.

"I'm good, how about you?" He still had the same sweet innocence in his voice.

"Are you free this weekend? Let me know where you live and I will pick you up," I said.

"I am still at the same place," Phong said.

I couldn't believe that after all those years, they hadn't moved out of the Bronx. They were still living in the same area with those bullies – the area that I still disliked. I prayed that Phong didn't have to go through any bullying. I asked him if he had any problems being bullied. Phong told me that Di Yen enrolled him in a private school next to the Catholic Church where I once went for the free sandwiches, hence he didn't have a hard time being picked on. It was a relief to hear that, and I thanked Di Yen for making that decision since it wasn't cheap to put him there. Our conversation went on for another twenty minutes until he had to go to bed.

Just when I hung up the phone, I heard Chi Trang knocking on my door, telling me to come up for a late-night snack. I opened the door, and seeing the tears in my eyes, she asked me what happened. Not knowing how she would feel about Phong after many years apart, I figured I shouldn't drop a bombshell on her, so I lied and told her that I had something in my eyes. After eating, I went back to my room. I lay on my bed but couldn't close my eyes to sleep. All kinds of thoughts ran through my mind. I was excited yet nervous to meet Phong that weekend. He probably had so many questions for me, but I was afraid I couldn't give him a proper answer. What worried me most was his curiosity about Ba's whereabouts. How could I explain to him that Ba had moved to Virginia? How could I make him understand the complicated series of events that forced us to leave him all those years?

That Saturday morning, I woke up early, got ready, and drove to the Bronx. As I walked up to his building, memories of living there came rushing back. The images of us sharing our lives made me feel emotional. I treasured those times as everyone treated me like their real family. I got to the apartment and my heart hammered as I rang the doorbell. I stood there shaking, wondering how to greet them appropriately. Within seconds, the door opened and there was Di Yen. I was afraid she'd slam the door in my face and tell me to go away, but she gave me the same smile as when I first met her and invited me in.

"Chao Di Yen. How are you?" I nervously greeted her in Vietnamese.

"Hi Linh, you got so much taller, I couldn't even recognize you." She laughed.

Di Yen told me that Phong had been waiting for me the whole morning. Anh Bao told her of our plan to hang out and she was happy we were going to spend time together. I walked in at the same time Anh Bao and Phong entered the room, and to my amazement, I couldn't believe how much Phong had grown. A little boy whom I once carried to the playground was now almost my height. For many years I looked at his picture in my wallet and wondered how he had changed. The chubby cheeks were gone, but his big eyes remained pure as ever, gently smiling at me. Without hesitation, I hugged him. The moment that I had been waiting for finally happened. I reunited with my brother.

We all sat down in the living room – the room we all once sat making hair clips while watching Chinese dramas. I looked around the house and it seemed Di Yen changed all the furniture. I asked about Anh Dung since I didn't see him, and Anh Bao told me he had moved to Houston, Texas a few years ago. I still felt uneasy about how we said goodbye the last time he moved out of our apartment. I hoped to have a chance to talk to him in the future.

During our conversation, Di Yen asked about my siblings, but never once mentioned my parents. I somehow appreciated it because I didn't want to tell her that my family had moved to Virginia. I didn't know whether it would make the situation worse, but I was sure it wasn't a pleasant thing to hear, especially for Phong. I didn't want him to feel confused. After exchanging stories, Phong, Anh Bao, and I got up and said goodbye to Di Yen. We got into my car and drove to Long Island to spend the day together. Throughout the ride, it felt like old times. We brought up memories; of the times we spent at the park playing basketball, days that we practiced karate at the botanical garden, and those days making hair clips while Phong was sleeping in a hammock that Ba tied from one corner to the other. As Anh Bao and I were talking, Phong seemed interested in our stories and even chimed in to share his opinions. He wasn't a little kid anymore now that he could carry on a conversation.

After driving around the beach on Long Island, we decided to do some sightseeing at one of the Botanical Gardens. While walking along the park, Anh Bao was subtle and volunteered to buy us drinks, giving Phong and me some alone time to talk. I showed Phong his picture from my wallet, telling him how it helped me cope every time I missed him. I also told him that I still had his favorite gloves that he left in Ba's car. I apologized on Ba's behalf for not being there for him all those years, and also for not being able to answer any of his questions although I knew he must have had so many. I promised I would tell him everything once he became a little older. I was surprised that Phong took it very well. He wasn't mad or incriminating any of us, but instead, he simply told me he was happy he got to see me again.

It was nice spending time with Anh Bao and Phong. Whether it was out of respect for my privacy or understanding my difficulties, Anh Bao didn't bring up our last conversation at the park about my family matters or our disappearance. I told them I graduated from college and that I also received a job offer. Anh Bao was happy for me that I finally achieved my goal. We drove back to Queens in the afternoon and ended the day with a meal at a Chinese restaurant in Flushing. After dinner, I drove them home, and we planned to see each other again the following weekend.

I didn't tell Chi Trang about meeting with Phong. I didn't know why I was reluctant to tell her. Maybe after the incident with Ma reading my diary, I became very cautious with everything and everyone. I needed to talk to Chi Trang first before having her become involved in this. I needed to be extremely careful in handling this matter, or else this could be the end of my relationship with Ma. That meant the same for Ba as well. I couldn't tell him either, or his marriage would be over. I wanted to reunite with my brother, but I never wanted to break up my family. Ba's move to Virginia was supposed to put an end to Ma's doubts about his honesty. He had to bear the reputation of being an irresponsible father to one child, so he could fulfill his duties for the other seven. The guilt that he had to live with tormented him every day. I couldn't bear to see him suffer more, knowing that there was nothing more he could do for Phong. After pondering attentively, I decided to keep this meeting to myself. I hoped for a day when I could tell everyone my secret without hurting any of my loved ones.

28 The Move: Virginia

As promised, I picked Phong up at his place the following weekend. When I arrived, Anh Bao suggested Phong and I spend time together just the two of us since Anh Bao had to attend another event in the early afternoon. While driving Phong to get breakfast, I thought of bringing him back to the house. I figured since Chi Trang and Bryant were in Virginia visiting my parents for the weekend, I could take him home and introduce him to Anh Robert. There were numerous times that Anh Robert had witnessed my parents arguing and he seemed to understand my family's situation. Based on his character, I was sure he wouldn't tell anyone of my secret.

Anh Robert was in the living room watching TV when Phong and I entered the house. He was surprised that I brought home a young guest, and based on the perplexed expression exhibited on his face, I didn't want him to guess any further.

"This is Phong, our brother. And this is Anh Robert, Chi Trang's husband," I told both of them.

"Hi Anh Robert," Phong said.

"Hi, Phong, welcome. You are such a handsome young man." Anh Robert smiled.

I breathed a sigh of relief to see Anh Robert happily greeting Phong, though he still displayed surprise when I brought Phong home. We sat at the dining table and Anh Robert asked Phong about school and his family. Phong politely answered him, and they seemed to have a good chat. I didn't know what Phong was thinking about, seeing only Anh Robert and me at the house, but he didn't ask or even show signs of curiosity. Anh Robert suggested we grab something to eat since it was almost lunchtime. We headed to a restaurant within the neighborhood. While we were eating, Phong abruptly asked me the names of all the siblings. I was surprised why he asked me that question all of a sudden and wondered if he would ask about Ba next. I looked at Anh Robert and saw the same reaction as mine. I stopped eating and slowly told him the name of all my siblings. As I responded to his request, many thoughts ran through my mind as I prepared myself for the toughest question I knew I had to answer one day. However, that question was never asked. I wouldn't know how to respond in a way to make him understand if he asked me why Ba left him. I silently hoped that those questions would be answered directly by my father. He was pleased with being reminded of his siblings' names and asked me to tell him more about Edgar, a brother he had never met. I felt pain in my heart looking at his innocent face while telling him about Edgar. We spent the whole lunch talking about funny stories of all the siblings growing up. Phong excitedly listened to me as he wanted to catch up with the times he was apart from his siblings. After lunch, we went to rent some movies and spent the rest of the day at my house watching them. Although Phong didn't seem to need any clarification about the last eight years, I felt the need to let him know of Ba's whereabouts now. I owed at least that much to him.

That night, during the drive back to the Bronx to drop Phong off, I told him that Ba moved to Virginia with the entire family a few months ago. He gave a reaction that I couldn't seem to read. There were no emotions shown or further questions about why Ba left New York City. He sat there quietly and looked at the road ahead as if he didn't hear anything from me. I knew he tried to control his emotions, and that hurt me even more. At his age, he should be able to freely express his feelings, but instead, he kept everything inside. I cleared my voice and told him that Ba had his own difficulties and had to move. I wasn't trying to ask him to understand Ba, but to at least have peace of mind knowing where Ba was. I continued to tell him that I was hoping one day Ba could explain everything to him and ask for his forgiveness. As of then, I would be here for him, and he could count on me if he ever needed me. He remained silent, eyes turning red, and I could see him trying not to let his tears fall. At that moment, I made another promise to myself—to have him and Ba reunite.

After dropping Phong off, I drove home unable to contain myself. I burst out in anger and sobbed, with one hand on the steering wheel and the other wiping away my tears. I screamed as I was driving on the Triboro bridge. *Why me? Life is not fair.* I wanted to call Ba and tell him about everything. I wanted Ba to be the one driving Phong around and making up for the lost time. As my tears dried up, my mind came back to its senses again. There was no way Ba could know about Phong at that moment. Ma would get angry, turmoil would once again resurface, and the entire family would deal with more chaos. I continued to drive and hope that one day Phong would understand the dilemma that Ba had to go through.

Anh Robert stopped me at the door when I got home. He told me it was nice meeting Phong and wondered how I got in touch with him after all these years. I told him about my encounter with Anh Bao at the party and one thing led to another. He was happy for me that I finally reunited with Phong but reminded me to be cautious with my actions or else the outcome wouldn't be what I wanted.

"I won't tell anyone your secret, but be careful with whatever you do, especially with your mom. If she finds out, you will be in a lot of trouble," he said.

"Thank you. I know. This is why I didn't tell my dad either," I replied.

"Are you planning to tell him?"

"I don't know. They seem to be doing very well in Virginia. I don't want to mess things up for them."

I went back to my room and thought about what Anh Robert said. I loved Phong but I loved my family too. I told myself I needed to be very mindful of everything I did and not cause pain for anyone, especially Ma. Every time I thought of those years when Ba and I were in America, she was home taking care of my siblings and grandparents by herself. She had gone through her own pain and suffering while missing her husband and son. As life seemed peaceful for Ba and Ma in Virginia, I didn't want to do anything hasty and thoughtless to ruffle their relationship.

After that day, I continued to see Phong on the weekends, just like the old times when Ba used to bring him to the apartment, except he didn't stay overnight. I picked him up on Saturday morning and dropped him off at night. I called him during the weekdays just to check on his studies and asked if he needed my help with anything. Although it was a relief that Phong was a very smart kid and was always at the top of his class. He was currently a seventh grader in junior high school, and Di Yen told me of his diligence when it came to studying.

I had been working at Pall Corporation for almost two years and there was only a minimal salary increase. I felt stuck as my career didn't go anywhere. I wanted to look for a better opportunity where I could grow, so I went back to job hunting again. During one of my visits to Virginia, Ba mentioned his agency was hiring and I should consider applying. Ba had been promoted twice in the last two years since he was hired. It was a guaranteed promotion based on work productivity. Conversely, I didn't get the same opportunity at my workplace. The only way for me to get promoted was by the discretion of upper management. After hearing from Ba, it sounded like what I was looking for, but I was apprehensive because I had to leave New York City and Phong if I applied for the job. It took me several days, but I couldn't make a decision. I talked to Chong about it. Chong had found a job at a food company and was their marketing representative. Chong encouraged me to go for it. He suggested that I should at least have a stable career to take care of Phong. He said that I could always call him or drive up for a visit since Virginia was only four hours away. After deliberating over his suggestion, I took his advice and sent my resume to the Patent and Trademark Office (PTO). One month later, I got a call from them requesting I fly to Virginia for a job interview. Within the next two weeks, I received a call from PTO Human Resources and got a job offer. When I called Ba to deliver the good news, I heard the excitement in his voice. He was already planning lunchtime schedules as he reminisced about the times we ate in his van at CCNY.

Although I accepted the offer and was happy that my career was boosted one step higher, I still hoped to hear from those companies in New York City that I had applied to. I wasn't fully committed to the PTO or moving to Virginia yet. By the end of June 2000, Phong invited me to his junior high school graduation. I asked

Anh Robert to go with me since Chi Trang always took Bryant to visit my parents during the summer. At the ceremony, I stood next to Di Yen as we watched Phong walk up to the podium and receive his diploma. I couldn't have been prouder of him. He did it! He didn't let anything hold him back. I turned to Di Yen and saw the happy tears of a proud mother of her son's achievements. She must have been waiting for that moment for so long. Anh Bao and Anh Robert stood by our sides and continued to scream Phong's name. At that moment, I wished Ba was there so he could celebrate his son's first milestone and be proud of him.

    The following weekend, I came to pick up Phong for our usual hang-out. While we were driving, Phong broke the news to me that he would soon be leaving New York City. Di Yen had planned for him to move to Houston to stay with Anh Dung and attend high school there. According to Di Yen, the education there would be better for him. I was saddened by the news but had to agree with Di Yen. At least the bullying would be out of the picture, and so was the chance for him to associate with the wrong crowd. I shared the news of me getting a job in Virginia as well and told him that I hadn't made up my mind yet. Phong congratulated me and told me that I should go for it if it was a good opportunity. I couldn't believe the little kid that I used to stroll to the park was now giving me advice. Right then, I knew he was ready to enter the next chapter of his life: moving to Houston and spreading his wings. Moreover, I was sure Anh Dung would be there to guide him along the way. After hearing his plans, I felt easier making my decision to move to Virginia.

    In July 2000, I packed my clothing and fit everything into the trunk and back seats of my Honda Prelude. Before leaving, I drove over to Chong's place, and both of us took the subway to meet up with Tang for dinner. I couldn't believe the four-plus years that we had known each other flashed right by us. These two guys had become brothers to me. They were always there when I needed them. We had a wonderful time eating Thai food at a restaurant, but I could guarantee it wasn't as good as how Tang would have cooked it. The next morning, Anh Robert and Chi Trang prepared breakfast for me before getting ready for the long four-hour commute. A couple of days prior, I told Anh Robert about my plans to move to

Virginia and Phong relocating to Houston. He was happy for me and promised to keep our secrets.

As I drove away from their house, I couldn't believe eighteen years of my life in New York City was coming to an end. I coasted down the neighborhood and waved goodbye to my neighbors. When I got to Chinatown before entering the Holland tunnel, I remembered the days Ba took Ma there for Asian food shopping. New York City Chinatown was always one of my favorite places on the weekends if I needed or craved Asian foods. Upon entering the Holland tunnel, I knew that my life would change, and I was ready to begin a new journey in Virginia.

When I arrived in Springfield, Virginia, where Ba bought a one-story home, I felt happy. The thought of living with my family again after two years of separation eliminated the loneliness I felt. Although there were three bedrooms in the house, once again I found myself sleeping in the living room since all the girls took one, the boys took another, and the last one was for my parents. It was difficult to sleep at night with Trinh, Anh, Vu, and Ly in college. They got home late and would do their homework in the dining room which was right next to where I slept. With the lights on and them talking on the phone with their friends, I was constantly disturbed every night. Besides that, Edgar would ask to sleep with me sometimes since he hadn't seen me for two years. It was nice to embrace my baby brother as we shared a full-size mattress in the living room. However, once he was knocked out, he spun in his sleep and would either kick or elbow me all night. I was amazed by how he fell asleep so fast with all that noise from my siblings.

Since Ba and I worked at the same agency, we traveled together every morning. I couldn't believe that after eighteen years in America, Ba and I ended up working together. The PTO was in Crystal City, Arlington, and it took about thirty minutes to get there. During the drive, Ba constantly reminded me to stay focused on my productivity at work. He kept reminding me that the promotion would be based on the production numbers during the bi-week. I sat there listening to him and realized that regardless of how old I was or even when I was done with school, Ba would always be Ba, guiding me every chance he could.

Working at the Patent Office was different from Pall Corporation. At Pall, my job was to test filters until I got enough data. It usually took days, and sometimes it would take weeks. There was no due date or deadline. In my job as an examiner at the Patent Office, I had to read to understand the inventions followed by searching for similar existing inventions to show if the patent application was valid or not. Unlike at Pall, I had to make sure my productivity was above expectations on a biweekly basis. I was constantly on my toes getting things done timely.

    I shared an office with a coworker, Kevin. He joined the PTO two weeks after I did. He reminded me of myself when I first started at PS122. He was very shy and nervous around people, even though he had no problem speaking the language since he was American. However, it didn't take long for him to feel comfortable around me, and within months, we became good friends. Kevin had the attributes of Bang, Eliazo, and Rufus, and that made me feel easy to talk to him. I shared with him about my journey to America and my family's matters. He admired our determination to stay the course to get to where we were and felt for our dilemma as well. He encouraged me to hang in there and not lose hope for a better tomorrow. Kevin also had his own obstacle that he needed to overcome. He grew up with both of his parents being schoolteachers—his dad was a history teacher in high school and his mom was a math teacher in middle school. They were strict with Kevin and his younger brother's education. Hence, Kevin spent most of his time studying, so his playtime with other kids was limited, and thus he didn't have many friends growing up. In addition, there was an incident that happened in elementary school where one of his classmates accused Kevin of spilling milk on him. Kevin claimed his innocence, but sadly no one believed him. In the end, he was sent to the principal's office. Due in part to that incident, he lost trust in people as well as interest in expressing his feelings. Gradually, he had a lot of self-doubts and didn't feel the need to make friends. Despite that, Kevin and I grew to be like good brothers and not just coworkers who shared the same office. He helped me when I had problems at work. I helped him gain confidence and become more outgoing. We looked out for each other, whether it was at work or in our personal lives. I was happy to gain another great friend who was like family.

    In August, I called Phong to inquire when his moving date was to Houston. Phong told me that Di Yen had changed her mind and decided to delay it until the fall of 2002. I didn't want to ask for further details because I was sure Di Yen would always act in Phong's best interest. I told Phong to call me anytime he wanted to talk or needed my help with anything. I also promised to drive up to visit him often until he moved to Houston.

    Later that week, Ma asked me to drive her and Edgar to a Vietnamese Temple in Annandale which was fifteen minutes away from our house. I hadn't been to a temple in a long time and had no plans for the weekend since I had no friends besides Kevin there, so I gladly took her. When we got to the temple, I told Ma and Edgar to head into the main hall first as I wanted to check out the Temple. I walked around the front yard to enjoy the peaceful scenery with the trees and Buddha statues alongside the walkway. I stopped at the Bodhisattva, Quan The Am statue, and prayed to her for the happiness of my family. As I turned around after praying, I saw an SUV pulling into the parking lot. Two ladies and an older woman got out of the car and as they spoke to each other, I knew they were mother and daughters. Among those two ladies, one of them caught my attention. She had long hair to her shoulders, and I noticed her gentle smile as she talked to the other lady, who I assumed to be her sister. They entered the temple, and I decided to come in to find Ma as well. I saw Ma and Edgar in the main hall talking to some of her friends and the two ladies with their mother were seated behind Ma. I walked to Ma and sat next to them. While waiting for the weekly ceremony to start, I overheard the ladies' mother calling one of her daughters' names, and I was shocked that she had the same name as me, Linh. In Vietnamese culture, Linh is a unisex first name. The way Vietnamese distinguish gender through the name is by having a middle name. I thought to myself, what a chance to meet a Vietnamese lady who had the same name as me on my first day going to the Temple. I laughed at my silly thought, thinking if it was fate that the Bodhisattva Quan The Am had brought to me.

    Shortly after, the ceremony started, and we were asked to stand up and chant along with the Buddhist scripture. It was my first time at this Temple, so I didn't know what page to turn to. As I flipped through the pages to find the right one, a soft voice whispered to me the page number. I turned to my right and there she was, the lady who had the same name as me. She smiled at me, and I could feel my heart beating at double the beating pace. I smiled and nodded my head as a gesture of thank you then slightly turned to the other side to hide my embarrassment. I didn't know what it was, but her smile made me feel warm and comforted. The entire time, I wanted to turn around just to see her, but I knew it would be awkward. The ceremony ended, and I was about to approach her and show appreciation for helping me earlier, but she left the room quickly to help serve lunch in the dining hall. It looked like her mother and sister were regulars at this temple. They seemed to know everyone there. I wanted to stay and wait for her, but Ma needed to go home for a prior commitment. We left the Temple and I was disappointed that I couldn't talk to her.

On the way home, I kept wondering about the lady who shared my name. For some reason, I wanted to get to know her. Although we didn't have a chance to talk, I felt close. The following weekend, I was hoping that Ma would ask me to take her to the Temple again, but instead, she had other plans. For the next two weekends, Ma went somewhere else instead of the temple. I didn't want to ask her to go, afraid she might find it strange as to why I wanted to go. One month later, on a Sunday morning, Ma gave me two tickets to a banquet that she bought a few months ago. It was a fundraiser event for some of the temples in Northern Virginia. Ma couldn't go because she was sick that day and didn't want to waste the tickets. I didn't want to go but since I had nothing to do anyway, I asked Ly to go with me. We got to the banquet and while we were taken to our table, I looked up on the stage, and to my surprise, I saw Linh, the lady at the Temple. There was a moment of euphoria that I might have a chance to talk to her.

As the show started, the emcee greeted everyone and then introduced the next part of the entertainment. To my surprise, I saw Linh walk closer to the stage. I wondered if she had anything to do with knowing the committee of this event. But instead, she slowly walked up the stairs of the stage, wearing a gorgeous traditional Vietnamese Ao Dai (*dress*), and approached the emcee. She took the microphone, greeted everyone, and then the band started to play. Delighted to see how she would perform after seeing a loud and inviting applause from the audience as though they had heard her sing before, I turned my chair directly facing the stage to embrace this moment. At the very first verse, I was mesmerized and captured by her sensational voice as though she was singing for me. The entire song was approximately five minutes long, and I was immersed through the entire performance. There was a moment when she looked over at my table, and I could see that we locked eyes. I told myself that I had to seize this opportunity and at least get her phone number.

After her performance, she walked to each table carrying the raffle tickets and sold them for the organizer. As she made her way to my table, I turned to Ly and inquired how many tickets I should buy. Based on my enthusiasm, Ly could sense that I was falling for this girl. When she was a few feet in front of me, I couldn't help but stare at the radiance she exuded and wait for her to finish selling the tickets before she could turn to my table. Once she turned to me again, I stumbled on my words, forgetting to acknowledge her beautiful voice, and went straight to saying, "Thank you for helping me last time at the Temple. By the way, my name is Linh as well, Vinh Linh," I continued.

"How interesting! I'm Phuong Linh," she said.

As I didn't know what else to say, since I still felt lost in the abyss of love at first sight, Ly bumped on my shoulder to remind me of the raffle tickets.

"Oh, yeah, can I have an arm's length of raffle tickets?" I happily asked.

As she tore the tickets, I mustered the courage and said, "I recently moved to Virginia. I was hoping you can show me some of the temples here."

To my amazement, Phuong Linh agreed to exchange numbers. The entire night, as she continued to perform, I didn't seem to care about my hunger while my table of ten was full of food; I was focused on her singing.

A couple of days later, I called Phuong Linh. We got together and before heading out on our first date, we went back to the temple where we first met. I thought that this would be appropriate to thank Buddha for bringing us together.

Phuong Linh came to America with her parents and an older sister in 1990. Both she and her sister graduated from George Mason University and were working as web developers in Washington DC. The whole family were musicians and singers. To my surprise, her dad played the guitar, her mom sang, and her sister played the drums, while she played the keyboard and sang. They had their own band while living in Vietnam and performed professionally. No wonder she had that amazing voice. I felt a bit left out since I knew nothing about music and couldn't carry a note.

As I got to know her more, I found myself sharing more about my life. I told her how Ba and I came to America and how we overcame some of the obstacles in New York City before settling in Virginia. Our conversations became amiable, and I opened up to her about Phong. She understood my situation and encouraged me to stay strong. I loved hearing the optimism coming from her. It was the reassurance that I needed each time I felt gloomy from my thoughts. After we dated for a few weeks, I invited her home to introduce her to my parents. I felt a little bit embarrassed to tell her that the living room that she was sitting in was my sleeping area once everyone went to bed.

It had been almost three months since I moved to Virginia to be with my family. I saw the life transition to Virginia had some benefits. The fighting between Ba and Ma subsided during my stay. I was happy thinking Ma finally found her inner peace and Ba made the right decision moving there. Nonetheless, I was happy too soon, as Ma suddenly became intensely irritated just like back in New York City, and no one knew the cause. She picked fights with Ba again when Ba and I got home late from work, or when she called and he wasn't in his office to answer. Ba's other relationship was brought up and once again, the same episode went on and on for days until she was emotionally stable. Ba kept his silence, not even trying to defend himself, and I could not understand why. Whether he didn't want to agitate her more or he just wanted to have peace in the family, but for me, I just couldn't take it anymore, so I moved out. I talked to Phuong Linh and she supported my decision. She helped me look for a place, and since I wanted to save money, I rented a basement in Annandale which was ten minutes away from my parents. Once again, I was back living in the basement, but this one was three times bigger than the one in College Point. Although I lived alone, I still came over on the weekends to visit my family.

One weekend, I went home for a visit, and the minute I entered the house, Ma was already waiting for me at the door. Ba was at work trying to get his work done since he didn't meet his quota for that bi-week. I didn't know what was going on, but I was astonished to see Ma's furious eyes gazing into mine. Suddenly, I relived the diary incident and it gave me chills. She didn't scream at me this time but accused me with hurtful words for the same old thing: not stopping Ba from being with Di Yen. She considered that my biggest sin for betraying her. Sadly, all my siblings were there listening to it, and they seemed to agree with her. She continued to rant that Di Yen and Phong were the cause of her misery, not her self-destructive thoughts that brought her pain. It didn't matter how much I tried to explain, using the same words and the same reasoning that I told her for years - all of that went out of her ears. The truth was, I was just the scapegoat for her to release her anger on Ba's unfaithfulness each time she remembered it. I felt hurt and broken. Instead of continuing to defend myself, I exploded with emotions, telling Ma that I was fed up with her accusations. Ba got home right that moment and the argument escalated. It was just too much for me to bear and I left the house.

Later that night, I got a call from Ba asking me to go grab something to eat with him. We met at a restaurant near my place and had dinner. The whole time we were eating, Ba didn't talk much, although I knew Ma must have driven him beyond his tolerance for him to leave home. I didn't know whether I should admire his level of patience, or I should be angry at his timidness that he could not stand up for himself, and even for me in front of Ma.

"Why do you always keep quiet and let Ma be unreasonable?" I asked.

Ba did not respond to my question and kept eating with his head down. I couldn't take it anymore and divulged what was on my mind.

"I met Phong," I said angrily.

Ba dropped his spoon and looked up with a shocked expression on his face. I supposed I took him by so much surprise that he needed a few seconds to regain his composure.

"How? When?" Ba asked rapidly.

"I met Anh Bao two years ago and he asked me to see Phong. We have been seeing each other ever since," I said.

Ba took a long pause and looked down at his plate again. He asked me as his voice cracked, "How is he doing now?"

I told him Phong just finished middle school and was a freshman in high school. He was doing well in school and was also a good kid. I wanted to tell him more, but he looked so pitiful as every word out of my mouth was tormenting his conscience, so I stopped. Ba picked up his tea, took a sip, and slowly revealed his emotions. "The reason I've been putting up with your mom was that I wronged her and that caused her great pain. To be honest, there was a time she had driven me over the edge and I just wanted to leave. However, thinking of what she went through to take care of Ong Noi, Ba Noi, and all your siblings in Vietnam when I wasn't there, made me feel guilty and I wanted to make it up to her. Also, Edgar is too young, I don't want to leave him like the way I left Phong."

I couldn't say another word or stay mad at Ba for another second after listening to his heartfelt confession. I felt sorry for him that he had to live carrying the guilt, whether to Ma or Phong, for the rest of his life. What a fate he had. At that moment, I told myself that I would be there for Phong in Ba's place as much as I could. I told Ba not to worry as I would continue to look after Phong.

That night, Ba stayed with me at my place, and I told him he could stay as long as he wanted. I was hoping that since Ba wasn't at home Ma would realize how angry he felt and maybe she would reconsider and not keep on bringing up the past. Ba told me as he was leaving, Edgar cried and pleaded with Ba not to leave. I could hear it in his voice, feeling guilty that he had to leave Edgar. During dawn, Ba woke me up and said that he needed to go home and attend to Edgar. I understood his feeling, but at the same time, I was afraid another fight would erupt if he saw Ma again. However, I knew it was the right thing for him to do at the moment. After Ba left, I couldn't hold my tears and wondered why after all these years, Ma still couldn't let go and couldn't forgive him, although he had proven over and over again that he loved this family.

In the late fall of 2000, after being with Phuong Linh and getting to know her more, I asked her to join me on a trip to New York City to visit Phong. She was always there to lend an ear, cheering, and encouraging me whenever I had problems with my family. I felt as if I wasn't alone in this chaos, and there was someone who understood my intentions. When we arrived in NYC, I immediately called Phong to have lunch with us in Chinatown. The two of them met, and instantly I saw the connection. After our lunch, I drove Phong back to the Bronx, and I showed her the place where I grew up. As she looked at the streets of Fordham Road, it was nothing similar to northern Virginia. When I pointed to the building where I grew up, I could see how she realized the pain I went through. After dropping Phong off, I drove to College Point to visit Anh Robert and Chi Trang. Anh Robert knew we came there to see Phong, but he kept it a secret for me and did not tell anyone, even his wife, Chi Trang. Same with Phuong Linh, as she told no one, knowing how much damage it would cause my family and how Ma would never forgive me if she ever found out.

After dating for six months, I proposed to Phuong Linh. With our parents' permission, we got engaged in July and set our wedding in April of the following year. I called Mrs. McKeever to tell her of my wedding plans and would love for her to be there on my big day. I also invited Tang, Chong, and Kevin to our wedding. As for Eliazo, he moved a few months before I moved to Virginia and we lost touch.

Finally, the big day arrived. On April 27th, 2002, Phuong Linh and I got married in full Vietnamese tradition. It was completely hectic, as I didn't expect the formality of a Vietnamese wedding. We started the day with a tea ceremony at her parent's house, where I was introduced to her relatives. Then we headed to the temple where we first met for blessings from a Buddhist monk. We ended with another tea ceremony at my parent's home as we introduced Phuong Linh to my side of the family. Just that alone took almost six hours in the morning until later in the afternoon. By evening, the banquet was held at the restaurant when I first met Phuong Linh while doing the fundraising event. As we stood to greet our guests, I was ecstatic to see Tang, Chong, and Kevin. Adding to the excitement, when I saw Mrs. McKeever walking in with her husband, Larry, I immediately ran over and gave them that long-awaited hug.

About thirty minutes into the banquet dinner, the emcee asked both Phuong Linh and me up to the stage. She grabbed the microphone and all of a sudden, the band started playing a song. I was caught off guard and wondered what was going on. Then the melody started to sound familiar. It was a Chinese song that both of us liked to listen to. As soon as Phuong Linh raised the microphone to her mouth, she sang the song in Vietnamese. The entire time, I got to treasure the beautifully delightful voice of my wife singing me a song that she wrote herself. It was a moment of exultation as I looked into the eyes of this charming angel knowing that my life would forever be changed.

The next day after our wedding, Phuong Linh and I invited Mrs. McKeever and her husband to join us for breakfast. As we were eating, Mrs. McKeever reached into her purse, took out a drawing, and handed it to Phuong Linh. At that moment, I recognized the drawing. Eyes brimming with tears, I looked at Mrs. McKeever and wanted to thank her for her years of support through letters and phone calls. As Phuong Linh looked at the drawing, I described to her the house in Vietnam, and next to it a boy sitting on a water buffalo going across the rice field.

"This is the drawing that Linh drew for me when he was in my class in second grade. I've been keeping it, but it's your turn to keep it now and show it to your children later," Mrs. McKeever said as she acknowledged the drawing would no longer be in her possession.

I looked at the drawing and couldn't believe the transformation of who I had become. For more than twenty years, Mrs. McKeever kept this drawing. She laminated the drawing to make sure none of the pencil and crayon marks faded. Mrs. McKeever continued to tell Phuong Linh how I was one of her favorite ESL students. As I listened, even though it was more than two decades ago, her voice brought me back to the seat where I sat the first time I was in PS122. When she asked me if I remembered some of the things she mentioned, I immediately responded that it was impossible to forget that it was her words - her encouragement - that made me work so hard to become who I was. When I struggled during tough times, it was her letters that gave me the strength to overcome the pain and sorrow. I cherished those moments and held them dear to my heart. By the end of her story, she looked at me and still with that same warm smile, said, "You were a determined little boy back then."

"Thank you for everything, Mrs. McKeever. Thank you for believing in me," I responded to her.

29 Building My Own Family

While we planned our wedding, Phuong Linh and I wanted to have our own place after we married. We went house hunting and found a new townhome development site in Fairfax, Virginia. Although it was a long commute from this new place to work during rush hour, we fell in love with the community. As the house was being built, I planned to stay with my in-laws for approximately two months as the builder promised it would be completed by June.

I still talked to Phong on the phone and via e-mail regularly. Around May 2002, Phong told me that he would be moving to Houston once this school year was over. Anh Dung wanted him to come early to get used to the area. I told him that once I settled into my new home, I would make a trip to visit him and Anh Dung. I hadn't seen Anh Dung since he left Astoria. It would be nice to catch up with him and see how he acclimated to Houston.

By June, Phuong Linh and I moved into our new home. After a month, she was constantly nauseated and wanted to vomit. I thought that was a sign she was pregnant. Hurriedly, I drove to the nearest pharmacy and grabbed a home pregnancy test kit. While waiting for the result, I couldn't stop thinking of becoming a dad. When she told me to go into the bathroom and check the result, I slowly walked through the bathroom door, took a deep breath, and reached over to see the tiny window on the test kit. I saw a solid line on the window but didn't exactly know what it meant. I turned to her and saw a smile with tears streaming down her face. With that, I knew we were about to have our first child together.

As I had promised Phong, Phuong Linh and I traveled to Houston to visit him and Anh Dung in late October 2002. Upon walking out of the airport, I saw Anh Dung and Phong waiting for us. At first glance, I recognized Anh Dung right away, although it had been more than thirteen years since I last saw him. He didn't change much except he had gained some weight. Nervously, I walked up to him and reached out my arms for a long-awaited hug.

"I can't believe you are married now and with a baby on the way," Anh Dung said. I assumed Phong mentioned to him that Phuong Linh was pregnant.

"I know, time flies. I was in high school when you moved out," I said.

Anh Dung also got married and had a daughter. It looked like his decision of leaving New York City to move to Houston was worthwhile. He built a new life and had a stable career. Seeing him become successful and happy in Houston made the guilt I had been carrying with me lessen. He had to move out of Astoria because of my family's reunion.

When we arrived at Anh Dung's home, his wife, Chi Lien, met us at the front door. Displaying an amiable smile, she stretched out open arms and greeted us. That night after having dinner, while everyone else left the house for dessert, both Anh Dung and I stayed behind.

"How is your family doing?" Anh Dung asked.

"They are good," I said. Before he could ask another question, I thought I wanted to take this chance to explain the situation back then to Anh Dung. I continued, "I wanted to apologize for how we ended things back then, and mostly, I wanted to apologize on my dad's behalf that he couldn't be there for Phong all these years. I won't ask you and your family to understand him, but he's living with guilt every day."

As I shared my deepest sincerity and gratitude that he took care of Phong while Ba and I were not able to help out during all these years, Anh Dung patted my shoulder.

"I understand. We all have our situations, but I'm happy that you reconnected with Phong," he said.

I was happy and relieved that he held no animosity against us. I'd always thought he would be angry and blame Ba for being irresponsible. Nonetheless, his compassionate response made me respect him even more. I wanted to explain further about our difficulties but realized it was my family problem that shouldn't be imposed upon him. Besides, what his family went through probably wasn't any easier than ours. I appreciated his understanding and moved on with the conversation. For the next three days, Anh Dung and Chi Lien made us feel like we were a family. They took off work to show us around Houston and its famous local Vietnamese restaurants.

On our last night before leaving Houston, I was in Phong's room having a brotherly chat. After I encouraged him to continue to do well in high school, I thought it might be a suitable time to tell him about Ba, but I was a bit hesitant fearing that it might disturb him after I leave. However, I was surprised when he asked, "How are my siblings?"

"They are all doing good. Chi Trinh, Chi Anh, Anh Vu, and Chi Ly are all in college. Edgar is growing big too," I said, still in shock that he brought it up first.

"Do you have their pictures? I wanted to see how they look now."

"Yes, I do. I will email their pictures."

Although it wasn't the first time he asked me this question, it got me every time, thinking that my siblings never once asked about him. I understood that they wanted to keep peace in the house and also respect Ma, yet it saddened me each time I answered Phong.

We said goodbye to Anh Dung's family the next morning and he took us to the airport. On the flight back to Virginia, I told Phuong Linh of the conversation I had with Anh Dung and was glad he was able to understand our circumstances. Seeing Phong getting older made me think that he deserved to know what happened and that he had the right to meet his dad. However, each time I stumbled upon the thought of bringing him to see Ba, I saw Ma and thought of how much it would hurt her knowing she still couldn't let go of the past. Moreover, the reactions of Di Yen and her family about this matter were also a concern for me. I wasn't sure if it would be fine for Phong to see Ba after all these years, but mostly, I was more worried about Phong's reaction. I was at an impasse between my thoughts and didn't know what to do. With words of encouragement as always, Phuong Linh told me to stay positive believing that I could make that day happen.

A few weeks after the Houston visit, Phuong Linh's company downsized and she was let go. After a few interviews and four months into her pregnancy, Phuong Linh's job search was not fruitful. She was disappointed and worried since we just bought a house. Fearing that she would be stressed out, I told her to take a pause from job hunting and nurse the pregnancy until the due date. I knew it would be tough for me to pay the mortgage alone while expecting a baby on the way, but I didn't let the impediment hold me back. I reached out to my boss and asked for maximum overtime. There were numerous times that I had to work many hours beyond my normal eight hours per day schedule, including weekends. However, having Kevin share an office made the late evenings and weekends seem less daunting. I was able to get work done and felt as though working hard for my family was rewarding.

April 12, 2003, Phuong Linh gave birth to our baby girl, Lara Tran. I was in the delivery room as Phuong Linh was experiencing excruciating pain without any epidural administered to her. She was one brave soul, withstanding the pain to deliver our daughter at eight in the morning. I was standing there, feeling helpless, watching the midwives assisting her to push the baby out. The only thing I could do was hold her hands as she squeezed four of my fingers so tightly that I had never felt this strength before. I felt the pain for her. After an hour of labor, my daughter arrived. The midwife wrapped Lara in a towel and handed her to Phuong Linh. I couldn't believe what I just saw. Being able to witness the birth of my child and seeing the display of happiness on my wife's face, I was in euphoria. I couldn't believe that I became a dad. Holding my daughter for the first time, I understood the importance of life. I didn't have to hear her call me "Daddy" just yet, but while looking into her eyes, I felt that deep connection. Right there and then, I promised to always be there for this little girl.

After enjoying three months of motherhood, Phuong Linh wanted to go back to work to relieve me from working overtime. Instead, I immediately told her to continue taking care of Lara, since I grew up without my mom and spent most of my time being alone at home. I knew how lonely it felt and didn't want Lara to grow up feeling the same. Although we could ask for help from either grandparent since they were close by, I preferred Phuong Linh to be with Lara. Moreover, I didn't want both of us to miss out on those precious times watching our baby grow. Being a stay-at-home mom wasn't an easy job. She was constantly busy around the house cleaning and feeding Lara. At times, I felt guilty for asking her to give up her career to take care of our daughter. However, we talked about it and both of us agreed it would be best for Lara. We worked as a team and appreciated each other for the sacrifice we made to build a happy life together with our child.

Having Lara in our lives made the time pass quickly. I would come home from an exhausting day of work, and there she was, waiting for me to play with her. It didn't matter how much work I had to finish, she became my priority when I was at home. The sacrifice that Phuong Linh made to stay home to take care of her was well worth it, as I could see how my daughter loved to be taken care of by her mother.

In June 2004, we took Lara to Houston to attend Phong's high school graduation. Upon arriving at Anh Dung's home, Di Yen and Anh Bao were there. It had been a long time since I had seen both of them. As always, they were hospitable and welcoming.

The following day, we all attended Phong's graduation. As much as I was happy to see him graduate, watching him walk toward the stage, I wondered when my entire family could witness his next milestone. The thoughts kept on bothering me, but I didn't want to dwell on them. I wanted to just enjoy this precious moment with him.

Later that night, all the boys went to a local coffee shop. It was the first time in a long time that all four of us were together alone. We all took turns congratulating Phong but mostly advising him to be ready and serious in college. As he listened, I could see he was feeling inundated with words of wisdom. Although he nodded, I sensed everything went in one ear and out the other. It was his moment to celebrate, and I thought we might have stolen the festivity away from him. As soon as we got back to the house, he was out the door with his friends, ready to party.

The next night when I was out with Phong getting food to bring home, once again, he asked me about the siblings. I answered him, but this time I entertained the idea of him visiting me in

Virginia. He quickly acquiesced to the idea. I didn't know what was running through his thoughts, but I said, "Finish college and I promise I will take you to go see Ba." Phong was silent as usual when I brought Ba up, and I immediately veered to talk about how different Virginia was compared to New York City and Houston. Somehow, I sensed he wanted to ask me if Ba would come to see him, but something held him back.

When we got back with several bags of food, I asked for Di Yen's permission if Phong could visit me. She hesitated with the idea, implying that it would cause problems for my family because of Phong's presence. I acknowledged her concern and promised he would only be at my house. Anh Dung and Anh Bao also chimed in and convinced her to let Phong go. She finally gave in but made me promise to keep my word.

The next day, as we all parted ways, I turned to Di Yen and reassured her that I wouldn't do anything to make her feel uneasy. More than anyone, the last thing I wanted to do was create chaos with my own family. Having Phong in Virginia visiting, I knew I was taking a big risk, but I was willing to take that chance to be with my brother. At the airport, I told Lara not to mention Phong's name in front of my mom. She looked at me befuddled by my sudden request. I couldn't find simple words or reasons to explain to my innocent child. Lara looked at her mom and tried to understand my logic. It was indeed a complicated situation that I couldn't understand myself, let alone my one-year-old daughter. We stopped talking as we didn't want to puzzle her more and hoped that one day she would understand this difficult request from us.

After we got back, I immediately booked a ticket for Phong to visit in the next three weeks. One day at work, I got a call from Ly asking for help with some of her school assignments. After our conversation, Ly suddenly surprised me with an unexpected question. She asked if I knew about Phong's whereabouts. She said it had been on her mind for a long time, but she was afraid to bring it up. After all, she was the one who spent time playing with Phong the most back then. I was glad that Ly opened up to me, so I told her everything since the day I met Anh Bao. I also let her know that Phong would be there in three weeks if she wanted to meet him. Ly was a bit tentative at first considering Ma's feelings, but after mulling it over for a few days, she reached out to me and was ready to reconnect with her long-lost brother.

On the day that Phong arrived in Virginia, Ly told me that she would come over to visit. At the moment that Ly saw him, I could see the reconnection in the hug that they gave each other similarly back in 1990 when they used to play with each other. Watching them made me realize that it didn't matter how long they were separated, blood was always thicker than water. Those times being apart didn't cease the bond between them. I felt hopeful that the rest of my siblings would one day be able to hug him the same way.

Phong stayed at our house for a week, and Ly came by almost every day. As we spent time together, I was sure Phong questioned in his mind about the others not visiting him. I felt a bit selfish for not explaining to him. I just couldn't come straight out and say that the other siblings hadn't reached out. It was a time of confusion and fear for me. If I would have gathered my siblings and told them about Phong, I feared how they would react. I kept on thinking about what would happen if Ma found out. I was petrified and told Ly not to let anyone know. She understood my intention, yet she could sense my pain for holding this secret for such a long time. Luckily, whether Phong knew I was in a difficult position or didn't want to ask me further, he enjoyed his time with us during his stay. After dropping him off at the airport, I made a promise to visit him in Houston again soon.

Living in Virginia had been a drastic change for me. Not only did I find the love of my life, but my passion for karate also grew. I joined a couple of karate schools, but none of them gave me the drive and enthusiasm that Sensei Dombrowski and Sensei Hai had given me. I was there for training, but I wanted more. I wanted to share the philosophy of martial arts that I was taught, but I was prohibited by the instructors at these schools. One day, I met another student, Felix, who recently moved to Virginia from Miami, FL. After a few months of training together, we got along well and shared the same thinking of what a martial artist should be. Frustrated with the current school, I proposed the idea of opening up our own school. However, I recommended to Felix that I wanted to continue the tradition that I was taught by both of my senseis. I refused to charge any of my students. Felix was on board with the idea, and we proceeded to look for places. When I shared this idea with Phuong Linh, she understood this was my passion and was supportive.

I began to look for a space to open my karate school. Since I had no intention of charging my students, I didn't post any advertisements. I wanted to give back what I received from both of my previous senseis. I started to ask a few people I knew at the PTO gym if they wanted to learn karate.

One day, I was having lunch with Kevin, and I thought he could be my first student.

"You are going to learn karate with me," I cheerfully said.

"I am not a tough guy, and I don't think I can do it," Kevin responded.

"You can't give up before giving it a try!"

"Okay, I will but no promises."

I was glad Kevin agreed to it although I knew he didn't like it much, especially while being around people. He had always been shy and would prefer going to work and then heading back home. Convincing him to be outside of his comfort zone was daunting. Besides Kevin, I recruited a handful of co-workers who were working out with me at the gym.

In July 2005, I finally found a space at a local recreational center in Alexandria and started my school. By the time I had the school running, there were more than ten people in the class, including Vu. I told him about my class and wanted him to join me.

On the first day of class, while I was standing at the front instructing my students, I felt a moment of exhilaration. I couldn't help but look back on those dreadful days in the Bronx, waking up early on the weekends, and walking for miles to practice with Sensei Hai. I also remembered the days in a hot gymnasium, drenched in sweat from Sensei Dombrowski's military training. Their teachings molded me into who I became.

Since all my students were adults, in their late twenties through their forties, I couldn't be as strict and demanding as Sensei Dombrowski. I didn't forbid them to wipe their sweat, but only introduced them to the concept and told them the backstory, hoping they could understand the idea as well as my expectations. However, from time to time, I encouraged them to force themselves from touching their faces and just let the sweat drip onto the floor. I kept reminding them that the sweat was a distraction and that our minds must remain focused. The students appreciated the concept and during every class, we made sure the floor was drenched with sweat. After three months, the class doubled in attendance. I invited Sensei Dombrowski to come to Virginia and train us. After class, Sensei pulled me aside and was pleased that I was his only student who was willing to go beyond learning and open up a school to continue teaching our style, Shorin Ryu. His words further motivated me from being a karate instructor to thinking about being a leader. During the next two years, I learned that teaching working professionals was different than Sensei Dombrowski teaching college kids. I had to teach karate philosophically while encouraging my students to set goals. Besides teaching them how to punch and kick, I taught them how to be successful in their work. Through teaching them, I discovered that I also had a passion for motivating people. Over the next several months, I pondered on improving my leadership skills by taking management classes.

In the summer of 2007, I saw an opportunity to become a supervisor. Immediately, I applied for the position and got a job offer. I didn't expect taking this position would also increase my time staying at the office. The workload was different, responding to demands from upper management while dealing with problematic employees. Luckily, I could always count on Kevin to lend me his ears. We treated each other like family. Besides Phuong Linh, Kevin was the second in line I shared all my problems, including Phong's situation. He didn't get sick and tired of hearing me repeat myself. Although he had no solution to resolve my family's issues, his empathy comforted me on many levels.

Despite my busy schedule, in late September, Phuong Linh and I were blessed with a surprise; she was pregnant. Lara had turned four and been asking for another sibling to play with. When we broke the news to her, she jumped with joy and even asked if she could name the baby. Both of us were extremely happy with everything that happened lately. Having my karate school up and running, getting promoted at work, and now being granted another child, we couldn't ask for more. I moved my home office to the basement so we could turn it into a nursing room. We were ready to welcome this baby.

Two months later, while I was at work giving a presentation, my phone rang, and it was from Phuong Linh. She wouldn't call knowing I had a presentation since we spoke about it earlier. Then I remembered today was the monthly check-up for the baby. I suddenly had a strange feeling, so I told my employees to take a ten-minute break. I went outside the room and returned her call. She picked up the phone, but all I heard were sniffles coming through.

"Hi honey, is everything ok?" I nervously asked. "What happened? Are you okay?" I got more anxious.

"I lost our baby." She let out a cry.

It felt like I got hit with a ton of bricks. I stood there speechless while Phuong Linh bawled on the other line. I tried to hold in my emotions so I could comfort my wife. I told her to stay put and that I would meet her at the doctor's office. I hung up the phone, went back inside, and told my assistant to take over for me. I got in the car and drove off, but my mind was blank as I was clueless about what had happened. As I got to the hospital, the doctor greeted me at the door and took me to one of the exam rooms. There, I saw Phuong Linh sitting with her head down, crying. I walked over, held her tight between my arms, and told her that everything would be fine. The doctor looked at me and said that the baby's heartbeat couldn't be heard. It was the news that I wasn't ready to hear. Phuong Linh cried even more hearing the same words that the doctor had told her before I came. She looked at me and said, "Can you please ask the doctor to do one last check-up? She might find the baby's heartbeat this time. Please! Please tell the doctor, honey!"

I couldn't stand to see those tears in her eyes. The pain I felt was nothing compared to my wife's. She had everything planned out with Lara, from shopping for baby clothes to preparing the right paint color for the room. They were ready to welcome this baby. I held her hand and nodded my head to ask the doctor to check one more time. Understanding our feelings, the doctor ordered another sonogram. As Phuong Linh and I looked at the machine, praying for a miracle to hear the heartbeat of our baby, we didn't see the result we wanted. It was a reality that we wished never came true.

The doctor informed me that Phuong Linh had to be sent into the surgery room to remove the fetus. As much as I tried to deny the result, I didn't want my wife to continue to go through the pain. I turned to comfort her as they were about to roll her away for the procedure. As I waited in the lobby, I made a phone call to Ba. When he picked up the phone, I couldn't contain my words, but instead broke down. Ba panicked not grasping the situation. He kept asking what happened. After I got my composure back, I informed him about our baby. Ba asked for the hospital's name and told me he would be right there. I went back to the waiting room and soon Ba arrived. He sat down next to me as I grabbed him and cried on his shoulder. He didn't say anything, but just patted me on my back and let me cry my heart out.

After the procedure, we stopped by my in-laws to pick up Lara. On our way home, I looked at Lara sitting in the back and didn't know how to explain everything to her. How could I make a four-year-old understand what happened without hurting her feelings, knowing how much she was looking forward to meeting the baby? Phuong Linh and I agreed not to tell her at the moment, as both of us were still grieving.

30 The Conflict

As much as Phuong Linh and I thought it would be easy talking to Lara about the miscarriage, we found it difficult to find the right time and prepare for any of the questions she might ask. It was a tough decision to make, but we agreed not to let her know for the time being. About six months later, we decided to try again, but for months, the tests continued to be negative. After seeing the doctor, we were told to let the course happen naturally since both of us were healthy. She told us not to put too much pressure on ourselves.

After a year went by, I figured we should tell Lara since she had been asking about the baby. I felt obligated to give her an explanation. When all three of us sat down in the kitchen during our meal in front of the television, I turned to my innocent child and said, "Lara, it is unfortunate that we lost the baby." She was stunned, and I could see the eagerness in her eyes, wondering what was meant by "lost."

"Daddy, how can we lose our baby?" she asked as she was still guilelessly eating her meal.

"We had a miscarriage and the baby just couldn't live," I chokingly said.

"The baby died?" She placed her spoon on the table and burst out in tears. "Why? Why? Daddy?" I turned to Phuong Linh as she covered her face and sobbed.

"Why" was the same word Phuong Linh kept asking me after we headed back from the hospital. She bore the guilt of having the miscarriage; it didn't matter how much I assured her it was the baby's fate. She continued to ask "Why?" It took a while for her to overcome the remorse that she carried.

I tried to contain my emotions as both my wife and daughter continued to have their heads down with tears dripping onto their shirts. The television played and was the only sound I could hear for what felt like an eternity. When I finally got my composure back, I stood up and reached for the car keys, and said, "Let's all drive and get some fresh air."

The moment we got in the car, Lara, while sitting in the back seat with her mom, asked, "Are we going to have another baby, Mommy? I want someone that I can play with."

I looked into the rear mirror and saw Phuong Linh's eyes glance at mine. As we connected eyes, I nodded my head, and tacitly Phuong Linh knew the answer I wanted to tell Lara. She turned to our precious daughter and said, "Of course, Sweetie. We are going to have another baby."

As we promised Lara, we were trying to have another baby. In the meantime, I grew another family. I never imagined how my karate school would grow so much during the first three years. Half of my students were older than me, yet they showed respect for me and my teachings. In return, I did the same, never crossing the line while remaining humble. Throughout these years, we would gather outside of the karate class, flying to Florida and Okinawa to visit other karate schools, which created more of a family practicing karate than just a regular dojo.

At the end of 2009, we were starting to look for a single-family home as we planned to expand the family. Phuong Linh wanted a bigger bedroom for Lara and a yard where we could grow a garden. As for me, I was hoping for a space in the basement where I could dedicate my time to karate. After a few months, we found a house nearby. As we toured the place, Phuong Linh fell in love with it as it had everything she wanted. I was sold when I saw the unfinished basement. It was a large open space that I could turn into a dojo. I could visualize myself training there with my students. The minute we drove away from that house, I told Phuong Linh that I loved the neighborhood, the ample parking areas, and especially the basement. When she agreed, I immediately called our real estate agent and submitted an offer.

On April 27, the day of our eighth wedding anniversary, we moved into our new home. Within a few weeks of moving in and unpacking most of the stuff, I invited some of my students to come train on the concrete floor of my basement. Seeing Felix and other students enjoying their time training with me, I was convinced that I made the right decision to buy this home. I told Phuong Linh that I needed to get the dojo built immediately. Teaching karate was an outlet for me to release stress at work and have fun with my students. I felt fortuitous for having dedicated and loyal students joining me on this karate journey.

One day, while sitting in my office, my cell phone rang. I looked at the screen and saw a call from my sister Trinh. When I answered the phone, she responded with a poignant greeting. She asked if I could be free that evening for a talk. I didn't know what to expect but agreed for her to come to my house in the evening. The entire day I felt puzzled and anxious to leave the office to hear what she had to say. By evening, she rang my doorbell, and the minute she walked in, I could see a strange expression on her face. As we entered the kitchen, she immediately asked, "Do you know where Phong lives nowadays?" Taken aback by her question, I didn't know how to respond. As she looked into my eyes, seeing my confused expression, she continued, "I was working at the hospital today and saw a name, Phong Tran. This patient only has a few days to live. I immediately thought of our half-brother. Life is fragile and I wanted to connect with him before it's too late." I was shocked, but I could hear the genuineness in her voice as she told me the story and request. Before I could say anything, I walked to the cabinet and reached for two cups. As I poured water into the cups, I told her that Phong and I had been in contact for years. I continued to tell her about the first time I reached out to him after I graduated from college. She was pleased to hear that Phong was doing fine. At the end of our conversation, I pleaded with her not to tell anyone or Ma about this. She gestured a sealed lip and promised me this was between us two. However, she also asked me to give her his contact information. I was delighted that another one of my siblings wanted to reunite with Phong. Now, I had one less to conceal the secret.

Seven months after moving into the new home, Phuong Linh was constantly feeling nauseated, especially after waking up or eating a meal. The persistent sickness led us to surmise that she might be pregnant. Once again, I hurriedly and excitedly drove to a nearby pharmacy and grabbed a pregnancy test kit. I handed her the kit and walked away as she went into the bathroom. While I waited anxiously, I prayed to let it be positive this time. Suddenly, I heard a scream. I immediately rushed to the bathroom as she opened the door with tears running down her cheeks. She embraced me with both arms around my waist and whispered, "I am pregnant." At that moment, I felt our prayers were heard. It took us three years, and we became superstitious by deciding not to let anyone know until after the first trimester.

Building a karate dojo in my basement was my plan ever since we moved into the house, but I had put it off due to the increased workload at the office. However, knowing Phuong Linh's due date would be sometime in mid-September, I decided to get it done before the baby arrived. I wanted to get it out of the way so I could dedicate my time to our newborn. To save money, I took on the project myself and estimated four months to finish. My students offered to help, from carrying heavy stuff to putting up drywall and tiling the floor. Although I taught them for free all those years, the time they put into helping me fix the basement was priceless. Since I had a deadline to meet, I scheduled when certain parts of the basement needed to be completed. After arriving home from work at about 5 PM, I immediately changed into my construction clothing and spent time fixing the basement until at least midnight before I would shower for bedtime. Having my father-in-law help me with some renovation work expedited the process. His knowledge of construction work put me at ease at times when I scratched my head about what to do next.

One day, Edgar called to offer help with the basement since his school was nearby. He attended George Mason University, which was ten minutes away from my house. By then, he was a sophomore in college and was the only one left living in the house with Ba and Ma. Everyone had gotten married and moved out but were still within ten to fifteen minutes away from our parents. After working in the basement, we took a lunch break at a nearby sandwich shop. I asked him how Ba and Ma were doing at home.

"They are fighting again," he said.

"What are they fighting about?" I asked.

"You know, it's the same thing about Dad's past."

"Edgar, it's been years now that you have heard Mom mention the name Phong. Do you wonder who that is?"

"Yeah, Mom said his name so many times and I kinda guessed it was Dad's kid."

"Would you like to hear the story about Phong?"

"Yes."

As much as I was surprised to hear his answer, I was so happy to hear it. I gathered my thoughts and told Edgar the background as to why we left Vietnam in the first place. I wanted him to understand that Ba's decision of leaving Vietnam was not impulsive. When I mentioned how Ba met Di Yen, I told him I wasn't fond of it either, but I was too young to interfere. Edgar looked at me and responded maturely, "Sometimes, you just can't control love." As he continued to listen, in the end, he said, "I wished Ma could let go of the past so she could find happiness."

"Do you want to meet Phong someday?" I asked after seeing his reaction.

"Yes, he is my half-brother and I don't see why I shouldn't."

Again, I was extremely happy to hear this from him. I was afraid after growing up seeing Ba and Ma fight about Phong all the time, he would be mad and wouldn't want to have anything to do with Phong. Instead, he didn't hesitate to get to know his long-lost brother, a brother he had never met before.

That night, I called Phong. At that time, he was working for Apple in Austin as a sales manager after graduating from the University of Texas with a business degree. When I told him about Edgar, he immediately wanted to connect. I gave him Edgar's contact information and within a few days, they were chatting away. Although similarly to how I told Ly and Trinh, I preemptively told Edgar to be careful and not let Ma know about Phong, since I wasn't ready for any commotion with Ma. Knowing that three of my siblings reconnected with Phong, I felt elated. I was hoping the other three would soon reach out to me as well. In the meantime, I was rushing to finish the basement, since the baby's due date was near.

On September 20, 2011, at around 8 AM, I drove Phuong Linh to Fair Oaks hospital in preparation for a C-section delivery of our baby boy. The moment felt so surreal as we had waited so long. After Phuong Linh changed into the hospital gown, she was rolled away to the delivery room while I remained outside anxiously waiting. After about thirty minutes, the nurse asked me to go into the delivery room. In contrast to when Lara was born with everyone in the family being present in the room and watching my wife give birth, I was the only one allowed in the room for my baby boy's arrival. As I sat by Phuong Linh while holding her hand, her midsection was covered by a hanging curtain. I couldn't see or tell what the doctor was doing on the other side, but I knew the process had begun. Within about twenty minutes, the anesthesiologist tapped my shoulder and told me to stand up to take pictures. I got up and looked over the hanging curtain and saw my baby boy being pulled out of my wife's stomach. I turned my head to Phuong Linh as she was numbed on the lower half of her body and told her our boy looked big and healthy.

When the midwife handed Phuong Linh our son covered in a blanket, I leaned over and said, "Welcome to this world, Leo." That was the name we planned for him. I wanted this little boy to be like a lion, having that brave characteristic of protecting the family when he grew up. After she passed Leo to me, I looked into his eyes as he struggled to keep them open. I couldn't hold back my tears thinking both Phuong Linh and I tried many years before finally being able to hold this precious little boy.

That night in the hospital, while Phuong Linh was resting, Lara and I took care of Leo. As I was holding him, I realized Ba, Leo, and I all had the same Vietnamese zodiac sign of a cat. However, what was amazing was that Leo and Ba had the same birthday. Looking at him, I thought to myself that Ba was now sixty. How much longer would he have to wait until he could reunite with his son? I had made a promise to Phong that once he graduated from college, I would bring him to see Ba. It had been two years since he graduated, and I still hadn't done anything. I still couldn't find courage.

When we brought Leo home, I was surprised by our first few nights with him. Unlike Lara, who was constantly up every few hours during her first week, Leo was sleeping more than five hours. He was such an easy baby—eating and sleeping were never an issue. Lara was the most excited as she finally got her wish to have a sibling. She was happy to play with him the minute she arrived home from school. Since Lara was eight years older, she was a big help when we needed her. I showed Phong Leo's picture and he couldn't wait to see Leo.

When Leo was six months old, Phong visited us. I thought it would also be a good opportunity for him to see Edgar and Trinh. Upon his arrival, I told Ly, Trinh, and Edgar to come over. I thought there would be some awkwardness as Edgar and Phong had never met before, but once I opened my front door, Phong reached out his arms for a brotherly hug. Throughout the months of them speaking with each other on the phone, it felt as though they knew each other for a long time. On the other hand, Trinh stood by the door trying to process if this moment was true. When Phong turned to her, immediately she was aghast to see a transformation from a boy who was four years old when she last saw him to now standing almost a foot above her. The weekend that Phong spent at my house, I was glad to see him connect with Ly, Trinh, and Edgar. Seeing all of them together, I had a sense of hope that one day I would be able to have him reunite with Ba.

As Lara was about to turn nine on April 12, 2012, we were planning a birthday party for her. Shockingly, I received an irate email from Trinh reviling me for how I disrespected Ma by not accommodating her. Since I was unable to change Lara's celebration date to the following weekend as requested by her, I was accused of accommodating other people, but not my own mother. I felt bamboozled with the entire thing. I made plans with Tang and Chee Chong who were coming in from New York City a month ahead of time and couldn't change the schedule. As much as I wanted to respond to the email and clear up the misunderstanding, I felt insulted by the choice of words and felt disparaged each time I re-read the email. I kept asking myself, *how could it be? How could Trinh misunderstand me?* It didn't take long for me to receive the same type of email from Anh and Vu the very next day. Neither one of them held back as they denigrated my actions.

I was sad and confused as to why they would say such things. My only wild guess was after all these years of listening to Ma rant about how Ba and I had caused her pain, they took her words and misjudged me. Although I was heartbroken at how my siblings thought of me, I could understand. Growing up knowing what Ma went through to take care of our grandparents and five young children back in Vietnam after Ba and I left, they felt for Ma just like how I felt for Ba knowing what hardship we had faced when we first came here. After a couple of days of contemplating what to do, my resentment subsided, but I felt forlorn. I decided to isolate myself from the family thinking my presence would cause more distress. As for Ma, I explained to her the situation and my intention, and she didn't seem aggravated that I had to stick to a specific date. However, even after making amends with Ma, I felt perhaps that without me being around, everyone would have their peace.

After months of not seeing my siblings, there were times I was sad and lonely. I wished that Trinh, Anh, and Vu would reach out to me so I could tell them my side of the story. As for Chi Trang, Ly, and Edgar, they thought that I should speak to Trinh, Anh, and Vu to resolve the conflict. However, I told them that this misunderstanding would be beyond just a conversation. I wanted to allow everyone time to ponder what went wrong.

I continued visiting Phong at least twice a year in Houston. As usual, when he asked me about the siblings, I told him of the conflict that caused me to be away from my family. In response, he apologized for being the culprit of the problem. Immediately, I cut him off from saying anything further and told him this was not his fault. Although I couldn't find a better way to quell this problem, I told him that family matters always happened, and eventually, there would be a way that this conflict would be resolved.

Over the next two years, I continued to keep my distance from Trinh, Anh, and Vu. Although I missed out on family gatherings, I maintained hope that we could solve our problems someday. During that time, I was starting to have pain in my elbow. After visiting an orthopaedic surgeon, I was told that I needed elbow surgery to remove bone spurs. I was scheduled to have the surgery in December 2014. While recovering at home, I was astonished to get a text from Trinh asking about my healing progress. I guessed she heard it from my parents. After back-and-forth texting, she apologized and wanted to put our misunderstanding to rest. Phuong Linh and I were happy that she wanted to mend the past conflict. We invited her over for dinner to reconcile.

A few months later, I received a text from Anh. She reached out to ask for a favor regarding work. I thought this would be a good time to put our misunderstanding behind us. We went to her house and the first thing she did was hug me, saying let bygones be bygones. I felt at ease to hear her opening up to me. The truth was, I was ready for peace.

Vu was the last one to reach out to me. We had a long chat and resolved the misunderstanding. After all, he was my younger brother who I spent the most time with playing video games and training karate. Reminiscing those days sharing the basement in New York City with him made me want to reconcile our relationship.

Although it took us four years away from each other, I was content that Trinh, Anh, and Vu finally came to me and let me tell my side of the story as I had been hoping. I reassured them that I would always love and respect Ma and also had done nothing to hurt her. In the end, we all agreed that Ma should let go of the past to find peace.

At the beginning of 2017, Anh came to me and, just like Ly and Trinh, wanted to know more about Phong. I was jolted with happiness. Finally, it wasn't only Phong asking me about his siblings, but now it was the other way around. I gladly told her that Phong was working in Austin and finishing up his MBA. Having that conversation with Anh, I realized that each one of my siblings had been living with the thought of finding out more about their half-brother. I gave Anh his contact information and within a week, Phong called me and said that Anh sent him an email. Happy to hear that almost all of us had now reached out to him, I wondered when Chi Trang and Vu would do the same. Right before we hung up, he surprised me again with a plan to get married in the fall of 2018 after finishing his MBA. I couldn't believe how time flew right by, and Ba had missed every minute of Phong growing into a fine young man.

During that summer, Chi Trang took Ma on a trip to Vietnam. Ba, for some reason, didn't want to go. One day while at work, I looked outside my window and saw gloomy, dark clouds. The rain hit the windowsill and random thoughts of Phong throughout the years overtook my work duties. I contemplated visiting Ba and telling him about everything, but part of me was afraid to see my family go through another prolonged period of conflict. One weekend, I came over to help Ba install a recess ceiling light in the living room. After a couple of hours of working, we took a break and sat in the kitchen to have lunch. The moment of silence with us two eating in the kitchen took me back to our apartment in the Bronx. I chewed my food and looked at Ba while he scooped rice with his spoon. It had been a while since I got a long glimpse of him without saying a word. I noticed the dense white hair on his head, the wrinkled skin on his hands and face, and the brace on his back to control the pain. I immediately wanted to walk over and hug him as I realized he is getting older by the day. I didn't want him to miss the chance to reunite with his son.

At that moment, I took the courage and asked Ba, "Do you want to meet Phong?" My lips tightened as my heart pounded. "You know I've been in contact with him since the last time I told you."

Ba stopped scooping the rice with his spoon and slowly looked away from me. His eyes clenched and his lips folded. I knew my question made my father's heart drop. Ba stayed silent for a few minutes. I kept quiet and waited for him as I knew he needed time to process his thoughts.

"You have? How is he doing?" Ba asked quietly.

"He's doing great. He graduated from college, got a good job, and will be finishing his MBA next May. Also, he will be getting married next fall."

Ba got up from the chair and told me that he would be back. I thought he didn't want to cry in front of me, but instead, he went to his office upstairs. Within five minutes, he came back carrying a thick, red hardcover dictionary. I was confused as to why he needed a dictionary for our conversation. He then took a paring knife from the kitchen and slit the corner along the edges of the front cover and the first page. I watched him carefully split the pages trying not to damage what was inside. When the pages were severed, he pulled out two strips of film negatives. He held them delicately on the corner of the film and raised them to the light above.

"Do you remember these pictures?" He smiled.

To my surprise, one of the negatives was Phong's fourth birthday and the other one was his baby picture. I didn't know how he got them, as I remembered the last time we were at Di Yen's house was right after Phong's birthday, and they were arguing in the room. I still wondered how he was able to get them.

"Of course I do, but why didn't you develop them so you can look at them better?" I asked.

"You know how your mom is. There will be chaos in the house if she sees it," he said. "I could still see him through the films whenever I miss him," he continued, still smiling while looking at the negatives.

I felt shattered listening to him. The agony that he had been carrying was bigger than I thought. I couldn't imagine the pain that he had endured.

"Do you want to see him, Ba?" I asked again.

"I don't know if it is the right time. Your mom will explode if she finds out."

"I understand, but you are getting older, Ba."

"I am just happy and fortunate to know that he is doing well."

Hearing what he said, I didn't want to corner him with further questions. Ba carefully placed the negatives back in the dictionary, then left to bring it back to his office.

Leaving Ba's house that day, I felt unsatisfied. I thought I could undo a knot, but instead, I left it more entangled. As much as I felt guilty about Phong and not keeping my promise to have him see Ba, I felt Ba's dilemma and also Ma's pain. I was stuck as I had no solution on how to bring everyone together without hurting someone along the way.

The next morning, I received a call from Ly telling me that Ba was admitted to the hospital due to a mini stroke. Luckily, Ba called Vu when he didn't feel well, and Vu was able to get him to the hospital in time. I was shocked since he was doing fine when I left. I thought about it, and it must have been our conversation the day before that triggered his emotions. Ly told me he was released t morning after his medical tests were confirmed, but the doctor ordered him to rest. I was thankful he recovered, otherwise, I wouldn't be able to stand the guilt if something happened to him. However, it saddened me to think that I may never bring this subject up with him again, since I feared it might cause him another episode. At the same time, I was pleased by now that Ba knew his son grew up well and became successful.

31 The Moment

As Ba was recovering at home, all of us frequently visited to take care of him, especially my sisters. Since they lived nearby, they brought him food every day while Ma and Chi Trang were still in Vietnam. I shared with Ly about my conversation with Ba, which may have triggered his stroke. I told her that I might never be able to tell him about Phong again given his condition. She comforted me and told me to think on the bright side that at least Trinh, Anh, Edgar, and herself have been connecting with Phong. I felt a sense of relief hearing this from my baby sister. I was grateful that they were willing to put aside our parents' complicated situation and bond as siblings. Although Chi Trang and Vu hadn't reached out to me yet, I believed they would once they were ready.

Two months before Phong's wedding, I called him and asked if he needed help with the planning. While on the phone, I had the urge to ask him to invite the siblings to the wedding. Without hesitation, he responded excitedly. "Please have them be at our wedding." However, he also mentioned that it would be a courtesy to inform Di Yen that they would be present. I certainly understood his concern and commended him for taking into consideration his mother's feelings. After a few days, he called me back with Di Yen's fond welcome to have us there on his special day.

Thrilled by the possibility of the siblings being at Phong's wedding, I didn't waste time and immediately reached out to Anh,

Trinh, Ly, and Edgar individually. When I entertained them with the idea, none had any objection and was more than delighted to be there for him. Indeed, Phong also reached out to them with a formal invitation. Although it was nice to have us there, I felt incomplete since Chi Trang and Vu were not aware of this. I was reluctant and apprehensive to approach them. I didn't know how they felt about it and didn't want to impose on them.

Upon discussing and planning with Phuong Linh and my kids, Leo suddenly asked, "Is Uncle Kevin coming with us to the wedding?" Kevin had become an added family member. A few weeks after Leo's birth, Kevin's lease at his apartment expired. He was looking for places to move to, but after several weeks of searching, he didn't like any of the areas that he found comfortable living. After listening to his struggles of being unable to resolve his lease soon, I offered my basement to him. Although I had built the dojo in the basement and intended to have a room there for me to work, I didn't mind having Kevin occupy the room in the meantime. When Kevin decided to move in with us in the fall of 2011, we treated him like a family member. He was just a door away from the dojo, and I would grab him at any moment when I wanted to practice karate. As for my kids, they got along with him instantly, and after a few years passed, Kevin became Leo's favorite uncle as they would always play video games together.

As I was contemplating whether to ask Kevin to go along with us to Houston for the wedding, fearing that he might feel like an outsider, my cell phone rang, and it was from Anh. Instead of asking me to book the airplane tickets, she caught me off guard and decided to back out from the planned trip. Apparently, she talked to Ly and they both felt guilty toward Ma as though they were betraying her. As a result, they both changed their minds of going to the wedding. I told her that I respected her feelings as she continued to tell me her concern.

"I understand. You go see him whenever you are ready," I said.

"Yeah, I am sorry, but I do hope to meet him someday," she said.

After I hung up the phone, I called Trinh and Edgar to make sure they were still on board. They told me they were fine and wanted me to proceed with the plan. That night, after talking to

Kevin about the trip to Houston, he cheerfully wanted to attend the wedding with us. I booked the tickets for my family, Kevin, Trinh, and Edgar. It was disappointing that Anh and Ly were fickle with their decisions. However, I understood how they felt. I knew I couldn't force it and had to let things happen in due course.

The following morning, sitting at my desk at work, I opened the bottom drawer and saw Phong's pair of gloves that I had kept for twenty-eight years. It was the pair of gloves that he left in Ba's car when he was four years old. I didn't have a place to store them when I first moved to Virginia, so I kept them at work ever since the summer of 2000. The more I looked at the gloves, I realized how much time had passed. I wondered if Ba would ever have a chance to meet him someday. Still struggling with finding an answer, random thoughts flashed through my mind. I fumbled with the idea of returning the gloves to their owner after the wedding. I brought the gloves home, and immediately Leo asked why I brought home a small pair of kid's gloves. Since Lara was much older, I remained silent to allow her to figure out why I was showing them the gloves. As I predicted, she asked, "Daddy, are these the gloves you have been telling us about? Is it Uncle Phong's gloves when he was a little boy?" Lara curiously asked. I just nodded my head as a proud father that my daughter had been listening to my stories. As Lara was still astonished and scrutinized over the aged pair of gloves, Leo took one of the gloves and tried it on.

"Daddy, look! It fits me." Leo waved his hand in the air.

"What do you all think? Should I return them to Phong after his wedding day?" I asked them, with Kevin and Phuong Linh in the kitchen.

Everyone acquiesced to the idea, and Lara said it would be sentimental to give this to Phong and his fiancée, Phoenix.

After putting the gloves away in a safe place to be wrapped, Phuong Linh sat me down in the family room and told me of her conversation with Ly that morning. She called and shared her concern that going to Houston would be betraying Ma. She asked for Phuong Linh's input as it was bothering her all night. After their conversation, Ly decided it would be righteous for her to attend the wedding. I couldn't be happier to hear this news.

Upon finishing my dinner, Anh called to say she felt unsettled since our last conversation. She asked me many questions regarding how to prevent Ma from knowing and getting hurt. I couldn't provide a strategic approach to avoiding Ma from finding out. As much as I had been keeping this a secret, I knew one day I would have to confront Ma if she questioned my honesty.

"Follow your heart and do what it tells you," I said.

After a long pause, she said, "Please book a ticket for me. I don't want to miss out on this."

I was elated to hear Anh's decision to go with us. Fearing the flight tickets might be sold out, I went straight to my computer and luckily found additional seats for Anh and Ly to sit next to us.

In September 2018, Trinh and her two-year-old son, Alex, Ly, Anh, Edgar, Kevin, and my family took off from Dulles Airport and headed to Houston. When we arrived in Houston, I showed them around Bellaire Boulevard, which had numerous Vietnamese restaurants along the streets. We spent that first day eating everything from main courses at restaurants to desserts until midnight. I booked a van that held all of us. While it may have been uncomfortable and tight, none of that bothered us as we bantered constantly with each other. Witnessing my siblings laughing and enjoying their time with my children, I felt all the familial joys I had missed in my life. With Ma blaming me for Ba's situation, I felt as if there was a wall between me and my siblings that eventually took away the bond that we once had when we were young. Because of that, we seldom hung out or took any trips together, and that made me feel lonely at times. However, for the first time in a long time, I felt that bond again. This trip was special as it brought us all back together, not only for Phong but for me as well.

The next day, we were ready for a two-hour drive to Austin. As we discussed Phong meeting up with Ba someday, we all agreed Ma should forgive Ba and let go of the past; that she should accept Phong so she could find closure. For that to happen, we needed someone who could convince Ma, since Ba and I had failed all those years. In the end, we all concurred that Anh should be that person since she was strong-willed and spoke her mind if she saw unfair things. She was known as a tough cookie in our family. Jokingly but somewhat seriously, Anh said, "Ok, after this trip, I will talk to Ma and tell her to get over it. Ba is too old to go back to any woman." As I drove, I smiled at her comment. Anh might be the solution I had been looking for. We all unanimously voted to have Anh talk to Ma when we got back to Virginia.

After we arrived in Austin, while checking in at the hotel's front desk, I noticed there were so many Vietnamese waiting to check in as well. Phong had registered us at this hotel, and I wondered if these people were his guests as well. However, I didn't recognize any of them, as they must be on Phoenix's side. As I turned around, I saw Anh Bao and his family in the hallway walking toward me. We hadn't seen each other since Phong's high school graduation. He was just married back then and now had three kids—two girls and one boy. As we talked, Di Yen and Anh Dung exited the elevator and saw us. I turned to greet her and so did everyone at our party. That was the first time all my siblings met Di Yen, Anh Dung, and Anh Bao after more than two decades. I was afraid it would be an awkward moment for everyone due to the situation, but I was relieved to see that everyone had put aside unsettled matters and was simply happy to be there for Phong.

We got into our rooms, and I rushed everyone to quickly change into their formal clothing for the wedding at 6 PM. Despite having only two rooms, ten of us were able to finish changing within an hour. While driving to the venue, I looked in the rear mirror and saw the nervousness in Anh's eyes. Trinh, Ly, and Edgar had met Phong before when he came to Virginia, but this would be the first time for Anh. Although I had shown her Phong's picture and they had been texting each other, I guessed seeing Phong in person would be a whole different story. To ease the mood, I asked Lara to go over the song that she would perform later at the banquet.

When we arrived at the venue, I told Phuong Linh and all my siblings to head inside first, while Kevin and I went to park the car. As I walked up to the entrance, I was blown away by the beautiful venue overlooking the city of Austin. However, my eyes caught something even more spectacular—I saw that all my siblings were hugging Phong. I stood still as I wanted to keep that image in my memory because it was the moment that I had been waiting for; a sight that I wanted to treasure forever.

As we reconvened in the wedding hall, Kevin and I stood in the back with Anh Dung and Anh Bao, while my family and siblings sat in the middle alongside the aisle. We reminisced about the past when we four boys were growing up in Fordham Road. Phong was a baby sleeping in his hammock while we were making hair clips and couldn't watch our Chinese drama, afraid it would wake him up. Just like that, Phong was now the last one getting married. As the ceremony began, I could feel the three of us trying to contain our emotions as we watched our little brother exchanging his vows with the love of his life. I looked over to see my family as they were wiping their tears and witnessing a lovely couple tying the knot.

After a break from the ceremony, everyone settled in their seats at their respective banquet tables. I approached Phong and told him that we had a surprise for him and Phoenix. He told me to give them ten minutes before heading to our table, which gave me plenty of time to talk to the DJ. I asked the DJ to give me a microphone because Lara would be singing a song while playing the ukulele that she taught herself. When I got back to the table, Lara nervously removed the ukulele from its case. With a smile and nudging some encouragement, she held herself together, took a deep breath, and said, "I am ready!" Phong and Phoenix arrived at our table, and I signaled to the DJ. With his announcement, "Ladies and gentlemen, Phong's niece, Lara, has a song that she wanted to sing for them," everyone at my table grabbed their phones and clicked on the video recording button. I helped hold the microphone to Lara's mouth as she sang *"Can't Help Falling In Love"* while playing the ukulele. Coincidentally, it was one of Phoenix's favorite songs. As Lara sang, the voice that she carried and the talent of her strumming the ukulele reminded me of her mom. It was a beautiful dedication that Lara displayed on Phong and Phoenix's wedding day.

The next morning, I entertained everyone with the idea of having a BBQ at a famous place. The last time Phong took me to Rudy's BBQ, I was amazed by the delicacy of the meat and wanted everyone to try it. Without any objection, I said it would be great to call Phong and Phoenix to join us for lunch. We arrived at Rudy's BBQ and to my surprise, Phong and Phoenix were already there waiting for us. While everyone gathered to find a table outside of the restaurant, Phong and I went to order the specials—briskets and sweet corn. Phong helped me carry the food to the table and I told everyone that this would be a meal that they would never forget. Right after we finished eating, I asked for everyone's attention as I had something to say. I cleared my throat and tried to gain my composure, then I picked up a gift bag from under the table and handed it to Phoenix. Lara knew what I was about to do so she quietly took out her phone and recorded it, as she didn't want that moment to be missed. Phoenix opened a box from the gift bag and Phong immediately said, "Wait, are those my gloves?"

"Yes, they are," I said.

All my siblings were curious as to why I was giving Phong his gloves that were not even his size. I looked over to Lara and saw tears come down her eyes as she continued recording. She made it harder for me as I tried to speak the words before tearing up.

"The last time I said goodbye to Phong was in Ba's car as we dropped him off. He left this pair of gloves behind and I had been keeping them ever since. I had made a promise to myself that I would find a way to give them back to their owner. Although Phong and I were able to reunite after eight years, I never had a chance to do it. I guess everything needs to have the right moment for it and today is that right moment. Twenty-eight years ago, Phong was separated from this pair of gloves as well as his siblings. Today, the gloves have found their way to their owner and we found our way to reunite with each other."

I paused as I couldn't contain myself anymore and just let out the tears. Then I looked up to see Phuong Linh, my siblings, and even Kevin all sobbing and wiping their eyes. I knew every single one of us had been waiting for this moment and those were happy tears. I took a deep breath and continued.

"Phoenix, I would like for you to have this pair of gloves now. I hope you will keep and cherish them as I have for all these years."

Phoenix thanked me for giving her such a sentimental gift and promised to take loving care of them. Although Phong didn't say much, I knew he was touched to see his old gloves were a keepsake for me. All my siblings were surprised to hear about the gloves for the first time. They wondered how I was able to keep them without anyone in the family knowing. I just smiled and told them I had my secret place. In fact, after the incident with my cousin, Oanh, and my diary, I became more careful with the stuff that could cause trouble in the house if Ma found out.

We spent one more day with Phong and Phoenix before flying back to Virginia. Phong promised to visit us the following fall. As we sat at the airport waiting to board, my siblings were happy they attended the wedding with me... not only to witness Phong's marriage but to hear some of the stories that Phong and I shared when they weren't around. Seeing how the love between my siblings had grown, I felt we were one step closer to my wish of having our family reunited.

One month after getting back from Houston, Anh told me that she spoke to Vu about Phong and our trip to Austin. Vu was disappointed that he couldn't attend, but he asked for Phong's contact information since he was going to Austin in a few weeks for a business trip. I was happy that one more of my siblings had found a way to reunite with Phong. Anh also let me in with more shocking news. She had told Ma as well. I was stunned by her words, but I guessed she wasn't joking when she said she would talk to Ma. I couldn't wait for her to fill me in with more details on Ma's reactions. She had been taking Ma out for walks every weekend, trying to ease Ma's mind with positive thinking, and the teachings about life from one of the Buddhist monks that she had been following on YouTube. Little by little, and week after week, she finally opened up to Ma about Phong's issue and slowly persuaded her to let go of the past so she could be free from her resentment. Surprisingly, Ma didn't get angry like she used to but calmly listened to her. We agreed that was a good sign and progress. Anh told me she would continue with the talking, and hopefully, Ma would change her mind soon.

In mid-November, Phong called me to share the news of reconnecting with Vu. He said Vu was in town and wanted to get together with him and Phoenix. They met up for dinner and had a wonderful time. Phong told me he found himself getting more siblings by the day. One thing for sure that Phong took after Ba was that he rarely expressed his feelings. However, I knew he was happy to reunite with all of us. As for me, I was happy that I could stop answering Phong about the siblings' status since he could ask them himself now.

Ever since Anh talked to Ma, I could see the change in her. She seemed happier and more relaxed. The fights with Ba at home were also reduced. Having someone on Ma's side to repair the situation was easier since I was a guilty one from Ma's viewpoint. Nonetheless, knowing all her kids chose to let go of the past to find peace must have affected her somehow. Most of all, Ba had been faithfully staying by her side for the last twenty-eight years and that should be enough to make up for the wrong he did to her. I just hoped and prayed that Ma could soon realize that all we wanted was a happy conclusion for everyone in our family.

In late July 2019, Phong called and let me know he was planning to visit us in September. Delighted to hear that he would be here with his wife in Virginia on Labor Day weekend, I phoned the other siblings to let them know. As I was debating back and forth whether to let Chi Trang know about Phong, Phuong Linh suggested it was time, since everyone met him already. One Sunday before Phong and Phoenix's arrival, Phuong Linh and I asked Chi Trang to join us for breakfast at a Panera Bread near her house. Chi Trang and her family moved to Virginia a few years after I left New York City. As we were eating, I said, "Chi Trang, I am sure you have been wondering about Phong."

With her eyes fully gazing into mine, she didn't say a word, then she looked to the ground and slowly asked me, "How is he doing?"

"He is doing good and just got married," I said. I continued to tell her how we met and told her about the incident when Phong called me while I was living in her basement in New York City right before she walked in. She responded by asking how I kept a secret like this for such a long time. I told her it wasn't easy for sure, but I was glad that she was the last to know about him. I told her that Phong would be here next week. Just like the others, she seemed nervous but eager to meet him. Driving home, I couldn't be more excited. Finally, we could all meet. I no longer had to endure holding a secret about Phong. As I drove along the highway, the stress that I held for almost three decades seemed to fall off my shoulders and mind. I could feel the heaviness in my heart melt away slowly as I passed each mile marker. The day I dreamt of was about to unfold.

The next day at work, Ma called to inform me to come over with Phuong Linh and the kids for Ong Noi's commemoration. It had been a tradition that on commemoration day everyone had to show up and pray for respect. Right after I hung up, I received a group text from my siblings concerning Phong's arrival being on the same week as Ong Noi's commemoration. After texting back and forth, I told them that I would feel guilty leaving Phong and Phoenix at home while going to my parent's house. The more I pondered, I concluded to ask for Ong Noi's forgiveness and skip that year.

On the Friday morning of Phong and Phoenix's arrival, I drove with Phuong Linh to Dulles airport to pick them up. Phong had been in Virginia a couple of times, but it was the first for Phoenix, so we took them for a tour in Washington, D.C. that afternoon. We had everything planned for their visit: having dinner on Friday night at Anh's house, having a barbeque on Saturday at the park near Ly's house, and then resting on Sunday at my house.

After the tour in D.C., we rested at my place until the early evening. When we arrived at Anh's house, all the siblings were there with their spouses, including my nieces and nephews. One by one, they greeted Phong and Phoenix, until Chi Trang was the last one exiting from one of the rooms, and loudly said, "Phong, is that you?"

She ran over to him, grabbed him by the hands, and said, "I can't believe how much you have grown."

Phong was still speechless, probably wondering who this lady was, since the last time he met her was when he was a four-year-old boy. Nevertheless, he continued to hold her hands as Chi Trang continued to rub his shoulders while tilting her head back to see how much taller he had gotten. She had taken care of him as a little boy and now almost thirty years later, he stood in front of her, about to give her that long overdue hug.

I couldn't believe it with my own eyes. The apprehension that I had conjectured in my mind for decades rang false. I feared that no one would accept Phong, yet in front of me was constant laughter exchanged from one to another. The stories they all shared, the comments they made to each other, to me silly, yet they all laughed. I was a few feet away witnessing a moment of jubilation seeing that we all accepted one another. We continued to enjoy each other's company the entire night.

Driving home from Anh's house, I couldn't help but think about Ong Noi's commemoration on Sunday. I didn't feel right for not going to show up considering how much I loved and respected him. Even back when I had a fallout with my siblings, I still came to pray and left before the others arrived. I still hadn't gotten back to Ma and she had been calling me and Phuong Linh, but we both were dodging her calls since we didn't know what to say to her. That night, I couldn't fall asleep—tossing and turning the entire night. It felt as if someone was telling me to do what I had set out to do as the moment had come. That voice kept on permeating deeper and deeper into my thoughts. At dawn, I got out of bed and went to get ready for a tennis match with a friend who I played every morning. As I washed my face, suddenly all the pieces of the puzzle in my head came together. I could feel Ong Noi's spirit surrounding and helping me end this unsettled matter and put things back in their right place. I could feel as though he brought his grandson, Phong, there that weekend. I sensed Ong Noi looking at me at that moment and saying, "Go ahead and do the right thing. Your parents should be waiting for this moment."

It was still early so I didn't want to wake up Phuong Linh since we got home late the night before from Anh's house. After finishing my tennis match, I called Phuong Linh and told her that I was on my way to my parent's house.

"We hadn't returned Ma's call, Honey. I'm going there to give my answer. I think they both deserve it," I said.

Phuong Linh was a little confused by what I just told her because I didn't have to drive to my parents to tell them I couldn't come on Sunday. Yet, respecting my decision, she didn't ask any further. I didn't want to explain it to her over the phone, so I told her I would talk to her more after getting back. When I got to my parent's house, I parked the car and took a deep breath before getting out. Ever since I got reunited with Phong, I was hoping this day would come, but I never dared to do it. That day, it must have been fate. Ong Noi must have wanted to see his descendants live in peace and harmony. I looked up in the sky and felt as if his spirit was watching over me, giving me the strength to put happiness back in our family.

I walked up the stairs and knocked on the door. Ba opened and was surprised to see me alone at eight in the morning without prior announcement. I quickly made my way in while greeting Ba, as I didn't want to give him time to ask the reason I came. Ma walked out of the kitchen and had the same look as Ba.

"Is the coffee ready, Ba? I want some coffee," I said.

Instead of asking me why I showed up so early, he went over to the kitchen countertop and prepared a pot of coffee. I paced back and forth while asking them random stuff about the house as I try to stay calm and divert their attention. I could see the confused look on Ba's face wondering why I was asking all these questions. When the coffee was done, Ma placed three cups on the table. I took the pot of coffee and gently poured it into three cups. After a few sips, Ba and Ma turned to me as they were ready for me to spill the beans, the reason I was there. My heart started to pound and the nerves kicked in. I had done this before with Ba, but never in front of Ma. Although I practiced what to say on the way there, my mind went blank sitting in front of them. *What happens if Ma stands up and screams? No, She won't. Ong Noi had me come here so he wouldn't let that happen.* I cleared my throat as well as those negative thoughts in my head. I turned to Ma and opened to her.

"Ma, I am forever grateful to you for giving me life and you are my only mom. What I am about to say, I know you never like to hear or to talk about, but regardless of what happens, I want you to know that I will always love and respect you. Ba, Ma, it has been almost thirty years and I think it's time to put this behind us." I paused to catch my breath and glance at Ma. To my surprise, she seemed calm as she just sat there listening to me. I continued. "Phong and his wife are at my house right now. They came to visit us. All the siblings met him at Anh's house last night."

I stopped there to see their reactions. Ba looked at Ma and to my surprise, she remained quiet. I seized the chance and took it further.

"We all felt your pain, Ma. We also know that it wasn't something to forgive and forget that easily. However, Ba and all of us had stayed by your side for the last twenty-nine years. Our family has gone through so much. I think we all deserve happiness and you are the one who could make that happen." I pleaded with her.

Ma still calmly sat there without a word and Ba finally broke his silence. "I know I have caused you pain all these years so I'm not going to ask you to do anything that makes you feel uneasy. I will accept whatever decision you make." Ba stood up and headed out to the deck.

"Where are you going?" Ma quickly asked Ba.

"I just want to get some fresh air," Ba responded.

Before Ba got to the door, Ma stopped him as she wanted him to hear what she was about to say, "If all the kids wanted this to happen, then let it happen. Your dad and I are getting older and Phong should see his dad."

I couldn't believe what I just heard from Ma. Thinking I was hallucinating from lack of sleep the night before, I pinched my hand under the table just to prove I wasn't dreaming. It was real! Ma just said that in front of Ba and me. No words could describe the jubilant celebration of my smile when she said that. I had been waiting to hear those words for years. I stood up and gave her a big hug as I said thank you for her forgiveness. Ba also turned around as he couldn't believe what his wife just said. I bet Ba was as pleased, and finally, he could put down his dilemma to atone for his past action toward Phong.

I told Ba and Ma about the barbeque outing at the park later and asked if they wanted to meet Phong there. Ma didn't object to the idea, so I gave them the location and bid them goodbye. Walking out of their house, I never felt the sky as beautiful as that day. I looked up and silently thanked Ong Noi for giving me the courage to complete the hardest task in my life. While driving home, I felt a ton of relief from my shoulders. Being able to talk to Ma openly about this was something unimaginable. However, another thing struck me. Everything happened so fast that morning as it wasn't my plan. I got carried away and just realized I needed to ask Phong if he was ready to meet Ba. I needed to respect his decision as well. Luckily after I got home, Phuong Linh asked me to buy more meat as she was afraid it wouldn't be enough for everyone although she had already gotten a lot the day before. I asked Phong to go with me because I needed to know how he felt about it; otherwise, I would have to cancel on my parents. I honestly told Phong that Ba and Ma would join us at the barbeque later. I told him there was no pressure if he wasn't ready to meet them and I would respect that. I didn't receive an excited or jolted reaction from Phong. Instead, his response was amicable to my suggestion of being at the barbeque with everyone. He didn't ask me further questions about Ba or seem overly concerned if he was ready to meet Ba or not.

After getting back from the market, we loaded all the stuff in my car and I drove my family, Phoenix, and Phong to the park to meet up with the others. On the way there, as everyone was talking in the car, my mind pictured the moment Ba would see his son again after twenty-nine years. I couldn't help feeling the excitement running down my spine. We arrived at the park around noon. Ly and Anh's family were already there setting up the tables. I took out the meat and got the grill ready, while Vu's family and Edgar pulled up to the parking lot.

About forty-five minutes later, I saw Ba's car pulling up. My legs shook, my heart throbbed, and my jaws clenched as though I was shivering from the cold. At that same time, I heard Vu and Edgar whispering to each other as they were standing next to me "What? Is that Ba and Ma?" Vu asked. Then all the girls stopped chatting from the table, ran toward me at the grill, and pointed to Ba and Ma walking toward us. Everyone, except Phong and I, was startled to see Ba and Ma. Phuong Linh looked at me wondering what was going on. With everything happening so fast that morning, I didn't have time to let Phuong Linh or my siblings know about the talk with Ba, Ma, and Phong earlier. I winked and smiled at Phuong Linh as if it would be okay.

Ba and Ma approached closer. Finally, the moment arrived. Ba stopped in front of Phong as he reached out his hand to hold his son for the first time after twenty-nine years. Every one of us stood there with tears in our eyes, frozen as if we wanted the time to stop so we could capture that moment a little longer. After what felt like an eternity, Ba let go of Phong and said with a smile, "You are grown."

Phong nodded his head while containing himself. He turned to Ma and greeted her with a bow and then introduced Phoenix to both of them. All my siblings gathered around Ba, Ma, Phong, and Phoenix, as we didn't want to miss any minute of this heartfelt reunion. They all had stopped crying but replaced it with talking and laughing, although they were still wiping their tears. Finally, those sleepless nights wondering how Ba and Phong would meet and the worries of Ma filled with indignation slowly drifted away from my shoulders. I stood there breathing in the nice breeze of a wonderful day.

While everyone settled down to enjoy the food, I walked to Ma and embraced her with a big hug. I thanked her for letting this day happen. There were times I questioned Ma for taking things to the extreme and blamed her for not understanding the pain that Ba and I went through. However, she had been enduring her pain and may have felt no one understood her. Only we, ourselves, can perceive our true affliction and understand our way of coping. For Ma, Ba was her everything. She lived her life for him and loved only him. She went through an ordeal being in his role by taking care of the family he left behind. Therefore, the betrayal she felt went even deeper. Nonetheless, I was grateful that Ma finally was able to let go of those thoughts that plagued her emotionally and destroyed her happiness. She willingly acknowledged that certain things couldn't be changed and accepted the reality for the sake of her family.

Ba and Phong sat at the table next to Ma and me. With a smile, Ma told me to join them as she had the girls to keep her company. I walked over and sat next to Phong. Immediately, the image of the three of us living in Astoria, Queens, on the weekend was like a movie playing in my head. Those times we went to eat Phong's favorites, Chinese fast food and McDonalds—when Ba didn't have time to cook for us. Phong's chubby cheeks and those big eyes always got him out of trouble whenever he spilled his food. Ba never yelled at him even when he drew on the wall. Ba would clean his mess over and over again and not punish him even once. It didn't matter how much Ba had to study late at night, he tirelessly took care of both of us once we woke up. Phong probably wouldn't remember those days, but maybe that wasn't a bad thing. It was time to let go of the past and look to the future. I hoped Ba and Phong could create new joyful memories together moving forward so they could replace those unhappy ones.

As for me, I wouldn't have changed a thing, as Ba was my world. The journey to America with him was the greatest gift that he had given me. I still didn't know why he chose me instead of the others, but I was grateful he did. It wasn't an easy journey from day one as we faced one obstacle after another. However, witnessing all the curveballs that life threw at us and sharing all the hardships with him throughout our time in a new land brought us closer and also helped make me become who I am today. I thanked him for guiding and constantly pushing me to achieve my goals.

In 1982, our family was split up by the sea not knowing if we could ever see each other again. Luckily, we were blessed with a chance to reconnect in 1989. Then, we were tested with another challenge and as a result, were forced to face another separation from one of our loved ones. However, through love and forgiveness, we found our way back to each other. I believe every family has its own stories to tell, as one might be different from others. As for ours, we encountered quite a bumpy road along the way, but in the end, the happiness of our family mended us all together.

    I looked up in the beautiful blue sky and looming in the distance, there was a kite flying high with its tail flapping vigorously in the wind. It reminded me of the one I used to fly with Ong Noi back home. As it got closer, it kept gliding above my head and didn't want to fly away. At that moment, I felt like it was Ong Noi looking down, smiling to see our family get our happy reunion.

The End

Afterword On Hope

For the Vietnamese people who left the country on a small fishing boat in search of freedom, they knew hardship would be faced in the open water. The South China Sea became the sea of hope for so many Vietnamese. Even knowing there would be obstacles ahead, we were ready because only by taking risks could we change our lives. Opportunity doesn't come often, and even knowing that our chances for survival on the open water were slim, we just couldn't wait for our home country to become better.

    Vietnamese lives changed after the Vietnam War. Many lost everything, from hope to their vision of the future. People lived day by day, hoping to have enough food for their families to survive. But with everything in life, when you feel at your lowest point, with no future and no sense of direction, you will automatically get on your feet to find means for survival. Hope was the only thing in the minds of the Vietnamese people, whether those who left the country on a boat or those who stayed behind to bear the changes from the new political party of communism. We all hoped for a better future.

    At the refugee camp, we celebrated by conquering our greatest obstacle of the South China Sea, overcoming the lonely cold nights, begging for help during the mid-day hot sun, and surviving the non-stop waves. Hope was what kept us alive. We looked forward and prayed for divine intervention to give us hope of survival and strength to see another day.

None of us at the time would have thought life in a new destination would also bring us another challenge. The challenge of communication and trying to fit in were extremely difficult for a foreigner. We had to endure endless teasing and ridicule. While not exactly understanding what was being said to us, the mocking laughter in people's voices hurt our hearts and soul. The only way to stand up and be respected was to be mentally strong and start all over again. We learned the new language, built a strong foundation, and hoped we would soon blend in with the new culture.

With every family, there seem to be conflicts that either get resolved quickly or are prolonged through years of pain and suffering. In my instance, my brother Phong was apart from us, but he remained close to my heart. For thirty-plus years of separation from his dad, I was the bridge between them, but my biggest fear was hurting my mother's feelings. I struggled for many years to give Phong faith that one day Dad would see him again. I gave him hope, and I needed hope so that my mother would one day accept Phong as my dad's son.

I prayed and practiced Buddhism so that I could have the inner strength to bear the hardships of today so that tomorrow will be better. Hope is important and it will guide us on the path of renewing energy so that we can overcome the present difficult moment. With every obstacle that we faced, there was hope if we remained persistent.

Reflection by Veronica McKeever

This is definitely not a "woe is me" book, but a story about bravery and courage. Linh stole my heart immediately with his straight black bangs and his soulful eyes. I was an ESL (English as Second Language) teacher when this beautiful boy was brought to Mrs. Powell's classroom. He spoke very little English, so ESL would be a big part of his school day.

One of my first sessions with Linh was to evaluate where to begin lessons with his second language. I was informed he spent time in Hong Kong and the Philippines where he had English classes but had no record or notes of his progress. Deciding that "colors" was an unintimidating topic, I got big fat crayons and used them for the lessons. Linh knew his colors but mixed up the blue and green crayons. After calling the blue-colored crayon "green" a few times, he got annoyed at himself. The next day, he did it again, except he informed me that the blue-colored crayon was "green" in the Philippines. I held up the blue crayon and said, "In the United States, 'BLUE'." Linh smiled a big smile from ear to ear with a quiet chuckle. He got my message with humor, and I knew we were going to be good friends. Linh was exceptional then, and he became more exceptional as he grew up. Also, that day he won my heart instantly.

Linh made wonderful progress through his first year in New York City public school. As Linh's second-grade ESL teacher, I knew how much he progressed both academically and socially. When I saw his third-grade class assignment, I thought it was unsuitable for him. Waiting a little while, I approached his teacher and told her of my connection to Linh. She was kind and understood my concern. I was certain his third grade would be a good year. His advancement through PS 122 was very good up to and through sixth grade. Thinking of his graduation, I remember being both happy and sad.

Upon graduation, students always say they will come back to visit their "old" teacher, but it seldom happens. Linh's graduation was a mixed-feeling day for me. I went to the graduation and stood in the back of the auditorium and clapped loudly when they called his name, "Linh Vinh Tran." I did not know then that Linh would be moving away. He had lived in the Bronx (my old neighborhood) since coming from Vietnam. Their new apartment was near a good college so Mr. Tran could continue his studies for an Electrical Engineering degree, and Linh could attend a better junior high school and high school. With all his other tasks and responsibilities, Mr. Tran made certain Linh kept in touch with me. I will always be thankful for Linh's dad for that.

Being invited to Linh's wedding to Phuong Linh was such an honor for me. I was so happy and excited to make the trip to Virginia with my husband, Larry. He talked about the wedding any chance he got. After all this time, I would finally get a chance to meet all of Linh's siblings and friends that I felt I already knew. It was a very big wedding with friends and relatives from all over the country. Linh's dad got up on the podium and thanked everyone for coming, especially those who traveled far. Then suddenly, he introduced me, "Linh's first teacher in the United States." I received a standing ovation. Never in thirty-eight years of teaching did something like that happen. I would never forget it.

I feel that Linh and his dad should be getting the praise and recognition, instead of me. I am pleased that Linh wrote this book to show how the Vietnamese people struggled and sacrificed to come to this great country.

Ba and me in 1983. Our first snow

Graduation in 1998

From L to R: Ly, Anh, Chi Trang, me, Ma, Ba, Vu
Front Row: Bryant, Edgar

Our Wedding Day, April 27th, 2002

Lara and me with Leo
2011

Our Family
2021

My Karate Family

Mrs. McKeever and me, 2020 in D.C.

L to R: Felix, me, Kevin in Florida for Karate seminar

Phong's 4th Birthday

1st Row (L to R): Ma, Ba;
2nd Row (L to R): Ly, Chi Trang, Trinh, Anh, Phong
3rd Row (L to R): Vu, me, Edgar

Phong's Wedding in Austin

Phong visiting us in Virginia
L to R: Edgar, Phong, Ly, Vu, Anh, Trinh, me, Chi Trang

ABOUT THE AUTHOR

We hope you enjoyed this book. Please consider writing a review to help other readers enjoy **Split Up by the Sea**. Thank you!

Want to know more about Len Tran's next project?
Follow Author on social media!

https://www.facebook.com/len.tran.7106
https://www.linkedin.com/in/len-tran
https://www.LenVTran.com

Len Tran was born in Hue, central Vietnam, and immigrated to the United States in 1982. After receiving a Chemical Engineering degree from City College of New York in 1998, he worked for the Department of Environmental Protection in New York City and then later moved to Virginia to establish his career at the United States Patent and Trademark Office. Len is a speaker, trainer, and coach at Kinetic Mind, LLC. His goal is to inspire and engage his audience with techniques that will make them RISE from their seats.

www.ingramcontent.com/pod-product-compliance
Lightning Source LLC
Chambersburg PA
CBHW030334010526
44119CB00028B/400/J